# PRAYING
# DAY BY DAY

## *a year of meditations*

# PRAYING
# DAY BY DAY

## *a year of meditations*

FORWARD MOVEMENT
Cincinnati, Ohio

COVER PHOTO
The Little Miami River
Cincinnati, Ohio
taken by Greg Buening

COVER DESIGN
Albonetti Design

Published 2009
ISBN 978-0-88028-321-2

FORWARD
MOVEMENT

300 West Fourth Street
Cincinnati, Ohio 45202-2666
USA

1-800-543-1813
513-721-6659
FAX  513-721-0729
Email  orders@forwarddaybyday.com
www.forwardmovement.org

# Foreword

*Forward Day by Day* celebrates its seventy-fifth anniversary in 2010. Hundreds of authors have written for the publication since 1935, most of them anonymously, offering guidance and counsel to Episcopalians and all people of faith on discipleship, prayer, and Christian living.

In this volume, we feature twenty-four of our most popular and gifted authors. Here we invite them to range more widely than is possible in *Forward Day by Day*, with its limited space and lectionary-based format. These meditations, one for each day of the year, are not tied to any particular calendar year or lectionary. Some are based on a scripture passage. Others cite a liturgical or hymn text. Many simply tell a story of faithful living or the presence of God.

As we celebrate our heritage and move into the next seventy-five years of serving the faithful, we offer this book as a supplement to *Forward Day by Day*. May it become a treasured source of spiritual wisdom to which our readers turn again and again.

Richard H. Schmidt
*Editor and Director*
*Forward Movement*
*Cincinnati, Ohio*
*October 2009*

# *New Year's Day*

I have started this new year as I hope to continue: I got up early (well, reasonably early), read the Daily Office, did my exercises, had a healthy breakfast, wrote a newsy e-mail to a friend. It's time for a walk.

Walking, as in exercise, is not that simple for me. I have to stretch, strap on a knee brace, and lace up special shoes before I set out. But it's good for me: it clears my head, gets my heart going, and gives me time to think without the usual indoor distractions.

It's a clear, cold day in the Midwest. The sky is a pale blue, the grass crunches beneath my feet when I leave the sidewalk, and hardy birds sing from bare branches. In terms of people, I might as well be alone in our subdivision this morning as I stride past houses with blinds still closed, newspapers uncollected in driveways.

I'm not much on New Year's resolutions. They're a popular cliché, and in any case, most resolutions don't make it to Valentine's Day. Still, a new year is a new beginning, and I am making new beginnings of my own.

My resolutions this bright morning are to be a better mother, daughter, friend, colleague, employee; to keep reading the Office; to watch my health—mental, physical, and spiritual; and to walk in faith, whatever comes. These, I think, are not just doable; they are necessary.

I will not always succeed, but I will always make the effort. I walk on, past the sleeping houses, and as I walk, I pray.
—*Sarah Bryan Miller*

# Two kinds of change

The workshop speaker was talking about change: "Say you want to lose ten pounds." That caught my attention; I could do with change like that after the holiday excesses.

"Losing weight is an example of *incremental* change," she went on. "As the adjective implies, incremental change is limited in scope. It doesn't disrupt our patterns radically." Incremental steps toward shedding ten pounds might include eliminating white flour from one's diet, cutting back on sugar and Big Macs, and making a pact with Jim across the street to meet early every morning for a forty-five-minute walk. Such steps are burdensome but hardly drastic.

"Here's an example of non-incremental change. Jesus said to Peter and Andrew, 'Follow me.' Immediately they left their nets and their boat and followed him. The term for that is *deep* change."

That caught my attention even more powerfully. Do I really want that much change? Deep change challenges us to our core. It is major in scope, discontinuous with the past, and risky. It disrupts existing patterns of action and entails surrender of control.

In projects of incremental change, we ourselves are in control of the process. *We* envision the goal, design the steps for reaching it, and retain the option of stopping when things threaten to go further than we like. Deep change means surrender of control; we have no way of knowing how far it is going to take us.

"New Year's resolutions generally have the character of incremental change," the speaker said. "There's nothing wrong with that. We could all do with some self-help type improvements. But the gospel isn't about self-help. It's about being radically remade."

There was deep silence in the room. Most of us Christians, it seemed, were more comfortable contemplating the loss of ten pounds. —*Bruce Birdsey*

# *Waiting*

Have you ever waited for a word? There's the kind of waiting that takes place in the hospital hallway or waiting room, waiting for a word from surgery or the delivery room: "The operation was a success." Or "It's a girl." There's the waiting for a word from a traveling loved one saying that she has arrived safely. There's the waiting for a word from a college or university or prospective employer that admission is granted, the job is yours. We wait for words about the stock market or the weather or the traffic conditions—countless things that affect our daily lives and our futures.

Prayer is waiting for a word from God, and often it requires that we open ourselves to the myriad ways God speaks. It is easy to miss God's word because we have limited the category of possible messengers.

Perhaps the most passionate waiting is the waiting for a word of love. We all want to know that we are loved, and we need to be told. Wondering won't do.

*In the beginning was the Word, and the Word was with God, and the Word was God.* If you are waiting for a word from God, if you are waiting for a word of love, look to Jesus. In him they are one and the same. —*James L. Burns*

# *Lighting the way home*

When I was a young boy in mill town New England there was a church service that involved lighting small candles that had cardboard wax-catchers around them. A great candle would be passed to the people at the end of the pews and the flame passed in turn to each individual candle. We kids then tried to get our candles home, still lit, after the service. It was impossible to do on an early winter's night in New England. A sudden gust of wind, a slip on the ice, a bump, or a quick blast of snow or rain, and the flame was out.

Until one year a group of us boys discovered that if we stayed huddled together as we shuffled along on our journey from the downtown river valley, up over the hill to our homes on the other side, we could make it. As a group we provided shelter for each other's candles from the gusts and the cold and the elements. And if one candle was blown out, we could relight it from one of the others that had been in touch with the original fire. Together we kept our candles lit, all the way home.

It strikes me now, well into my life, that those candles taught me my first real truth about our life of faith and about the church. On our own, as individuals, the gusts and cold and hardships of life can blow out the frail flame of our faith. But together, with others on the journey, God's Spirit provides us shelter from the storms and reconnections to that original fire in our hearts. Together we can make it—all the way home. —*Leonard Freeman*

# *Light in the darkness*

I remember once coming home from choir practice when I was a child. My house, an old Minnesota farmhouse, was on the top of a big hill, with a dirt driveway leading up to it. It was dark and cold, and the friend's mother who had given me a ride dropped me off at the bottom of the hill because she didn't want her car to get stuck.

As I walked up the hill in the dark and looked through the big picture window into our kitchen, I saw my mother inside that warm room making dinner. Light in the darkness. Warmth from cold. Safety. Home. That, I think, is a picture of what Jesus offers to us— light in the darkness. Warmth from cold. Safety. Home. An invitation, if you will—"Come in here by the fire, by the light. Stay where it is warm. Come back here when you've been out in the cold. This is your home, with me," says the Lord. "Follow my light."

As the wise men followed the bright light of the star, so are we invited to do. It's a pretty clear choice—follow the light, follow Jesus; walk in the light, or stay in the darkness and the cold. "The light shines in the darkness and the darkness has not overcome it. ...The true light, which enlightens everyone, is coming into the world" (John 1:5, 9).

May we be so filled with the light of Christ that we never walk in darkness again, but shine as beacons to others, inviting them to know the light of Christ in their hearts as well.
—*Lindsay Hardin Freeman*

# *Taking down Christmas*

"Need some help?" a visitor offered.

No, I didn't. It was the Feast of the Epiphany, the day I appoint for taking down all the Christmas decorations, one of my very favorite and most solitary housekeeping rituals. Now, why is this? I love decorating for Christmas, but I am happy to delegate getting the tree, trimming it, putting up lights; glad to have help hanging the ornaments, to talk about the provenance of each one.

Taking it all down is different—I want it all for myself, want to contemplate the quiet re-emergence of a sparer way of life on my own, without conversation. I want to put it away in silence, respectfully closing the lid on that bright beauty.

In past years the boxes of glass globes, angels, and birds and the bags of light strings have all gone back up to the attic. This year, though, I realized that there were empty drawers in the little secretary in the living room, that the hall closet had a space on its shelf just the size of three stacked wreaths.

And so the Christmas things will now go there. Sometime in July, if I want to, I can open one of the drawers and catch a Christmas flash of red and gold, or look at all the glass hummingbirds.

The seasons are not far from one another, not any more. A year used to crawl by, but now they race to their ends ahead of me, one yielding to another in disorienting succession. That may be why the taking down of Christmas appeals—the stretch of ordinariness feels more timeless than the dizzying race of all the festivals. I move gratefully through our simpler house and acknowledge the promise of its blank slate. The year is new and clean and fresh. All is still in order. I have not lost any of it yet. —*Barbara Cawthorne Crafton*

# The thread that runs so true

*There's a thread you follow. It goes among*
*things that change. But it doesn't change.*
*People wonder about what you are pursuing.*
*You have to explain about the thread.*
*But it is hard for others to see.*
*While you hold it you can't get lost.*
*Tragedies happen; people get hurt*
*or die; and you suffer and get old.*
*Nothing you do can stop time's unfolding.*
*You don't ever let go of that thread.* —William Stafford

I resonate with the image of the thread. Countless threads, of course, are woven together in the fabric of my life. Some of these threads are wonderful. Some are not. But there's one particular thread that I follow. I've always sensed a profound continuity in my life—both a direction and a presence—that is undisturbed by the warp and weft of any particular day or season. This thread, I have discovered, is the love of God. This is the thread that runs so true.

"You don't ever let go of that thread." That is obvious, yet deliciously ambiguous. Is it a statement of fact, or an expression of intention? Is it a gentle word of encouragement, or a terse warning? Does it speak of divine grace, human will, or some inscrutable interplay of the two?

As you make your way into this new year, you may be striding forward with confidence, lightly running your fingers along the thread, just enough contact to remain adequately oriented. Or you may be stepping gingerly, feet slipping here and there on the loose stones or the wet moss, holding onto the thread with whitened knuckles. The thread may feel as thick as the rope lashed to a ship's mast, or as thin as the filament of spun spider's silk. "You don't ever let go of that thread." —*Charles F. Brumbaugh*

# Snow day

It snowed last night and into the morning. Six inches in New York City, where I live—merely a dusting to some northern regions that reported over eighteen inches, but a big deal in a city where every inch must be removed at a cost of about $300,000 an inch and the year's budget is already spent.

City schools closed for the first snow day in five years. Offices cut back their expectations. Children and parents flocked to Central Park with sleds and saucers in tow. Dogs got frisky. By tonight the park will be populated with snowmen. Frolic wasn't the mood at New York's three airports, where a thousand flights were canceled.

I took my camera out into the storm to record snow scenes for an essay series called *God in the City*. What did I see of God? Children, of course, that holy breed who can find fun in almost anything, especially in snow. Snow plow operators, for whom today will be a long grind. Able-bodied people paying special attention to the frail and housebound.

I also saw reality as God may see it: changeable, balmy one minute and frigid the next, dry and then icy, manageable and then hazardous, streets empty of children and then suddenly full. We like to think of God as languid, slow-moving, as if eternal meant changeless, and everlasting meant ever-slow. But there is little in scripture that affirms such an image. God responded promptly to the Hebrews' cries in bondage, to Moses' plea, to David's adultery, to Israel's apostasy. Jesus stopped immediately to heal Bartimaeus. He lashed out at Simon Peter.

We might prefer an endless succession of days without change. But that is us, not God. A storm changed a city overnight; and so God can warm a human heart and change a world.
—*Thomas L. Ehrich*

# *Like little children*

*Let the little children come to me,*
*and do not stop them;*
*for it is to such as these*
*that the kingdom of heaven belongs.*
—Matthew 19:14

Our church sponsors a preschool. The kids often go to the city zoo for field trips. It is right around the corner, close enough that they can walk there. One day the children lined up on the church playground to come inside for lunch. A little boy looked out over the fence and said, "I see a lion." The teacher hushed him. He said again and again, "There is a lion over there." Finally the teacher demanded he be quiet, and then everyone went into lunch. The next morning the headline in the newspaper read "Animals Escape from Zoo!"

When Jesus said that we must become like children, he was not speaking metaphorically. He knew that children often see the world more clearly, in simpler terms, uninhibited by the burdens and distractions that plague adults. Jesus knew that children often see the kingdom unfolding before their eyes and are unafraid to share what they have discovered. It is an approach to life that Jesus wants for all people. Stop and pay attention the next time you hear a child say "Hey, look over there!" You may be surprised by joy. —*Jason Leo*

# *Optimism or hope?*

Our culture seems to regard Christianity as a soft and sentimental view of life. That is because it does not understand the distinction between optimism and hope. Christians are not optimistic. Because our faith is rooted in the cross, we understand that things can go wrong and end badly. We are fully aware of human malevolence; we know that innocence has a hard time surviving in the world.

So Christians are not optimists. But we are hopeful. We live fully aware of life's tragic possibilities, but also open to the action of a God who promises that all will be well.

This means that we are called to live in a kind of doubleness, to approach life in a way that is both hard-headed and open-hearted. We are open both to disappointment and surprise. Novelist Flannery O'Connor once said, "To expect too much is to have a sentimental view of life and this is a softness that ends in bitterness." What makes life not only bearable but wonderful is that we do not have a sentimental view of life. We are open to our own pain, the pain of those around us, the pain of those in the world. We approach the easing and healing of that pain knowing that disease and poverty and aggression may win the day. But we also know they will not ultimately prevail.

Approach today with hope, without optimism or despair, without expectations. God is at work in you, in those around you, and in the far-flung and nearby places of your concern. Act on those concerns, and trust that God will act on them, too. And let what comes forth both illuminate and surprise you. —*Gary Hall*

# *Hezekiah*

Hezekiah is not exactly a familiar name. Few children are named for him, but he was a reasonably successful king of Judah from 716 to 687 B.C. He won a few battles and is best known for cutting a conduit into Jerusalem to guarantee a supply of fresh water, which is important during a siege. You can still walk through that tunnel today. He got along tolerably well with the prophet Isaiah, which was no mean feat. There would be nothing to bring him to our attention but for a remarkable act of selfishness near the end of his life. Isaiah told Hezekiah that after his death the kingdom and city would fall to Babylon and that all, including his sons, would be carried away into captivity. Hezekiah said, "'The word of the LORD that you have spoken is good.' For he thought, 'Why not, if there will be peace and security in my days?'" (2 Kings 20:19).

Did we read that correctly? Did he really admit to thinking that way? It was OK if disaster fell on his family and his community after his death, as long as he enjoyed peace and security. A person that selfish would be capable of almost anything. Polluting rivers and streams, endangering species, dissolving the ozone layer, or contaminating the skies would not be beneath him as long as he had a nice car. National debt beyond imagination would not faze him as long as he got his perks and his grandchildren got the bill. His church could avoid appealing to a younger generation as long as the customs of his generation were continued. He could let his local school system rot, knowing that the bad fruit would not fall until after he was gone. A person as selfish as Hezekiah is almost beyond imagining. Almost. —*Francis H. Wade*

# Your money or your love

I understand that many lottery winners end up worse off than before they hit the jackpot. Their families and their friendships fall apart. They fall prey to addictive excess. Sometimes they end up broke. It all sounds so dreadful that I don't play the lottery—I can cross winning $27 million off the list of terrible things that might befall me.

When you're poor, it feels as if everything would be good if you just had money. So many things are so hard, but easy for people with money: you don't have a car, so getting to and from work takes two hours each way on the bus. You can't go to a supermarket, so you buy not-very-good food for too much money at a neighborhood grocery. You can't get your teeth fixed, so you always cover your smile with your hand. You can't get orthotics for your shoes, so your feet always hurt. You can't save. You have to refuse your children every time they want something. You are always exhausted, and you never take a vacation. Some preacher on the radio tells you that money doesn't buy happiness, and you want to slap him. "Maybe not," you say, "but it buys plenty of other things."

Money is a tool. It buys things we need, and the lack of it is terribly painful. But it can't take the place of life. Husbanding it doesn't make a good life's work. When money becomes anything beyond a tool, it grows monstrous, a sorcerer's apprentice that leads a person to places he probably wouldn't want to go.

The main reason for having money is to give it away. After there is enough to get your teeth fixed and buy sturdy shoes, money can be a powerful agent in the service of love. You can ease people's pain with it—not all of their pain, but some. You can save people's lives with it. You can use it to make the world safer and more beautiful. You can learn the peculiar pleasure of saying "No" to yourself in order to say "Yes" to someone else, and wonder why you never realized before how much fun that is. —*Barbara Cawthorne Crafton*

# *A little direction, please!*

A friend recently made his first automobile trip to one of the New York airports. A Midwesterner, he was unfamiliar with New York. He became disoriented as he approached the airport. "I went this way and that, ran a couple of red lights, and finally stopped in my tracks to consult a map, which didn't help."

Suddenly, he saw a gumball light in the rearview mirror and a large policeman gaining on him. "I rolled down the window and began to recount my plight, my having never been in New York before, much less the airport, the wrong turns, my confusion. The policeman listened until he could take no more. He interrupted me, asking: 'Do you want to go on telling me where you have been, or do you want me to help you get to where you want to go?'"

Hearing the story brought to mind moments of bewilderment in my own life: the day it first dawned on me that high school graduation was approaching and I was anxious about my future—I needed a guidance counselor, and quickly! The prospect of marriage and wondering if there were a blueprint or road map to negotiate that unknown terrain. Approaching a job change or retirement and praying, "O God, help me!" You've been there a time or two?

There is no road map or counselor to provide guidance at many of the major confluences of our lives. It comes down to a degree of self-reliance, and a large measure of trust that whatever we encounter, we will be all right. This, of course, puts us squarely in the realm of faith.

Jesus says, "Do not worry. I am the way forward. Trust me."

—*Richard L. Shimpfky*

# *Living faith*

Twenty-eight years ago, I had the great privilege of baptizing our second son at a church in Indiana. Four dear friends stood up as his godparents. Our paths separated not long afterward. One godmother stayed in touch for a few years. The other three godparents drifted into blessed memory.

Then yesterday I was discussing a possible consulting engagement in Indiana. One of those interviewing me by telephone was the thirty-two-year-old daughter of one godparent couple. How strange! And how wonderful! We exchanged e-mails afterward; her mother wrote, as well. We all hope to connect on an upcoming visit to my family home and reintroduce godparents to godson.

In the many baptisms I performed, I always counseled godparents to take their role seriously. Two of my own three godparents were exemplary. I myself have been a dud as a godfather, but I always appreciated the potential joy of being connected to someone solely by faith.

What does a good godparent do? My godfather taught me to play bridge at a tournament level. My godmother saw me through childhood and young adulthood, and threw a party for me and my new bride so that we could meet other young people.

None of that is overtly about church, of course, but it is entirely about faith. These godparents gave me the best they had to give. I always knew I was the object of their affection.

This is what faithful people do. They give the best they have, sing a song, play a cello, walk with you through a time of trial, bring food after death, ask about your health. None of it is heroic, and yet it makes all the difference. —*Thomas L. Ehrich*

# Try the impossible

Do you remember the story of Jesus walking on the water to reach his disciples in their boat, which a storm had carried far from shore? They are terrified and think he is a ghost. He says, "Take heart; it is I." Then Peter, ever eager, wants to walk on water also. He starts, but soon he begins to sink. It's OK. He has had a failure of faith, but it's not fatal. Jesus reaches out a hand and catches him.

Sometimes our boat gets knocked over by a storm. We're not anchored and we're drifting away. On my office wall is a sign: "All who wander are not lost." Tossed about, perhaps, and frightened, but not lost. Leaving the shore means taking a risk, moving into unknown territory, meeting sea monsters, and experiencing the miraculous. Young people often need to wander; older people may also. In the process, our faith may falter. Jesus says to Peter, "Come," and in that moment Peter is capable of beginning. None of us can maintain a miracle and so he starts to go under, but what an adventure!

May we be empowered to attempt the impossible, in our personal lives, in our church, and in our country. The impossible must be tried in order to make it possible. Women had to push their boats far from shore to obtain voting rights, employment rights, marital rights. Slaves organized insurrections whose benefits they would not live to see. Now gay people have achieved some political rights on the road to full equality. Athletes at the Olympics break records that once seemed beyond human capability. At the beginning, many things look impossible. Try anyway. God is reaching out a hand to you to hold you up and push you forward. —*Lee Krug*

# Gifts

*Now there are varieties of gifts, but the same Spirit;*
*and there are varieties of services, but the same Lord;*
*and varieties of activities, but it is the same God*
*who activates all of them in everyone.*
—1 Corinthians 12:4-6

My wife will tell you that she knows nothing about gardening. The truth is that I know nothing about gardening, but she is famous in our neighborhood for her annual crop of sunflowers. The stalks grow nine feet tall and the flowers look like hubcaps. People approach me all the time and ask, "How does she do it? How do they get so big?" They walk by our yard and cannot help but stop and stare. Some have asked for seeds to plant them at their homes, but for some reason no one has had the same success.

Paul reminds us that there are varieties of gifts, but the same spirit. It is often the case that I am envious of another person's skills or gifts. The message we are given is that we all have a part to play, a gift to share. All of us can help build the kingdom in our day and time.

It is the middle of January and there are ten inches of snow on the ground. My children are playing in the snow in our yard, right near the flower beds. Before long, I know there will be enormous sunflowers, pointing to heaven, for all to see, and that we can all point to heaven with the gifts and blessings God has bestowed upon us. —*Jason Leo*

# *Expectations*

What does God expect of me today? What do others expect of me today? What do I expect of myself today? These three questions may not always pose themselves in precisely that order, but some version of them emerges in our minds as we rub the sleep from our eyes each morning.

One of the most remarkable things about Jesus and his life was how he could be present to the unique reality of each situation in which he found himself. Jesus took account not only of the opportunities and problems which a moment presented him; he also was attentive to the needs and concerns of the people involved. With some he was warm and pastoral; with others he was compassionate and inviting. With still others he was authoritative and appropriately judgmental. Paul may have tried to be "all things to all people," but Jesus was particularly present and authentic with everyone he encountered in a characteristically unique way.

At the end of Shakespeare's final play, *The Two Noble Kinsmen,* a character steps forward and addresses the audience. At the end of his speech, he makes this demand of his listeners: "Let's go off, / And bear us like the time." In the context of the play, it means living in a way that is appropriate to the comic and tragic events which have transpired. In the context of our lives, it means living in a way that is responsive and fitting in the circumstances we encounter.

What God expects of me today is no more and no less than that I will bear myself with you, others, and God "like the time." God asks no more—and no less—of us than that. —*Gary Hall*

# Peter and Paul

The New Testament gives us clear, well-rounded pictures of just two of the apostles, Peter and Paul. They were both formidable, but very different.

Simon Peter was an illiterate fisherman from backward Galilee. Saul, later known as Paul, was a scholar and an intellectual. Peter was among Jesus' first followers, present at most of the important events in Christ's life. Saul was a Pharisee who actively persecuted Christ's followers. Peter was married, with a family; Paul was unmarried, by choice. Peter often doesn't seem to have a filter between his mind and his mouth. Paul always has a filter in place, an argument at hand, and a point to make.

In other words, Peter and Paul are night and day, black and white, yin and yang. But their very differences exemplify the inclusive nature of Christ's love for us. They remind us that the church has never been completely unified, never of one mind, and yet the faith has stood through the centuries.

For God made us all, Jesus saves us all, and the church needs us all: the physically strong and the physically weak, those who live by their minds and those who live by their hands, those whose faith is simple and straightforward, and those whose faith is more complex and nuanced. God needs those who will stand up for tradition and those willing to look beyond it, those who come easily to faith and those who need convincing, those who come early and those who come late, those who weigh their words and those who speak their minds.

When you see principled people disagree and despair of their ever finding common ground, remember the examples of Peter and Paul and, as they did, have faith. —*Sarah Bryan Miller*

# *Going to jail*

When I was a young green curate full of self-righteousness and certainty, God gave me the gift of friendship with a wise old bishop. One day over lunch he said, "If you are a parish priest long enough, you'll end up in jail!" He went on to talk about the fact that the United States is the world's biggest jailer. "Parishioners won't tell you about a family member in prison until they really know you and trust you, but if you are in the parish long enough," he said, "you will learn there is a father, a husband, a son, or family member in prison. The question will be, will you be courageous enough to visit them?"

For a number of years my answer was no. Funeral homes, emergency rooms, and nursing homes, yes, but prisons, no. They were usually out of the way and always frightening.

And then it happened. A quiet, widowed school teacher, one of my favorite parishioners who could always be counted on to know my literary references and appreciate a creative turn of phrase, invited me for coffee at her home. She told me about her son and the mistakes he had made. She didn't ask me to visit him, but I found myself volunteering.

Initially my fear was physical as heavy iron gates clanged shut behind me. What if there were a riot while I was in here? But soon my uneasiness changed to something more frightening as I talked with the widow's son and realized how much we had in common. We shared the same list of things done and left undone. There really wasn't that much difference between us except he had been at the wrong place at the wrong time, while I always went home early.

Prison ministry is extremely hard—and one of the best things I do for my soul. —*David L. James*

# My problems, your problems

*Sometimes I lie awake at night and ask why me?*
—Charles M. Schultz

A young woman finds out she is pregnant, and she would rather die than tell her parents. A man is laid off from his job, and on the drive home he wonders how he's going to tell his wife and kids; they're one mortgage payment away from foreclosure. A mother opens the door to find a solemn-faced police officer telling her that her son has been seriously injured. A man and his wife hold one another as they listen to the doctor explain what stage III means in a cancer diagnosis. A young student calls home to say she's being asked to leave a prestigious school after being arrested for possession of drugs. A homeless man is told he can stay at the shelter for only another week without a job, and it's the middle of January and no one has come close to hiring him.

The scenarios could go on. The point is, at some time in every life, there comes a moment when everyone wonders, "Why me?" It's pointless to wonder why bad things happen to good people because, like it or not, they do.

It is human nature, when these burdens are upon us, to perceive our troubles as far worse than other people's, but maybe that's not so. Someone once told me that if we could all walk into a room and toss our chief problems on a big table with the only requirement being that we take someone else's problem with us—a problem they tossed up there themselves—we would soon all be back at the table fighting to get our old problems back. —*Bo Cox*

# Hard roads

*I am ready not only to be bound
but even to die in Jerusalem
for the name of the Lord Jesus.*
—Acts 21:13

After I concluded my first burial service, I lingered by the gravesite and asked my mentor priest, "How do we ever bury a child?"

He responded with no hesitation, "We do it because we have to."

Three weeks later, when he was on vacation and I was alone in the parish, I got a call from the hospital that an infant had died. The mother was asking for a priest. I did that burial with the senior warden standing beside me holding the processional cross. Every time my voice cracked, I remembered the words of my mentor and leaned harder on my senior warden's shoulder.

Paul knows he must go to Jerusalem. Though Agabus, the Caesarean prophet, and the members of that young church beg him not to go because they foresee his destruction at the hands of the authorities, Paul will not be deterred from his march to the holy city (Acts 21:10-14). It seems the old apostle sees something they cannot see. Paul has processed through the new churches now dotted all about the Mediterranean. He has witnessed the mighty work God is doing. Therefore, when Paul is warned of the torturous route that awaits him, just as Jesus was warned before him, he can remain obedient to God's call. He can lean on the love of Christ's new disciples planted both near and far.

What hard road are we being asked to take? Where do we find the courage? We find it by leaning on Christ's faithfulness and the love of our brothers and sisters who kneel with us shoulder to shoulder at the altar rail. —*W. Patrick Gahan*

# *Getting in spiritual shape*

My sweaty forehead pressed against the floor, I reach behind me for a leg I know is back there somewhere—if only I can reach it. Our "prayer in motion" retreat leader's voice is steady and soothing—"That's it... turn...and reach...feel the stretch...don't forget to breathe..." I am turning and reaching and feeling, but breathing is something I have forgotten to do. I gasp. How can anyone breathe in such a contorted position? How can such physical torture have anything to do with spiritual formation?

Combining contemplative prayer and yoga might be considered a stretch, but few practices have better clarified for me the truth about spiritual formation. Like any physical discipline, spiritual formation is not necessarily easy or pleasant; it is often challenging, even painful.

Forget the official definitions. Spiritual formation is nothing more than answering Jesus' command to the deaf man: "Ephphatha!" That is, "Be opened!" Opened to hear the sandaled feet of Christ come closer. Opened to feel the radiance of his Spirit grow warmer. Opened to encounter the divine, healing nature of God even in the dark depths of our human reality.

I let go of my leg and lift my head for an ant's eye view. Some are calm. Others grimace. Still others lie flat in quiet resignation. Clearly, though, I see that all of us have at least answered that command, opening ourselves to the God who stretches, molds, forms us into who we are called to be. —*Jerald Hyche*

# *Gallantly*

My friend is dying. She's had cancer for eight years now. Some would say she's already cheated death. She was only "supposed" to make it to five years. As recently as two weeks ago, she had color in her cheeks. Now that color is gone. She can talk, with effort, but she can no longer move. Nurses need to turn her in her bed.

She didn't want to be bathed yesterday. She doesn't want to see friends anymore; she doesn't seem to notice flowers; she doesn't seem to have the energy, or interest, in hearing about cards and letters friends have sent. Her thoughts have turned elsewhere. Maybe systems are just shutting down.

But maybe there is something else going on as well. Her soul is about to go on a new adventure, a journey into eternity. Maybe her soul is using what energy it has left to prepare for that flight—and for its separation from loved ones, dearly loved ones, in her own way.

"If I am to lie low, help me to do it patiently. And if I am to do nothing, let me do it gallantly," I quoted to her from the Prayer Book. "You're being gallant," I said. "That's you. Gallant." She laughed. Who doesn't want to be gallant, especially in the face of death? True to the end, spirited, brave.

That same prayer ends: "Make these words more than words, and give me the Spirit of Jesus." *The Spirit of Jesus.* God, I ask that for her: Your Spirit, your promise of new life. Your presence with her now, as she suffers, and your presence with her then, at the moment of death. And forever, keeping her next to your heart. *The Spirit of Jesus.* Thank you. —*Lindsay Hardin Freeman*

# *A God who moves*

In 2007, I flew to New York City to take possession of our first apartment here. I set up camp with an air mattress, folding chair, lamp, and tray-table. It felt cold and unfriendly. I wondered what I was doing moving my family here. I went to a local market, D'Agostino, to buy supplies. It felt cramped, dirty, and unfriendly. I vowed never to shop there again.

Much has changed in two years. Thanks to my wonderful wife and the arrival of furniture, the unfriendly apartment became a warm home. Every day I see abundantly why we moved here. And today, I returned to D'Agostino and thought it was great: spacious, clean, and friendly.

What changed? I changed. My perspective changed. Thanks to the stresses and strains, joys and adventures of living here, I am a different person.

That's how life is. We change as we live. Some of the changes feel positive, some feel negative, but we are the sum total of both. We learn especially from our failures and disappointments.

I think of God in this same way. I know that for some people, it is an article of faith that God never changes. I don't want to trample on that belief, but I believe that God does change over time, in response to the creation God made and especially in response to humankind. That's the nature of love. Just as the birth of a child transforms two parents, so God hears our cries, sees our pain, knows our failings, watches our dreams, walks with us, and is moved to some form of response. Compassion and mercy, for example.

If we don't expect God to listen and be moved, why do we pray? —*Thomas L. Ehrich*

# Remember who you are

My parents were in later life when they had me. Mother and father were both forty when I was born, in an era before it was fashionable to delay parenting.

My folks guided me with gentle but sure hands. How they could be so confident with their first attempt is beyond me, but they were. They instinctively knew that I would never willingly do anything to disappoint them.

Since my father was a newspaper reporter, my family was widely known in the area. You could find us at all the major sporting events, political rallies, and town hall meetings. All this meant that I had to behave myself everywhere I went. If it takes a village to raise a child, it took the surrounding counties to raise me.

When I was old enough to drive a car, I wanted a little more freedom. This was fine. I knew where I could go, with whom I could go, and what time I was expected back home. As I left in the evening, the door never got quite closed without me hearing my father's voice saying, "Remember who you are." That was all, just four words, but they kept me out of more scrapes and more trouble than I could begin to recount.

Over the course of the past several years, as we have witnessed the shame of Abu Ghraib and the fallout of a massively flawed economic strategy, I have wondered how things might have been different if certain key people had been able to hear my father's words ringing in their ears: "Remember who you are."

Thanks, Daddy. That's one story I know you got right.

—*Gregory A. Russell*

# *Herod and Pilate*

When I read the Bible I do not always find myself in good company. King Herod was the one who beheaded John the Baptist (Mark 6), and Pilate ordered Jesus' crucifixion (Mark 15). While I have never actually given the command that took another's life, I have fallen to the same pressures that led my infamous companions to make those decisions. It is said that King Herod so admired and feared John that he resisted pressures to have him killed, but when his stepdaughter memorably danced at his birthday party, he publicly promised her anything she wanted. At her mother's instigation she asked for John's head on a platter. Herod was loath to do it, but was embarrassed to back out on the promise made in front of his guests, so John was killed. Similarly, Pilate was convinced of Jesus' innocence but "wishing to satisfy the crowd," handed him over to the cross.

You see my connection to these two. Perhaps you can feel your own. How many times have I gone along with a conversation, a joke, or a cruelty because I did not want to appear "uncool" or obnoxiously pious? How many times have I been silent when there were opportunities to bear witness to my beliefs and principles? How many times have I been Herod, embarrassed to do what I knew was right, or Pilate, more afraid of what the crowd might whisper than what my conscience was shouting?

One of the most subtle temptations we fall prey to is confusing virtue with a lack of opportunity. I have not ordered anyone's death, but then I have never had the power or responsibility to do so. I have many times, however, walked the path chosen by Herod and Pilate. —*Francis H. Wade*

# The good books

I'm spending these days in the Florence of the Renaissance, in a Yiddish community in Alaska, in sixteenth-century India, and in twentieth-century Istanbul. I read until I can't keep my eyes open, and then when I fall asleep I dream about what I read.

I study scripture, but I rarely read theology for pleasure. I read novels, history, biography, and other nonfiction, but not theology. My reason *is* theological, though: we find God in the conversation of history. God happens among us, steadily and with ongoing creative power. The traces of God become visible as we look around us. I prefer to see God there.

I prefer to write God there, too. To signal the happening of God in words, so that someone reading it can see: that is the theology of writing. Just as theatre isn't religious simply because actors appear in their bathrobes and call each other "thou," it is not only in books about God that we see God. It would be a paltry God indeed who could only inhabit places everyone already agreed were holy. A God incarnate walks our earth and steps in our mud, sees what we see, thinks and feels with us.

And yet, it cannot be that God is simply a supernatural being, a figure like Paul Bunyan who is like us except really big and strong. All religious language is metaphor. God cannot be "a being." God must be *being* itself, the fact of existence—or God cannot be at all. Visible in the events of history for those with the eyes and the will to see, God can never be contained in it. God is free, or God is not God.

I finished *The Yiddish Policemen's Union* this morning. It's my day off. Now I've started *The Enchantress of Florence,* and I have somebody's old copy of *War and Remembrance* on the shelf for a reread. Gorgeous. —*Barbara Cawthorne Crafton*

# Basset/Leviathan

A basset hound once stole my heart. It was frigid weather, "snow on snow" as the carol hymns it, and what with repeated meltings and freezings, the sidewalk near my friend's house was several sheets of ice, one on top of another.

We were standing near his drive when we looked up at the odd sound of an oncoming clack-thump—and there coming toward us was a neighborhood dog, a large, lowly basset hound. Bassets were bred to have short strong legs, low bellies, and large jaws so as to move easily through low brush and hunt rabbits. Their bellies often hit the ground between leaps, and in this case the clack-thump of claw and belly on ice was just for getting up speed.

Before our eyes the mighty beast gained traction, lifted his front and rear paws, and slid past us on his tummy, with that wonderful jowly, ponderous face gazing out oh-so-seriously, like a British butler on a banana peel.

The combination of utter seriousness of visage while engaged in so obviously a fun and funny task stays with me as a message of the lightness and sense of humor built into creation.

Our spiritual ancestors understood this. Speaking of the Lord's creation of the great and wide sea and its inhabitants, the psalmist said, "There is that Leviathan which you have made for the sport of it" (Psalm 104:27). Just for the sport of it, just for fun.

To play, to enjoy, to have a lightness of being amidst all the supposed seriousness of our lives is part of what it means to dwell in the image of God. —*Leonard Freeman*

# *Loving the unloveable*

He does nothing right. Stomps up the stairs giving me a seething, hateful look. Slams the door of his room that is cluttered with papers, half-eaten burgers, crunched CDs. Sullen, clumsy, overweight, did this child come out of my body? In my fantasies of a dream child, I had pictured a slim, happy, athletic boy. But this?

If only he were nice to me, if he appreciated the things I do for him, I could love him. But he doesn't. Ugly words spew out of his mouth. Hands over his ears, he screams for me to leave him alone with his games and the Internet.

What am I supposed to do? I dislike him, my only child. He makes my life ugly on a daily basis. I read books and columns and seek advice. Nothing works.

What does Jesus say? Heal the leper, befriend the friendless, be merciful, and feed the hungry. He tells me that this kid is a friendless, hungry leper. He urges me to let go of my parental pride, my fear of what people will think, my fear that this kid will stay like this until he is fifty, my dread that this kid is like the secret part of me that I hate. Jesus says I can feed this child with what he needs. Jesus says that I don't have to get advice from anyone else, that I already have the food this child needs. He says, "Find the good and praise it."

I look for the good in this child and the only thing that comes to mind is how he treats his lizard. He loves that lizard. I tell him, "You really love that lizard. You're a good pet owner and a loving boy." He looks at me; he hears me. —*Carol McCrae*

# What the wise man knows

*When all the trees have been cut down,*
*when all the animals have been hunted,*
*when all the waters are polluted,*
*when all the air is unsafe to breathe,*
*only then will you discover you cannot eat money.*
— Cree prophecy

What a quaint saying. It was written by someone who, I am sure, never rode across a crystal-clear lake on a waverunner that cost more than a couple of semesters of college tuitions, or skied behind a boat that cost more than most U.S. families make in a year. I'm sure the author of those words never held the keys to a million-dollar house or sat back after a Sunday spent manicuring a seven-acre, $500,000 lawn, sipping tea and gazing out over his domain. This person was never in charge of a budget. He never had to meet production deadlines, manage a stock portfolio, or ponder the mysteries of commercial finance.

This person might, however, comprehend domination from the bottom side. He might see very clearly the dichotomy, the either/or it creates. He might recognize that the world is comprised of haves and have-nots, not people who work and study hard and those who don't. This person sees that, at its core, true religion points toward less, not more, and wisely shakes his finger at false religions that push a heavenly endorsement for personal prosperity.

This person understands that if you throw a rock in a pond there will be a ripple, no matter how big or small the rock or the pond. And he knows how destructive it is to look at the world through self-centered and short-sighted eyes.

This person knows that a culture built on "Manifest Destiny" will someday crash. —*Bo Cox*

# Taking in the Word

*Blessed Lord, who caused all holy Scriptures*
*to be written for our learning:*
*Grant us so to hear them, read, mark, learn,*
*and inwardly digest them...*
—The Book of Common Prayer,
Collect for Proper 28

"Hear, read, mark, learn, and inwardly digest" are among the most oft-repeated words from *The Book of Common Prayer*. They refer to all we have been given in the biblical text, and counsel everyone to attend to it frequently and with due diligence. No direction is offered—about the means of interpretation to be used, about what is historical fact and what is myth written to encourage and guide—only that we should attend with care to what has been given to us through the record of God's involvement with his people.

As we hear, read, mark, learn, and inwardly digest, we learn not only of God's acts in times gone by, but we also become more aware of God's continuing presence among us at all times.

All things that matter, matter for all time and become ingrained through repetition. Once is never enough. The words "I love you" need to be repeated, again and again. They cannot be said often enough. What the Bible has to say to us bears repetition, requires repetition, demands repetition. What it has to say may be complicated or disarmingly simple, but it will not be available to us unless and until we have made it part of the basic and essential fabric of our lives. —*Edward S. Gleason*

# *What motivated Dr. King?*

*There is no longer Jew or Greek,*
*there is no longer slave or free,*
*there is no longer male and female,*
*for all of you are one in Christ Jesus.*
—Galatians 3:28

February is Black History Month, and my daughter's third grade class studied Dr. Martin Luther King, Jr. I was surprised and saddened that nowhere in the material did it mention that Dr. King was a Christian and the pastor of a church. Nowhere did it mention that he baptized people, officiated at weddings and funerals, taught Sunday school, struggled over sermons, and wondered why the people in his congregation could not get along. I shared with my daughter that Dr. King's work and ministry were a reflection of his faith in Jesus and a hope for the kind of world that Paul described to the church in Galatia. She seemed surprised, and then a little proud.

Jesus declared again and again that the kingdom is at hand, so close that we can all reach out and touch it, a kingdom that Dr. King learned about from Jesus. —*Jason Leo*

# *Not for everyone, and that's okay*

Big day at the mailbox today! My tickets for the 93rd 500-Mile International Sweepstakes, also known as the Indianapolis 500, arrived in a plain blue envelope.

Again this year, our six seats are across from the Start/Finish line, near the end of Pit Road, a term that means everything to race fans but little to anyone else. I had requested seats closer to the First Turn, but they weren't available. "How many years of upgrading would it take to get to Grandstand E in the First Turn?" I asked a Speedway clerk. "You won't live long enough," she said.

As we watch from Box 65 of the Paddock, surrounded by 400,000 fans, race cars will go by at 220 mph. A bit fast for noticing details, but exciting, deafening, powerful. Pure heaven if you like it; torture if you don't.

One great joy of the human adventure is that we don't have to enjoy the same things. I would find a dog show absolute tedium, for example, but would travel far for seats at the Final Four in college basketball. When I tell friends that my family will be trackside on Memorial Day weekend, some roll their eyes in disbelief.

It might seem odd, perhaps unfortunate, that the United States has over three hundred distinct Christian denominations, not to mention thousands of one-of-a-kind, nondenominational churches. But as with sports and romance, we don't have to agree on the nature of God. Nor can we compel anyone to accept our views. God seems larger than any of our belief systems. We each see an aspect of God, and if Christians could stand to listen to each other, we might learn more about God.

Will we live long enough to see oneness happen? Probably not, but I sense movement toward acceptance of other beliefs and those who believe them. —*Thomas L. Ehrich*

# "No one can make you feel inferior without your consent"

Of all the remarkable things Eleanor Roosevelt said, none is more memorable than her oft-quoted remark, "No one can make you feel inferior without your consent." This was a lesson she learned early in life, especially in relation to her mother (who disparaged Eleanor's physical appearance) and to her stern and disapproving mother-in-law (who lived for many years with Eleanor and Franklin at Hyde Park). She went on to apply that lesson—"No one can make you feel inferior without your consent"—to the victims of discrimination, oppression, and systematic disregard. She stood for and with African-Americans when segregation was still national policy. A priest friend of mine has taken Eleanor Roosevelt's idea and made it her own in her prayer that we not become "agents of our own oppression."

To say that "no one can make you feel inferior without your consent" is not to blame the victim. There is real oppression in this world, and the responsibility for it lies squarely with the oppressors. Oppressors can subjugate me without my consent, but they cannot make me feel inferior to them unless I give them permission.

In Elizabeth Bishop's beautiful short poem "Filling Station," the speaker surveys the order and beauty of this shabby little place and concludes that "Somebody loves us all." Somebody does love us all, and that makes us worth a good deal both to that Somebody and to ourselves.

"No one can make you feel inferior without your consent." Today is a good time to start refusing to give it. —*Gary Hall*

# *Road rage*

One day in Britain, with my family in a small rental car with five-on-the-floor and driving on the left, I experienced the power of humility.

Humility is often misunderstood as a form of lying. The hero or heroine has just done something remarkable, but when it is commented upon tugs at a forelock and says, "Aw shucks, it was nothing"—when everyone knows it was really something! True humility on the other hand is knowing the truth about ourselves—what we have to offer and what we do not—and acting upon that truth.

As I entered onto a main road from a confusing roundabout on that Gloucester day, I felt anxiety pouring from my veins. In my anger and fear I honked loudly and long at a sports car that cut briskly in front of me while I labored at the gears.

That car abruptly stopped, and a young, strong, tough-looking driver climbed out and approached my car with fire in his eyes. Road rage personified. As I sat with my family, I wondered what to do.

The truth seemed simplest. Letting the window down a bit I said: "I'm sorry. Could you help me? I'm an American and I'm lost and I'm confused, and I'm not good at this car. Could you help me find my way?"

A blank pause, then "What?" I repeated my request for help, and the moment changed from challenge to aid. He gave me directions. I followed him to the next roundabout and then waved a thank-you goodbye.

Scripture tells us that the truth will make us free. The truth of our own vulnerability—some humility as to who we are and who we are not—can often "change the game" in a saving way.

—*Leonard Freeman*

# *Finish the work*

Jesus says in John 14:16 that he was completing his work and passing it on to us. We are the body of Christ, the chosen people, not to be above others, not to be glorified, not to receive special favors, but to serve.

Every time I lie down in the muck and whine about the trivia of my life, Jesus prods me with a stick, tickles my ribs, and says, "Get up, woman! Get up and get moving!

"Cry if you must. Cry, as I wept over Jerusalem. But let your tears be over the ruinous events of your country and the world. Then dry your eyes and go do something about them. Finish your piece of God's work. Pray and then go practice."

I think about this as I get up, and I hear a further voice: "Don't forget to laugh. Laugh at the ridiculous situations you bring on yourself. Laugh at how seriously you take yourself. And laugh for the sheer joy of life, as I did at a wedding. God prefers a dance down the aisle to a solemn procession. God delights in all people who refuse to remain victims, who get up and move on."

Amen, Jesus. It's not always easy for me to stand on my own feet. I have problems. I can get locked into self-pity. Thanks for reminding me that my work is to help those who also want to stand.

What other hands does God have in this world but our hands?
—*Lee Krug*

# *Giving thanks*

Ten lepers cried out, "Jesus, Master, have mercy on us!" as Christ entered their village (Luke 17:13). Ten lepers asked for help. Ten lepers were healed. Ten lepers went skipping off to a new life, transformed from untouchables to normal healthy men, suddenly returned to membership in their old world. One leper came back to thank Jesus and to give God praise.

"So where are the others?" asks Jesus. Ten were healed; only one bothered to acknowledge the miracle to the miracle worker. That's human nature for you. We can focus pretty tightly on our prayers when we need something, when we want something, when we're in pain, when we're afraid. But when that pain or fear has dissipated, it's easy to overlook giving God our thanks. Maybe we forget how it felt. Maybe we assume things would have gotten better anyway, without the power of prayer. Maybe some part of us doesn't think it's important.

It is, though. The thanks themselves are important. The balance is important. The very understanding of what is a blessing is important. It may not always be obvious. My grief over my mother's death is visceral. Understanding that her relatively brief decline and her lack of pain at the end were blessings needs a more intellectual acknowledgement, and in the first days and months after such a loss, I didn't feel particularly intellectual. It all takes time to sink in.

Sometimes we have to sift through the gravel of life like a prospector searching for gold. When our prayers are answered—when we find a brilliant nugget amid the rough rocks and sand—we owe God our thanks. It's worth making the trip back to say so. —*Sarah Bryan Miller*

# The extra mile

The story is a famous one. Jesus was teaching from a home in Capernaum. The crowds were thick as usual. Some enterprising fellows, concerned that their paralyzed friend would not get close enough to be healed, cut through the roof and lowered the stretcher literally onto Jesus' lap. It is a great story of ingenuity and healing, until we recall that Jesus was an itinerant preacher.

He probably did not own a house in Capernaum, so his teaching venue was borrowed, as his crib had been and his tomb would be. Did the person who let him use the house think he was agreeing to have the roof ripped off? I doubt it. He could have foreseen the crowd stepping on his wife's begonias, maybe pushing the livestock around, but the roof? He did not sign on for that!

We all know what it feels like when we find that we are going to have to be a lot nicer, more generous, more tolerant than we thought we were volunteering to be. Lead the stewardship campaign? Chair the bazaar? Have your spouse's college roommate and family visit "for just a day or two"? "See what you can do with the financial records—it shouldn't take long." Nobody sets out to deceive us. It is just that sometimes, to paraphrase Hamlet, there are more things in a job than are dreamt of beforehand.

Jesus healed the man on the stretcher. What could he do to heal the consternation of his benefactor? Thank him for his unplanned generosity? Explain that the extra mile is not always a chosen mile? Remind him that life is not predictable? Point out that love's required forbearance takes many unexpected forms just as love's joys do? That would help—but the roof still has a hole in it. —*Francis H. Wade*

# The albatross

Ever since the publication of *The Rime of the Ancient Mariner* by Samuel Taylor Coleridge, the albatross has gotten a bad rap. We don't normally find these wondrous creatures hung heavily around our necks; they roam gloriously free over the oceans of the world. Uniquely adapted to gliding on a locked wingspan nearly twelve feet wide, these seabirds can soar on oceanic winds for years without touching land.

But despite their remoteness, albatross feel the acute impact of fishing fleet harvests and the far-reaching drift of pollution. The web of life, while magnificent, is also exceedingly fragile. Even the smallest event can ripple out with a negative and often unforeseen impact on the delicate balance of nature.

We also experience this rippling effect in human society. The recent economic upheaval, for example, has shaken everyone from Wall Street to Main Street, Peru to China. All life on this planet is intricately interwoven. And our keen awareness of this fact lays a solemn responsibility upon us all—*Homo sapiens*, the species richly blessed "with memory, reason, and skill" (*The Book of Common Prayer*, p. 370).

A common misconception is that Christianity's sole focus is the personal relationship between God and each individual. Holy Scripture, by contrast, teaches that we live within a wide-ranging, complex web of important relationships. We don't belong to ourselves alone, but to God, one another, and all of creation. Therefore, God calls us to take great care as our words and actions ripple out into the world.

The albatross has survived by adapting over the past twenty-five million years. May the human family continue to seek new, creative, and loving ways to adapt in the swiftly changing environment that is our habitat—"this fragile earth, our island home" (*The Book of Common Prayer*, p. 370). —*Charles F. Brumbaugh*

# *Here today, gone tomorrow*

Just seven years ago, Gene, my youngest brother, age thirty-eight, retired to his bedroom for his customary Saturday afternoon nap and died. My family was devastated. Yet it could have been worse. A few months before, Gene had confessed his alcoholism, successfully completed residential treatment, and became an ardent, two-meetings-a-day member of Alcoholics Anonymous. For the first time since he was seventeen years old, Gene was sober and fully himself in the presence of his family. He began truly to experience his days, and we began to experience him in genuine ways again. But then, far too soon, he was gone.

James tells us we are here today and gone tomorrow. "You are a mist that appears for a little while and then vanishes" (James 4:14). Sincere humility should be our only posture at the beginning of each day and at the inauguration of any extensive future plans. James insists that each day is a gift from God. Human beings will never change that fact. What's more, our humility in the face of our own tenuous life here should lead us, if need be, to change the direction of our lives and the way we treat others. James states, in effect, that we are always preparing to die, so that we can fully live.

Acknowledging we have no lease on life is a spiritually sobering act. —*W. Patrick Gahan*

# Homeless for a night

For years our parish provided food and clothing for the homeless in New York City through what we called the Midnight Run. One day the director of that ministry challenged me to experience homelessness for thirty-six hours. I was to dress in old clothes, take no more than five dollars, and spend two days and one night on the streets.

The first hours felt like a field trip with new and exciting sights and sounds on street corners, in subway and train stations. Then it became a bone-chilling, mind-numbing time of aches and hunger. I spent a terrifying night in a shelter with a hundred other men, many of them sick, drunk, psychotic, and smelly. But some seemed just like me, except perpetually down on their luck.

The next morning a man named Carley from the shelter came limping toward me. "You look pale, boy," he says.

"I'm hungry."

"Take up a collection."

"I don't know how," I said, shivering.

He told me to wait and limped off, stopping as people passed him. He spoke to people as they left the deli or subway. Most ignored him, some shook their heads, and a few placed something in his hand.

After twenty minutes he made his way back. He dug his chapped hand into the torn pocket of his coat and presented me with everything that was there. He admonished, "Take care of yourself, boy." He started off but then turned back, and I thought he was going to ask for some of it for himself. Instead he handed me an orange from the other pocket.

I said, "God bless you."

He said, "He does, every day of my life."

I counted the offering: a subway token, a crumpled one-dollar food stamp, and $3.40 in cash. Just in time for breakfast.

—David L. James

# Safe crossing

On my morning walk I turn a corner and see my friend Lorene, the school crossing guard, at her post. When I come near enough I hail her with a "Good morning!" I try to be heard above the wind. She answers, but the weather is noisy, and our words are lost among the snowflakes. With no children ready to cross the street, Lorene comes over to where I stand. I tell her that my wife's surgery was successful and there was no sign the cancer had spread.

"Well, thank God," she says. "My sister had breast cancer and they got all hers, too."

I say, "I appreciate your prayers."

Turning to go back to her post she tells me, "You're welcome, honey; you've got them every day." I believe her.

Lorene is at her post every school day, in all kinds of weather. She has been a crossing guard for twenty-two years, and at this corner for seventeen. Day by day she sees hundreds of children safely across two streets busy with I'm-a-little-late-for-work traffic. "I love this job," she once told me. The children and their parents obviously love her. A couple of years ago when there was a death in her family, third graders at the nearby school sent her notes of sympathy.

I have great admiration for Lorene and all crossing guards. They remind me of all the people in my life who have helped me across the treacherous parts, sometimes putting themselves in harm's way, walking with me for a little while, seeing that I get safely to the other side.
—*Robert Horine*

# Hope for new possibilities

A friend became severely depressed. He called his mother to inquire about depression in the family's history and she said, "There have been no crazy people in this family and you aren't crazy either. Get yourself together and get on with your business!" No wonder people keep their depression close to the vest.

Martin Luther King, Jr., described depression as "spiritual exhaustion." As a pastor I have dealt with a legion of depressed folk, one describing himself as "in a swamp of sadness." They speak of great anxiety and of everything gone wrong; the flavor of ground glass; feeling emotionally frozen and unable to make decisions, read, write, pray, enjoy company, or keep track of daily things; a pain in need of redress when no redress is possible; constant anger. Depression calls to mind Sisyphus and his endless climb, pushing a rock uphill knowing it will always roll back down and have to be pushed up again. Maybe depression derives from getting wise to the futility in pushing rocks up the hill again and again. Or maybe it marks the moment the rock we are accustomed to pushing lodges against another rock and stops, suddenly confronting us with the question of our purpose.

I hope for my depressed friends that contained within it all is a kernel of hope for new possibilities. The poet Rilke wrote:

> Were it possible for us to see further than our knowledge reaches, and yet a little way beyond the outworks of our divining, perhaps we would endure our sadnesses with greater confidence than our joys. For they are the moments when something new has entered into us, something unknown; our feelings grow mute in shy perplexity, every-thing in us withdraws, a stillness comes, and the new, which no one knows, stands in the midst of it and is silent.

—*Richard L. Shimpfky*

# *The power of love*

**W**hen I hear the guitar chords come pounding through from Huey Lewis and The News at the start of their 1985 hit single, "The Power of Love," the lyrics uplift me with their practical, obvious truth.

> *You don't need money, it don't take fame.*
> *Don't need no credit card to ride this train.*
> *It's strong and it's sudden and it's cruel sometimes.*
> *But it might just save your life.*
> *That's the power of love.*

Warren Buffett says the same thing: "I know people who have a lot of money, and they get testimonial dinners and hospital wings named after them. But the truth is that nobody in the world loves them. When you get to my age, you'll measure your success in life by how many of the people that you want to have love you actually do love you. That's the ultimate test of how you've lived your life."

Buffett is right. One way I know he's right is from hospital visits. In three decades of visiting hospitals, I have never yet heard someone tell me that he wishes he had done a better job with his career. Not once! What I have heard many times is someone wishing he had spent more time with his children, or treated his first wife better, or been less demanding with his teenaged son. People end up measuring their success in life not only by how many of the people they want to love them actually do love them, but also by how—and whom—they have loved.

That is, indeed, the power of love. —*Paul F. M. Zahl*

# *For love or money*

With my arm around my beloved, drowsily waking to the day, I thank God for the gift of the beautiful man beside me. This is the second man I have deeply loved. The first died seven years ago. I feel a pang of guilt. Isn't it greedy or unjust to have two? Many people don't have one, or, even worse, they have neglectful, angry, or demeaning relationships. Why? Inside us dwells the Holy Spirit, guiding us toward the people who are good for us.

I've always known whom I liked and whom I didn't. You have, too. As children, we ran to those we were attracted to, and no amount of cajoling convinced us to want to be with Aunt Prune or Uncle Should. We lose this connection with the Holy Spirit and the contact with our own joy when we listen to the world, our parents, our peers, the media, or popularity, and not to our own hearts. Our hearts tell us immediately whether we like someone. Our heads over time tell us whether that person is worthy of our love. Others may be impressed by social standing, money, power, or education, but attempting to love someone for these reasons will only dry up the soul.

Too many hurting people befriend, love, or marry someone for his or her potential or for the glimpses of good they see deep in that person. It's God's job to unearth that potential, not ours. We can't bet our love and our lives on the hope that he or she will change or that a mere spark of potential will produce a flame.

That is why Jesus said a person can't serve two masters—God and mammon. God is love. If you go where the love is, you will be blessed.
—*Carol McCrae*

# The conquest of space

Somedays I fret that my life has been too narrow—centered as so much of it has been on the parish church. Doesn't the very noun *parish* give us the sometimes pejorative adjective *parochial*?

My high school friend Mike tried college at Tulane for a month, hated it, and without a by-your-leave from anyone went down to the New Orleans docks and shipped out as a seaman on a freighter to Australia.

I saw him ten years later when he came back to the United States for a visit. He had been doing underwater demolition for harbor construction all over the Orient. "You always load the charge with this much explosive because if it backfires, you want to be sure to go with it," he told me. I was agog at such Hemingway-esque nonchalance.

Occasionally I mutter to myself, "He's sure seen a lot more of life than you have with your cautious career in Mother Church." But what if I were to tell him something I've learned? That the journey of the spirit is also perilous, that prayer is to my realm of life as dynamite is to his, that the divine reconstruction of the human self is an adventure involving the highest possible stakes? In short, that there is more than one kind of breadth to life, just as there is more than one kind of narrowness.

"One who knows distances out to the outermost star is astonished to discover the magnificent space in one's heart," observed the German poet Rilke. A person like Mike, who's lived in the wide-open spaces of the world's oceans, might understand. —*Bruce Birdsey*

# *A small thank you*

The table was set at the local nursing home for about twenty local clergy. A small bag of goodies sat at each place. Steaks were being grilled, the smell wafting through the room. Usually when I visit a nursing home, grilled steak is not what I smell. This was different.

I had rushed over after a staff meeting, seeing the event on my calendar but not thinking about it, just doing the normal dash to the next obligation. There are lots of meetings in this clergy life, too many. I expected this would be the normal monthly meeting for area pastors, but it turned out to be an appreciation lunch, sponsored by the nursing home chaplain, for clergy who call on residents.

I wasn't expecting that. I don't expect appreciation in this clergy life, for I figure our job is to serve Jesus and to appreciate *him*—not the other way around. If appreciation comes, that's great, but if it doesn't, it's not part of the deal we're promised or should seek. The clergy are supposed to help laity feel inspired, involved, and appreciated.

The chaplain got up and said thank you for our work, both in our own churches and the nursing home, then introduced residents to talk about their lives and ministries. We left renewed. And, as we found later, hidden amongst the candy and chocolates in the little bag was a $20 gift certificate to a local bookstore. Totally unexpected. But a nice surprise.

Such expressions of thanks are small when compared to the words we hope to hear at the end of our lives: "Servant, well done." But even small words seem large along the way. —*Lindsay Hardin Freeman*

# *A work in progress*

Since faith, like politics, is inherently contextual, I need to identify my context: New York City, Upper West Side of Manhattan, worst economic downturn since 1930; amid cascading bad news, living into my dream of supporting my family by writing, publishing, and church consulting; nervous about my prospects, working hard.

By the time these meditations appear, all that might have changed. We might have moved. The recession might be ending. My business venture might have gained solid ground or crashed. These glimpses might seem outdated, even quaint. But moments-in-time always shed light.

Further context: I am searching for God with new eagerness. The God-of-the-Church whom I knew faintly in childhood and served diligently for most of my adulthood needs freshening. It is a time of listening, in an awareness that God must be more than Sunday services and occasional arguments.

Mine is a faith in progress, not a finished product. I don't want to rehearse worn themes. That would waste my time, and yours as you read these words.

On Ash Wednesday, my seventeen-year-old son and I went to a neighborhood church that I had noticed while walking. Odd little place, I started to think—then caught myself and said, No, not odd, just different. Trying to be true to itself. Just as I, after many years of tilting at church windmills, am trying to be true to my quest.

I want to be free to bring the self that I am today before God. I must, therefore, accept that in others. We aren't called to be alike. We are called to find God in each other. Our journey isn't toward normalcy or sameness. Our journey is toward a light being refracted into countless bands. —*Thomas L. Ehrich*

# No ordinary days

*I will turn aside and see this great sight,*
*why the bush is not burnt.*
—Exodus 3:1-12

I've always liked Moses for saying this. There he is, minding his own business and his father-in-law's sheep, on an ordinary mountain on an ordinary day, and suddenly mystery breaks in—a bush, burning in the distance, is not consumed. I like his sense of curiosity—his almost scientific interest in this great and improbable sight.

What I like, too, is that when he approaches the bush, any sense of detachment gets blasted away. Mystery intervenes, a voice calls out his name. And in a flash, his father-in-law's ordinary acre of pastureland becomes a sacred spot, a mysterious place of divine encounter.

Stories like this make me wary of regarding any day as ordinary. We tend to occupy our place in the world as if mystery had long since fled. But you never know when the bush might start burning again. You never know when you, too, might step aside in idle curiosity to investigate some great sight, only to find yourself standing barefoot on sacred ground, hearing God calling you to a bold new life that you never would have imagined could be yours. —*Roger Ferlo*

# Everyone has a prison

*We who lived in concentration camps can remember the men who walked through the huts comforting others, giving away their last piece of bread. They may have been few in number, but they offer sufficient proof that everything can be taken from a man but one thing: the last of the human freedoms—to choose one's attitude in any given set of circumstances, to choose one's own way.* —Viktor Frankl

I was thinking that getting used to being out of prison was perhaps the hardest thing I'd ever done until one day it dawned on me that getting used to being *in* prison was no cakewalk. I had grown accustomed to prison. Never mind that it was something that at one point in my life would have been unimaginable. Never mind that prison was painful and real and scary. Never mind that it was one of the most traumatic events in a string of traumatic events in my early twenties.

I became so used to prison that when I was released I had difficulty adjusting. At times, I might even have found the familiarity of prison preferable to the unfamiliarity of the outside world. Both then and now, I have more peace when I'm helping others.

Prisons come in myriad forms, and I can tell you three things:

(1) Everyone has a prison.

(2) We can get used to our prisons and think they're the norm, so much so that when we step out, we want back in.

(3) In or out, solace comes by finding and helping others who have more troubles than we do.

If you are standing at the gate of your prison—little matter if you are going in or coming out—trembling at the unknown, take a deep breath and look for someone to help. —*Bo Cox*

# *Direct us*

*O God, because without you we are not able to please you...*
—The Book of Common Prayer,
Collect for Proper 19

What a deceptively simple thought! Imagine, a world without God. No boundaries. No definition. Endless nothingness. No beginnings and no endings. Nothing. Complete freedom surrounds you, but if you allow your imagination to take hold, you realize that absolute freedom is not freedom at all. What it brings is no meaning, nothing, which is quite the same as endless and limitless imprisonment. There is nowhere to turn and no reason to be. This is the world without God.

Jean Paul Sartre wrote, "Hell is other people," words describing our frustration with intractable, thoughtless persons who are sometimes placed near us. Hell may be defined in another way. Hell is a vacuum; hell is nothingness, the world where we are unable to please God, because God is completely absent. This is the reason we say, with thanks, "without you we are not able to please you." Nothing matters more.

As the number of my days increases, I discover that when I first open my eyes, I give thanks—thanks for another day, thanks for my best friend, my wife, lying next to me, who gives shape and meaning to this and every day, thanks for God who gave us life and our lives together.

It is not complicated. It requires but one thing—our willingness to accept God's presence, God's love and our dependence upon it. It all began with God and begins again, each day, with God, if we are open enough to say with thanks, that "without you we are not able to please you." —*Edward S. Gleason*

# Who's in charge?

*I came that they may have life, and have it abundantly.*
—John 10:10

We have a church cat named Elvis. He came from a shelter where he had lived for many years. His first few months with us, he hissed and ran every time someone came near him. Very slowly, Elvis started to warm up to the parish, allowing people to pet him, and even offered gratitude for cat treats and food. He is now loved and revered by all, and I often hear the children from the Sunday School shout down the hallway, "I love you, Elvis!"

The church has so much to offer people. We are a warm and welcoming community where there are no outcasts. We offer faith rooted in the conviction that God reaches out to each and every one of us. We claim a love so powerful, so contagious, that it can transform the heart of anyone and everyone, even the most skeptical and indifferent soul.

Our new bishop made a surprise visit one Sunday. Elvis climbed into the pew next to him and they stared intently at one another for some time. It was as though each was trying to communicate that he was in charge. We can give thanks that God is in charge, and that with God all things are possible, even the transformation of our lives. —*Jason Leo*

# *Cold night, warm heart*

It was a cold night in New York City. Against the chill, the lights down empty side streets seemed like a dim gasp against the dark. Before long it would be a deep-freezing night, and anyone trying to sleep on those streets, even over the steam grates, would be in danger of never waking.

The police patrol car turned onto the block where a bag lady shuffled down the sidewalk. Pulling abreast of the woman, the officers tried to get her to let them help her into the safety of the homeless shelter only a few doors back. She looked at them blankly, then fearfully. She wouldn't listen. She mumbled. The officers realized that she was one of New York's walking wounded. Released from some hospital's mental ward because she had been stabilized on medications, she was now back on the streets on her own, had lost or stopped her medications, and was back into her insanity.

Reason was not one of her current options. But the law was clear. A recent court ruling had said the authorities could not force a homeless person into a homeless shelter without consent. Legally, technically, the officers were supposed to drive off and leave her there to freeze or not on her own. And they almost did.

But one of the policeman said "Ah, the heck with it." He went back, picked her up, and carried her into the shelter where she spent the night in warmth. "She reminded me of my mother," he later told his partner.

This is a true story and a good one. We live not by the letter of the law, but by the spirit. And by every word to our hearts that comes from the mouth of the Lord. —*Leonard Freeman*

# No distinctions

*For there is no distinction between Jew and Greek;*
*the same Lord is Lord of all*
*and is generous to all who call on him.*
—Romans 10:12

It's easy to forget how radical Christianity was in its early days. The Jews disdained everyone else, but they were hardly alone in that. Every family, every tribe, every people disdained all others; each considered its religion and customs as superior and those of outsiders as grossly inferior.

And this has changed in the last two thousand years…how? Well, despite the fact that lots of people still despise and even slaughter outsiders, Christ not only gave us a reason to embrace outsiders, but also commanded us to do so. Any Christian who looks down on the other—whether that other is a foreigner, a member of another denomination, a member of another political party, a resident of another country or another part of this country, anyone who's different for any reason—is forgetting that very basic aspect of the faith.

As one of my Lenten disciplines this year, I am examining my own prejudices and seeing what I can do to undermine them. Few of those prejudices are the obvious ones, but that doesn't make them any less harmful to my spiritual health. The same Lord is Lord of all. Until I can see that clearly, I will not be living my faith as Jesus commanded.
—*Sarah Bryan Miller*

## *Angels unseen*

When my wife was studying at the University of Chicago Divinity School, Bond Chapel was renovated. Bond Chapel is an exquisite little midwestern-gothic jewel of a building, with dark wood, deep-toned stained glass, and a slate floor. It is one of the few places I have visited which immediately inspired my reverence; in fact, it drove me to my knees.

During the extensive renovation, workers discovered a series of medallions at the points of the arches that support the roof. On each of the medallions was a bas relief angel, each one different. They had been covered over by years of dust and ascending candle smoke. They were in fact so obscured that no one had known they were there. It was nice to have them back.

When it came time for the chapel's service of rededication, the preacher for the day mentioned the recovery of the angels and we all welcomed them home. He noted that the angels are not unlike those people who love us and pray for us and, in a sense, hover round us— people whom we may not notice or indeed even realize are there. They are our unseen angels.

It was a compelling point, and he then went on to say, "You serve that same function for someone as well, you know. You do realize that, don't you? There are people to whom you are kind and emotionally supportive, for whom you are their angel, perhaps recognized, perhaps not. It doesn't really matter whether or not you are recognized. Be kind and supportive anyway."

Which leads me to ask two questions: Who are your unseen angels? And, whose unseen angel are you? —*Gregory A. Russell*

# Life is lent

As part of our reflections during Lent we might ponder the fact that life itself is lent. Our lives are lent to us for varying amounts of time. The gift of life during that time belongs to us, and, as with any gift, we may choose to put it on a shelf, throw it away, share it with others, hide it in a closet, admire it, use it every day, or "return to sender."

I had a friend who died at thirty-nine, leaving a devoted husband and two young children. Was she given only half a life? No way. Into her years she packed a career of helping others, a happy home, and a church she delighted to serve. Hers was indeed a life full to overflowing.

Gifts do not bring obligations; they bring possibilities. How do you spend your time? Many of us say we are too busy; we just can't keep up with ourselves. We may get all the tasks done, but still feel we are falling short. We may have brains that are shackled to the past and losses that hold us hostage.

We forget that a gift is meant to be enjoyed. How can we enjoy the gift of life? The first way is to build into our routines space for what nourishes us. It may be just doing nothing for a while. We need to make room for whatever brings us peace and pleasure.

The first way prepares us for the second, which is to do something meaningful for other people. Life is not given us to be hoarded, but to be spread outward and connected in healing ways with other people. Lending some of our life to others is a way to say to God, "Thank you for the gift." —*Lee Krug*

# *A return to orthodoxy?*

A lot of people want the world and the church to shape up and fly right. They want to be told what's what—orthodoxy (right teaching). Theologian Kenneth Leech describes what he calls "the orthodox project" as "the holding together of apparent contradictions and ambiguities." That's not what you might think of right away as a definition of orthodoxy. Heresy longs for easy simplification and cannot stand paradox and ambiguity. Leech describes heresy as "straight–line thinking, preferring a pseudo-clarity to the many-sidedness of truth, tidiness to the mess and complexity of reality. Orthodoxy by contrast is rooted in the unknowable." Yet many who insist on orthodoxy are uncomfortable with the unknown.

Archbishop Rowan Williams tells us that orthodoxy is an exhilarating truth that makes us happy. "To speak of orthodoxy as a truth that makes us happy is not always the first phrase that might come to mind because we have, sadly, come to think of orthodox belief as a set of obligations to sign up to, rather than a landscape to inhabit with constant amazement and delight of the discovery opened up." *

I am attracted to Rowan Williams not only because of his articulation of theology as a converting conversation with mystery but also because he is deaf in one ear. He has to listen carefully. Theology is always an encounter with the unknown. We are called to stay together patiently in love, and to resist the urge to parade convictions and go off to do our own thing with the like-minded. True orthodoxy requires listening. That seems to be an art we have lost. It's time for us to return to it. —*Alan Jones*

* Rowan Williams, "To What End Are We Made," an unpublished address, April 7, 2005.

# Clean the windows

I live in a large city, and the living room windows of my apartment look westward on a beautiful park. Every spring I have the windows cleaned, and for a while the view is crystal clear. But the prevailing winds blow from the west, and gradually over the summer and fall the windowpanes begin to cover with pollen, dust, and exhaust from the street below. By winter, when the days are short and the darkness lengthens, my windows are the most clouded, and while I can still see across the park, the view is distorted.

This is generally the way sin operates in my life. Gradually, slowly, almost imperceptibly, the sins of my daily life—the self-centered desires of my heart, the casual dishonesties, my indifference to the suffering of others, all the ways I rebel against God—accumulate on the windows of my soul, clouding and diminishing my vision. And then when things are darkest and I need God's light the most, my ability to see and receive it is hindered. I have learned that I need to clean the windows of my apartment more frequently, and the same applies to my soul.
—*James L. Burns*

# Any day now, the quickening

Up through the snow they come, the first brave spikes of this year's daffodil crop. And the primroses' crunchy bright green leaves, sharp against the dark mat of decaying leaves that covers the ground. Soon it will be time to prune back the butterfly bushes and the lavender in preparation for the growing season, and any day now I can bring some forsythia into the house, where it will fill the rooms with bright yellow blooms as part of a process mistakenly called "forcing"—you don't have to force them. You don't even have to put a nickel in. They're eager. We all are.

I have visited in the South several times in recent weeks, breathed its softer air. There, I have touched actual azalea blooms. *Soon,* I have told myself, *soon we will have these at home.* Any day now, I will see a snowdrop. Azaleas in two months, the first daffodils in one. Then the tulips. Later on, lilacs. The cats petition to go outside several times a day now. It's windy and still brisk, but they're ready to go. "It's too cold," my husband says, calling to them in vain from the kitchen door. "They'll be fine," I remind him. Cats have fur.

All of us are coming out of hibernation. The scandal of an early Lent also means an early Easter—the penitential season seems to speed by when it comes early like this, a natural effect of the shorter days. Easter will be here in just a few weeks, and all nature knows it. Even the accountants will close a first quarter. "Just wait," I tell Anna. "Pretty soon you'll feel it. Soft, like butterflies. You don't even realize what it is at first. But then it will just keep coming." Like everything else in this pregnant season.

Oh, vegetable rising, animal quickening, both within me and around me, welcome! I did not know how I longed for you until I felt your flutter, began to smell your first humid stirring.
—*Barbara Cawthorne Crafton*

# The grip of suffering

Jack Kerouac was on to something when his character Ray Smith met his muse, Japhy Ryder, at the start of *The Dharma Bums* (1958). Ray tells Japhy that he is not interested in the "mythology and all the names and national flavors of Buddhism, but was just interested in the first of Sakyamuni's four noble truths, *All life is suffering*."

Almost the whole of Kerouac's prodigious output is a reflection on that "noble truth" that all life is suffering—and through a Christian lens, for Kerouac himself was always a Christian to a lesser or greater extent.

The author of Ecclesiastes understood this. Saint Paul understood it when he observed that "the whole creation has been groaning in labor pains until now" (Romans 8:22). And we believe the Lord Jesus was *the* Man of Sorrows, acquainted with grief.

I have on my study table the drawing by William Blake of a drowning man, his hand upstretched above the wave, going under for the third time, with Blake's handwritten title, "Help! Help!" I listen frequently to Fleetwood Mac's single, "Save Me." And the truth of Kerouac's view of life, buoyed by an Eastern phrase yet underlined poignantly within Christianity and Judaism, is something quite unarguable.

Everywhere I turn in ministry I come upon suffering, even acute suffering. I come upon memories of deceased daughters and estranged sons, resentment of absent fathers, neglect of aged mothers, fortunes lost and homes foreclosed. When the courtly old obstetrician in John Ford's movie-parable, *The Sun Shines Bright*, observes that he has brought several thousand babies into this "vale of tears," we murmur yes. Our lives confirm the fact of suffering, universally, without exception.

All the more comfort in the fact that Jesus saves.

—*Paul F. M. Zahl*

# *Among the missing*

What happens to enthusiasm? Why can't we sustain it, hold on to it and the energy it gives us? Scientists tell us that our senses are geared to change. This is why we notice odors when we first come into a room but not after we have been there a while. Maybe our spirits have a similar shut-off valve that protects us from whatever dangers may be lurking in sustained excitement.

Consider the story of Bartimaeus, the blind beggar of Jericho who cried out as Jesus and his entourage marched by on their way to Jerusalem (Mark 10:46-52). His need was so great that he would not be quieted by the shushing of the disciples. And when Jesus heard and healed him, he was awash in joyful enthusiasm and followed Jesus, undoubtedly "leapin' and dancin' and praisin' God," as the song says. But in all the lavish detail given of the last week of Jesus' life, there is no mention of Bartimaeus.

One would have expected him to be front and center in the temple, bearing witness to all that Jesus had done for him, testifying at the trial, weeping at the cross.

But he is absent. Why? Maybe his enthusiasm went where mine seems to go when it is simply engulfed by routine. The Bartimaeus in me gets excited about a discipline, an insight, a project, an experience of God, but it soon washes off. How many Ash Wednesday commitments actually make it to Easter?

How many altar vows crumble in day-to-day life? Jesus talked about the Bartimaeus in us when he told the parable of the sower (Matthew 13). It is a good story for meditation halfway through Lent when our Bartimaeus starts to slip. —*Francis H. Wade*

# *Freedom*

*O God, who art the author of peace and lover of concord,*
*in knowledge of whom standeth our eternal life,*
*whose service is perfect freedom...*
—The Book of Common Prayer,
A Collect for Peace

When I was in college, what mattered most was wondering, planning, praying about what to do with the rest of my life. Your life should matter, I told myself, not just for you, but for other persons. The professions—law, medicine, education, the church—pointed the way. I sought others who might have the same concerns but found few. The situation has changed little. What matters to most people is making money, getting ahead, doing better than the next person: go to a good college, then graduate school (preferably law or medicine because the pay is good), find the best job and highest salary. Sounds a great deal like "one damn thing after another." Until—until what? Death, that's what.

When Endicott Peabody founded Groton School in 1884, he chose a Latin translation of "whose service is perfect freedom" as the school motto. His goal was to civilize the barbarian rich. One student—Franklin Delano Roosevelt—listened carefully to Peabody and saved the lives and futures of millions of people.

One thing, only one thing, really matters. It is serving others, giving back in the name of God who has given you everything. How do you serve, where do you serve, whom do you serve? To whom much is given, much is expected, but it's more than that. It is realizing that everything you are, all that you have, everything you do, is a gift—a gift from God. We have been placed here by God to serve God's purposes. This is perfect freedom. Everything else is captivity and charts a straight path to death. —*Edward S. Gleason*

# *Be kind*

One of my favorite quotes, often attributed to Philo of Alexandria, is "Be kind, for everyone you meet is fighting a great battle." It acknowledges that life is difficult and that, while our individual battles may or may not be perceptible to others, we are all struggling.

So "be kind," Philo advises. Practice compassion. This isn't *noblesse oblige*, gliding through life reaching down to pat the head of another who is sputtering along. "Compassion" comes from a Latin word meaning "to suffer with." To be compassionate is to keep company with a fellow sufferer.

It isn't easy to practice compassion. After all, who wants to admit to being a fellow sufferer when only flawed people become entangled in addiction, go through divorce, lose their jobs, become dependent on others, or fall from grace? Who wants to sit helplessly in the presence of another's pain that we can't "fix"? And who wants to get sucked into the mire of another's problems when our own burdens overwhelm us?

And yet compassion is at the heart of the Christian mystery. God loved us so much that our Creator, in Jesus, shared the human experience with us—celebrating at a wedding, dining with sinners, holding squirming children, tending the sick, wrangling with the arrogant, wrestling with demons. But it was in Jesus' self-giving on the cross that God most clearly suffered with us. And to this very day the risen Christ's faithful companionship encourages us with the hope that our suffering will not be the last word.

Everyone is fighting a great battle. The dope dealer on the corner. The squad leader in Kandahar. The starving mother in Darfur, the financial advisor on Wall Street, the angry stone thrower in Gaza.

So be kind. Practice compassion. Suffer together. And the Risen One will be with us. —*Charles F. Brumbaugh*

# Never left behind

*Therefore, since we are surrounded by so great a cloud of witnesses,
let us also lay aside every weight and the sin that clings so closely,
and let us run with perseverance the race that is set before us.*
—Hebrews 12:1

Our neighbor's dog died recently. She and her husband are members of our parish and live around the corner from the church. A few weeks later, she walked by our house with the new dog she had adopted from the local pound. Lucy Brown was a real American mix with a lot of character and looked, as my son pointed out, "to be a little fat for a pound dog." It turned out that Lucy Brown was pregnant. Four of her puppies went to families in the church, and the runt of the litter joined our family.

Lucy died suddenly a few months after repopulating the neighborhood, and we were all very sad. When I walk through our neighborhood with our new puppy, we are often greeted by siblings from Lucy Brown's litter. I am reminded of how thankful I am for her short time with us and that her presence is still so strong.

The church's claim is that once you "buy the farm," you own a piece of the farm. Forever. In a way, this explains the communion of saints and the truth that those who have gone before us in their journey with Jesus are still present with us. We are never alone, never left behind. We are surrounded by a great cloud of witnesses. They continue to bless us, and even now cheer us on from the other side of the kingdom.

—*Jason Leo*

# *Who is he?*

Traffic was at a standstill, horns blared. "Lord, I'm late—help me, please!" The truck ahead of me wasn't moving.

A disheveled person lurched across the street in my direction. I rolled up the window and looked deliberately in the other direction. He kept coming and started tapping on my window. I rolled it down and he said, quietly, "The truck is parked." Sheepishly, I thanked him and proceeded on my way. Whoever he was, he had saved me in my distress.

Often it is a stranger who succors us and provides what we seek. The one we need is perhaps not out there somewhere, but among us, nearby, perhaps even within us. Because we look for salvation in faraway places, we fail to recognize the saving one in our midst. We miss, as Kierkegaard said, "the alarming possibility of being able." An important part of Jesus' being among us is to empower us to be able—able to be, to become, to stand in the storm; able to survive, to win the victory, to move beyond the hurts, pains, and losses that should devour us; able to stay afloat in our marriages, divorces, jobs, illnesses, and moments of loneliness, grief, and pain.

The derelict on the street woke me up to the traffic problem and to the grace of finding that what I need is provided, right where I am. It is often the stranger who mirrors the promise of God in Christ.
—*Richard L. Shimpfky*

## Connection and communion

Carol Hofstadter, aged forty-two, died of a brain tumor when her children were five and two. A few months later, her husband Douglas, a professor of cognitive science, was looking at her picture. "I looked at her face and looked so deeply that I felt I was behind her eyes, and all at once I found myself saying, as tears flowed, 'That's me. That's me!'"

What happens when a scientist asks a personal question like "What kind of creatures are we?" The mind is not, after all, a centralized thing. What's more, we send little flares into each other's brains. "Friends and lovers create feedback loops of ideas and habits and ways of seeing the world," said columnist David Brooks, writing about the Hofstadters in *The New York Times*. We flow in and out of each other more than we realize. We are permeable.

In Sebastian Faulks's novel *Human Traces,* there's a story about a priest traveling in a coach. One of the fellow passengers "was a coarse woman in plump middle age with a greasy bonnet who told a story of how she had been abandoned by her husband, taken up by another man, for whom she had borne a child, then deserted once more." The priest "felt a profound and disabling emotion pour through him. He experienced a sudden and irresistible feeling of identity with her…it seemed as though his blood were in her veins and that her despair was the charge that animated his perception of the world.…His obligation was not to diagnose her but to love her." This is the gift of connection and communion. We are all in this together. Our job is not to diagnose each other but to love each other. —*Alan Jones*

# Time outdoors

I read a while back that crayons are no longer made in natural colors. The new crayons display an array of electric or artificial colors instead. This change was made because, according to research, children no longer draw directly from the natural world. Instead of drawing grass, trees, and houses, they draw cartoon characters and superheroes.

Like our children, we adults are spending less and less time outdoors. Our work takes up an increasing proportion of our waking lives, and much of our work is done indoors. Our recreations have become more passive than active, watching and listening to others rather than acting and creating ourselves. It is easier and more comfortable to do passive work indoors than out.

One Lent I decided not to give something up, but rather to take something on. The practice I took on that year was simple: I resolved to spend at least some time of each day outdoors. While it may have sounded easy, it was in fact hard to do. The press of life's business made it almost impossible some days to stop and take a walk, even for a couple of minutes. At the end of that Lenten period, I understood more profoundly how much I was alienated from the natural world.

Nearly one hundred and fifty years ago Henry Thoreau experienced this need for daily connection with the natural. "In my walks I would fain return to my senses," he wrote. If my primary daily sensory reference is the artificial world of computers, televisions, and indoor light, I become disconnected from my bodily animal essence. It is only by maintaining daily contact with nature that I remain grounded in the real, that I return to my senses and am the person God made me to be.
—*Gary Hall*

# Drafting missionaries

We were taking apart the dryer at 10:00 p.m. last night. This was not my chosen task on a Monday night after returning from Austin only an hour earlier, but Kay thought we needed to seek out a malodorous varmint perhaps decaying somewhere in the entrails of the dryer's whitewashed metal body. After grappling with a score of metal screws and yards of colored wires, we failed to find the culprit, but I have learned these thirty years not to impede Kay's household missions. She is a 5'4" force with which to be reckoned!

Paul, too, confesses that his task of ministry began in the face of an overpowering force (Acts 26:1-23). Governor Festus sends Paul to King Agrippa so that the king might glean something damning from Paul's defense that Festus can then pass on to Emperor Nero. Paul, in one of his more flamboyant moments, stretches out his hand toward Agrippa like an esteemed Greek orator and presents his biography somewhat differently than he had done earlier before Tribune Lysias and the apostle's Jewish adversaries. This time Paul does not report his blindness, but he does elaborate on the words Christ spoke to him on the Damascus road: "It hurts you to kick against the goads," a familiar Greek quip meaning it is useless to contend against a higher power. Paul cannot impede Christ's chosen task for him to "open the eyes" of others.

Christ is not asking for volunteers. He is drafting missionaries.
—*W. Patrick Gahan*

# *Daylight Saving Time*

My computer clock has sprung an hour ahead. So has my cell phone. The kitchen clocks, however, require human hands to acknowledge the vernal switch to Daylight Saving Time. So in one room it is 7:30 a.m., while in another it is only 6:30 a.m.

This twice-yearly resetting of clocks is such an intriguing conceit: that we can control time. In a way, we do control time, of course, in that we define it, declare its markers, divide the globe into zones, and set the clocks that provide our sense of time.

On the other hand, time's meaning is elusive. Watch sand flow through an hourglass and wonder whether the present moment is real, or just the passing of sand from one chamber to the next. Religion talks vaguely about "end-time," "time-before-time," and "time-after-time," as if those were verifiable facts. Theologians and historians make common cause in presenting time as both linear (inexorable historical movement forward) and circular (cyclical seasons, repetitive dramas of apostasy and forgiveness), the difference being not so much in what is real as in what is sought after.

Some people take days to adjust to this loss of an hour in March. For me, it's just a matter of resetting a dozen clocks. Either way, the sun rises an hour later, and I feel cheated by that. As a "morning person," I care more about early conditions than late. Now I have to wait another month before the sun is rising at 6:00 a.m. again.

If something as basic as time eludes our control and leaves us in different emotional states, we shouldn't be surprised that faith leaves us even more at sea and at odds. Our work shouldn't be to force agreement, but to celebrate the countless "zones" in which we observe and respond to God. —*Thomas L. Ehrich*

# *Helen and the squirrel*

In midwinter we knew our friend Helen was losing a decades-long struggle with cancer. During my last visit we talked about many things, including her black belt in karate. We ended with a prayer entrusting to God all who are dear to us, for this life and the life to come. Helen was silent for a moment, then smiled and said, "There is life to come." A couple of weeks later she died at dawn on her birthday.

She had lived fully. Her obituary said, among many things, that she was an avid reader, a devotee of music from classical and opera to jazz and bluegrass, a storyteller, a gardener, a humanitarian, a good companion, an outstanding chef, a charming and gracious hostess, and a lover of dogs, guinea pigs, rabbits, and frogs. It also noted that she played the piano, flute, cello, and guitar.

In her last days, spent in a room looking out over the yard, Helen enjoyed watching a squirrel, and the squirrel seemed to be watching her. On the day Helen died, the house was silent for awhile and then a ruckus arose downstairs. Dogs were running and barking and moving furniture. The family rushed down to find the dogs chasing a squirrel—*the* squirrel?—which had apparently come down the chimney. The squirrel escaped.

My wife thinks the squirrel was looking for Helen. Another opinion is that the squirrel's visit was to signal that Helen was free and well. I still don't know what to make of the squirrel incident. In the end I guess we'll just have to accept it as it was or, more likely, as we wish it were. —*Robert Horine*

# *Reunion*

My parents used to upset me by "going home" for holidays. What did they mean by home? Home was us, our little nuclear family, not the huge group of older people speaking in weird ethnic tongues, barely understandable to us kids. At home we cooked our normal American food, not this strange-smelling, unpalatable food that we children hid under our plates or our napkins.

Why did we have to be uprooted from familiar places and people? We were annoyed. But we were only children, and the adults—sisters and brothers—wanted to be together. So we kids hung out together, all us cousins, telling on our parents, kid-gossiping, comparing notes on our lifestyles, scaring each other with ghost stories, and later talking about sex. Who better to talk to than a cousin?

As we grew up, there were annoyances and competitions, and we grew away from each other. Who had time? We locked ourselves into our own little nuclear families and celebrated major holidays alone, never leaving home. Our parents died; there were no more funerals or weddings to attend, and we felt dispersed, scattered, rootless, isolated. Then, luckily, one of us was going to a high school reunion, and we piggybacked it with a cousins' reunion.

We came from California, Vermont, South Carolina, New York, New Jersey, and as far away as Shanghai. We converged on the little coal town in which our parents had grown up. We delighted in the ethnic food we once abhorred. We shared photographs and videos of people long gone, and we felt "at home" in a way we had long missed but hadn't known we missed. We had the strong feeling that our parents were looking down and rejoicing with us. This was communion, and just a small earthly sample of our heavenly destination, our true home. —*Carol McCrae*

# *Who is Jesus?*

*But who do you say that I am?*
—Mark 8:29

Brother Ron Fender, a member of the Episcopal Brotherhood of Saint Gregory, saw Jesus one day. He wasn't "Brother Ron" yet, just Ron. If I remember the story correctly, he was doing his graduate work at Harvard when, walking across the campus one day, he happened to notice a homeless man digging through the trash for something to eat. Their eyes met and in that homeless man Ron said he saw his Lord rummaging for scraps. Right then he knew he was going to become part of a solution to help homeless people, as opposed to part of a system that regularly has folks—possibly Jesus himself—eating out of trash cans.

Not long after that, Ron began a ministry in which he cares for the feet of the homeless. In the beginning it was just Ron, some soap, and a bucket. Today that ministry includes a podiatrist and several nursing students.

You might think it would be difficult to be in the same room with Ron. After all, how could he not have the attitude of "what are you doing for Jesus?" Yet it's nothing like that. He's gracious and unassuming when it comes to discussing what one does with one's beliefs and, in the very end, service to others seems to stand silently as a sort of benchmark.

Still, if I fall prey to comparison, I find myself sorely lacking. It seems, most often, I am more consumed with who I am than with anything else, and Jesus will have to dig through a few more trash cans while I attend to my well-being. —*Bo Cox*

# *God and Caesar*

"Is it lawful for us to pay taxes to the emperor?" the chief priests asked (Luke 20:22). Jesus knows this is a trick question. Jewish law is clear: No, for God is our only sovereign. But if Jesus says this out loud, the Romans will nail him for rebellion. Either way, he loses—as his cunning antagonists expect.

Jesus says, "Show me a denarius." A coin is placed in his palm. He turns it over between his fingers, studying the engraved image and lettering. Then he locks eyes with his adversaries: "Whose head and whose title does it bear?" They answer, "The emperor's." Jesus flips the coin back. "Then give to the emperor the things that are the emperor's, and to God the things that are God's."

Jesus' answer is ingeniously ambiguous. He says nothing to stir up the Romans. Yet he knows what those "religious experts" also know: "The earth is the LORD's and all that is in it" (Psalm 24:1). Including the emperor.

And you. And me too.

It's one thing to chuckle over Jesus' slick repartee with his adversaries. But it's another to realize that Jesus is speaking to us too. Jesus gazes into our eyes, into our souls, and softly reminds us: "Give to the emperor the things that are the emperor's, and to God the things that are God's."

*Everything* is a gift from God: the wonder of the universe, the beauty of creation, the mystery of love. Our families and friends. Our food and our homes. Our cars and our clothes. Our jobs. Our time. Our skills. Our very selves. Blessed with such abundance, what does it mean for us to lock eyes with our Lord and respond, "With all that I have, and all that I am, I honor you"? —*Charles F. Brumbaugh*

# *When Jesus wept*

When I grew tired of the sound of my own voice and needed a Sunday off, we occasionally slipped off to Boston for a weekend and worshiped at Trinity Church, Copley Square, a rare parish of great preaching and great music under the same roof.

One Sunday in Lent I heard a communion hymn that mesmerized me. Following the dismissal, instead of walking to the door to meet the clergy and leave, we fought our way upstream toward the choir room to talk to the music director, who was an Oberlin Conservatory classmate of my wife.

I told him of my fascination with the hymn and asked about the piece. He said matter-of-factly, "It's a round in the back of the hymnal, #715, 'When Jesus wept, the falling tear.'"

I said I had been a priest in the church for many years and had never heard it. I wondered why. He said; "Although it's only twenty-four words long, it is very difficult to do well, so most choirs don't attempt it."

During the two-hour trip home, the words of the hymn and the words of the choirmaster kept running through my mind:

> *When Jesus wept, the falling tear*
> *in mercy flowed beyond all bound;*
> *when Jesus groaned, a trembling fear*
> *seized all the guilty world around.*

So short, so powerful, so hard. Just like forgiveness.
—*David L. James*

# A father's hands

*Father, into your hands I commend my spirit.*
—Luke 23:46

The young mother had come in, ostensibly to talk about her son's problems in nursery school. Before long, however, the conversation took an abrupt turn, to her sorrowful disclosures of an affair with a local workman. Along the way the young mother made a passing remark about how the workman's hands reminded her of her father's hands. The line stuck in the back of my head. As she was about to leave I repeated: "Your father's hands?"

Out poured her painful story, unspoken until then, a tale of incest and childhood betrayal by the one who should have protected her, but who instead was a predator.

We do not all get the fathers we need in this life. Some are abusive, some are cruel, some just don't care. When a father's love is absent, it creates an enormous, gaping hole that demands to be dealt with later, one way or another.

Deeply, primitively in the best sense, our human hearts ache for and need good fathers—protectors, guides, mentors. We long to know that the one who brought us into creation essentially loves us.

And this, when all else is said and done, is part of the deep grace proclaimed by our Lord Jesus Christ, when he taught us that "we are bold to say, Our Father..." That is the Father of all creation, but also our own personal father—my creator, my father—who will not betray me, but holds me in his love always, and who cares even at my darkest moments.

*Abba,* our Lord taught us to call him. Daddy.

Thank you. —*Leonard Freeman*

# Eighth grade confirmation

As lector this coming Sunday morning, I will read the epistle to a congregation enhanced by an unusually dressed-up group of eighth graders and swollen by the addition of visiting grandparents, godparents, and others. Our episcopal visitation takes place this week, and we will have confirmations during the eucharist.

Our eighth graders this year include my younger daughter. She had decided, not quite at the last minute, to be confirmed. I've retrieved a family heirloom cross from the safe-deposit box, had it cleaned and placed on a new chain; now I must prepare for the visiting grandparent and godparents.

Eighth grade is an odd time to ask our children to renew their commitment to Christ and make one to the church: awash in hormones and itching to be just a little independent, they are seldom greatly enthused about confirmation. I look at my daughter and remember that at her age I went through my own brief atheistic phase. I outgrew it in six months, but it's just as well that I was confirmed at eleven instead of fourteen.

Yet here she is, a part of a good-sized group. And here is the author of 1 Peter: "Come to him, a living stone...a cornerstone chosen and precious." We have brought up our children in the church, we have taught them our faith—or tried to—and now we present them as members of that chosen race, that royal priesthood, that holy nation.

Some of them won't take up residence in the holy nation. Some of them will drift away and return in a few years. I find hope in the fact that my daughter made this decision on her own, without coercion, despite doubts. May she live in God's marvelous light, may she know God's mercy, may she always taste that the Lord is good.
—*Sarah Bryan Miller*

# A suprising day in March

Sun poured down on the Upper West Side. Spring flowers peeked through the snow in Central Park. Runners toiled in shorts, impromptu soccer games ignored fresh mud, and everywhere, from the rhinoceros playground to walkways to benches, I could feel the mood lightening, elevating, positively soaring on this fifty-four-degree day in March.

Not that it has been a harsh winter in New York, weather-wise. But it has been an awful winter in the marketplace, as thousands lost their jobs, sales became elusive, and luxury stores suddenly found the word "luxury" a tarnish. Any change for the warmer is welcome.

Early spring can be cruel, of course, and the recession seems poised for a long run. But we enjoy what we can, while we can.

That's a solid biblical theme, isn't it? Hebrew history is a grim recital marked by occasional bursts of life, grace, song, and triumph. The ministry of Jesus began and ended in conflict, and along the way he endured betrayal, misunderstanding, and accusations. And yet there were moments of light, when his goodness brought glimpses of grace that no oppressor or nay-sayer could douse.

We live for these moments of grace. They not only lighten the momentary load, but they assure us that God isn't far away and humanity's lot, while challenging, remains bound in the heart of God. The storms won't destroy us. Our own folly won't be the final word.

So, I say to you on a surprising day in March: Go outside and enjoy the warmth of God's love! Dare to live, because God dares to love! Though the market is shaky, the ground of our being is solid.

—*Thomas L. Ehrich*

# *Another surprising day in March*

And so it happened, suddenly, yesterday's fifty-four degrees became today's seventy, and the park, streets, and playgrounds are brimming with life.

How could this be? That was the question they asked about Jesus. How could he just appear and speak with such authority that even the evil spirits submitted to him?

What little we know of God invites that question again and again. How could such grace suddenly appear in our lives? It's the element of surprise and also of extravagance. No one woke up this morning deserving what Haydn called "gentle spring, ethereal mildness." It just came, and we are blessed beyond our deserving.

Imagine a God who isn't bound by our standards of deserved and undeserved. Imagine a God whose life is brimming with a life to share. Imagine a God who looks at us with compassion and gives us what we had stopped imagining could be ours. Love, after all these years. Light, after all this darkness. Spring, after all this winter. Joy, after all this sorrow.

My wife and I went for a walk on this bountiful spring day. Our steps were lighter, and our hearts were open to all. The irritating seemed charming today. The gray seemed vivid. The way forward, so clouded by the current economic downturn, seemed hopeful. We became agents of grace ourselves, bearers of spring. —*Thomas L. Ehrich*

# *Jesus our night vision*

I still replay those first television images of the world at war in my mind. Captured in the emerald green glow of night-vision technology, fighter jets take off from the carrier. Tanks and armored vehicles caravan through the desert. Silent missiles hit their marks, leveling buildings, spraying debris, killing bystanders.

Even as the sunlight bathes my world, I still wonder when the true light will appear to break the darkness of this time over there. And almost as soon as I ponder that question, an answer arrives in the words of Psalm 119: "Your Word is a lamp to my feet and a light for my path." Of course. The Word himself proclaimed that truth: "I am the light of the world. Whoever follows me will never walk in darkness but will have the light of life" (John 8:12).

Through this and any dark hour, Jesus is our night vision. Through him, we see clearly through the darkness that shrouds our world in supposed peace as well as war. Through him, we see clearly ourselves as we truly are—sinners in need of a savior. Through Jesus, we clearly see hope even in the murky violence brought by war.

The night will pass. The sun will rise. But the night will come again. The light of Jesus, however, shines on, leading us to a place where night and day are both alike. The light of the world is an eternal, unchanging light, fueled by a love that never fades, a love that heals us inside and out, restoring the division within us—and between us. —*Jerald Hyche*

# *The shadow knows*

At the time I had no idea that I was the terror of the neighborhood, causing concern among mothers and other interested parties. It was wartime, and like other children across the United States we were playing war, slaying battalions and even regiments of our enemies. No one wanted to play the bad guys, so we had to imagine them as we stormed the beaches or fought our way through the narrow streets of French and Italian villages.

The mothers were worried because while their children were equipped with toy guns, I had a real .22 rifle, though it was broken and its firing days long past. The other boys were envious; they wished they had real rifles. And we all wished we were big enough to go shoot or bomb enemy soldiers. We were young savages. Why do you think the young are recruited to fight?

For the rare days we wearied of war, I also had a real sword to play Robin Hood or pirates—another source of concern on the one hand and envy on the other. It was my grandfather's lodge sword, bearing on the hilt the initials FCB for friendship, courtesy, and benevolence. Grandpa said it stood for fresh country butter.

And then there was the cape. My mother had been a nurse. Wrapped in her cape I became the Shadow, able to "cloud men's minds" so they could not see me. And able to know what "evil lurks in the hearts of men."

The rifle is gone. The sword, refurbished, hangs in our family room. The cape has a few moth holes but lives as a treasure in an upstairs closet. If I put it on now, would I know what evil lurks in the hearts of men? Sadly, I don't need it anymore. —*Robert Horine*

# *Rose*

In my first job after seminary, I worked at St. Paul's Cathedral in Boston. In that congregation was a woman named Rose, an older woman who seemed ageless. Rose had a great presence, energy, humor, and strength. You treated her kindly and with respect because that's the way she treated you. She kept all of us on our best behavior because she made it clear that she deserved no less.

Rose was in church every Sunday. And every Monday she made soup at the cathedral soup kitchen, warming the basement with both her presence and a savory soup that brought warmth to the city's homeless. The smells of poverty were lifted up and released by the smells of Rose's soup, like incense, carrying the grime of our daily lives to God, replacing it with something holy and life-giving.

One day after church, Rose invited me to her home. As I followed her there, I realized she lived in Roxbury, a poor section of Boston. Some of the houses appeared to be in good repair, but many weren't. Hers was on the border, both physically and economically. It wasn't a safe place. It was only then that I realized Rose was poor. There was no sense of poverty about her, for she was rich in so many other ways. Her soul was brimming with God's spirit and love, and nothing would stop that. She lived in a state of grace. Rose expected and brought out the best in us.

It is to that state of grace that Jesus calls us. Sometimes we just need people like Rose, the salt of the earth, to remind us.
—*Lindsay Hardin Freeman*

# Old and new: the beginning is the end

I'm listening to music that has been preserved in the twelfth-century *Codex Calixtinus*, some of the oldest polyphonic music notation that survives in ink on parchment. The interplay of choral voices would soon become more complicated, but if you go to Santiago de Compostela, you can read a page of that music written when it was new, the very latest thing. The people who heard it then had never heard anything like it before. They must have been thunderstruck.

The *Codex* is kept at the cathedral in Santiago de Compostela, a medieval pilgrimage destination, but it wasn't written there. It was written in France. Besides the music, it contains travel directions, descriptions of interesting places to see along the way between France and Santiago, and stories about the things pilgrims will experience once they get there. It's a medieval *Michelin Guide*.

I close my eyes and I can see the pilgrims: riding on horseback or in carriages, their servants walking. Stopping along the way at an inn, where they eat and drink heartily and then turn in early. Or maybe they don't turn in so early, not all of them; maybe they sit up late by the fire and tell stories. Maybe they sing some of the songs I'm listening to right this minute. Maybe their voices hang in the air, still.

In the domain of God, there is no such thing as time: the beginning and the end are the same. "Old" and "new" are our categories, not those of heaven. So yes, the voices of those first singers, trying to make sense of this complicated new music, *do* still linger in the air like the long ground notes of these ancient songs, while our descant trips and skips above them, for now. Yes, the long dead still live among us, in another way, a way we sense sometimes, but will one day know, because we will be living that way, too. —*Barbara Cawthorne Crafton*

# Nature's double-edged beauty

"And you were a liar, O blue March day."

On March 24, 1878, the British ship Eurydice foundered and sank when a sudden and violent hailstorm appeared out of a clear blue sky. Shortly thereafter, Gerard Manley Hopkins memorialized the wreck in "The Loss of The Eurydice." The startling line above speaks of the painful irony of the horrible happening on a beautiful spring day.

Preachers and film-makers tend to portray Good Friday as a darkly overcast day. We imagine the crucifixion happened in a thunderstorm; we know darkness covered the earth from noon until three. By contrast, we think, that first Easter morning must have been glorious.

We know, of course, that life is not like that. We know that exterior beauty does not always presage internal truth; weather and human suffering are not always coordinated. Part of life's poignancy is that tragedy can overtake us at any time, in any weather.

Another English priest-poet, George Herbert, described a similar day in his poem "Virtue," calling it: "Sweet day, so cool, so calm, so bright!" Like Hopkins, Herbert knew that the world's beauty was one sign of God's glory in the world. But he also knew that nature's beauty has a double edge.

To be sure, there is both hard and good news in that doubleness. The hard news is that nature's beauty is not always trustworthy; we human beings can always delude ourselves, especially in glorious surroundings. But the good news is that even on a cold gray day in a thunderstorm, something wonderful can be on the way. God and God's grace transcend our stereotypes. So in all times and seasons, be on the lookout for what God is up to. —*Gary Hall*

# Gabriel's mistake

The angel Gabriel is the production manager of the Christmas story. He tells Zechariah, the father of John the Baptist, and Mary, the mother of Jesus, what is going to happen and what their respective roles will be. His handling of the two is remarkably different, and I have an idea why. When he tells Zechariah about the birth of John, the future father asks, "How will I know that this is so? For I am an old man and my wife is getting on in years" (Luke 1:18). Gabriel takes great offense at having his message questioned and makes Zechariah mute until the child is born. When Gabriel tells Mary about the birth of Jesus, she asks essentially the same question, "How can this be since I am a virgin?" (Luke 1:34). Gabriel couldn't be sweeter to Mary, explaining that the Holy Spirit will come upon her and the power of God will over-shadow her.

Why the difference? Angels are known for their obedience to God and may have trouble understanding the doubting nature of mere humans. I think that when Gabriel got back to heaven and reported on what had happened with Zechariah, God took him aside and explained the human tendency for doubt. Chastened, Gabriel responded to Mary with a deeper understanding of people. This scenario is fanciful, of course. I picture it because I often make the same mistake.

I cannot understand why, when I explain something clearly and logically, people do not immediately grasp my truth. Why don't they see that my political opinions, theological positions, memories of events, perceptions, prejudices, insights, and understandings are absolutely compelling?

They are fortunate that I lack Gabriel's power to silence their questioning. I am fortunate when God takes me aside and reminds me that skepticism is human nature.
—*Francis H. Wade*

# The mystery of you

Renaissance doctors said that the essence of each person originates as a star in the heavens. How different this is from the modern view that a person is what he makes himself to be.

The Greeks told the story of the Minotaur, the flesh-eating creature with a bull's head on a man's body, who lived in the center of the labyrinth. He was a threatening beast, and yet his name was Asterion—Star. It is a beast, this thing that stirs in the core of our being, but it is also the star of our innermost nature. We need to care for this double identity with reverence so that in our fear and anger at the beast, we do not overlook the star.

When we try to be "normal," when we seek to become "a well-adjusted personality," we undercut another reality. Care of the soul appreciates the mystery of human suffering and does not offer the illusion of a problem-free life. It sees every fall into ignorance and confusion as an opportunity to discover that the beast residing at the center of the labyrinth is also an angel.

Belief can be fixed and unchanging, but faith is almost always a response to the presence of the angel, like the one who stirs the waters. Or it could be the angel who appears to the Virgin Mary and demands absurd faith in his message that she is pregnant with a divine child. Mary says to the angel, "Let it happen to me even though I don't understand." This angel, Gabriel, appears more often than you might think, telling us that we are pregnant with a new form of life that we should accept and trust. —*Lee Krug*

# "He answered them not a word"

Jesus' replies to Pilate and to the Sanhedrin on Good Friday are strong ones: *he did not answer.* Jesus' replies are strong because he says nothing.

As the Negro spiritual puts it, "He answered them not a word, Not a mumbling word." It is true that he answered one time, concerning the Son of Man who would come with glory on the clouds (Matthew 26:64). But the consistent and astonishing tenor of Jesus' "defense" at the point of critical accusation was…silence.

I wish I could be that way! What comes to me is defense and counter-charge, explanation and rationalizing. Jesus did the best thing. He made no answer, trusting God to justify and sort things out.

Did you ever see *The Life of Oharu*? It is a 1952 Japanese movie directed by Kenji Mizoguchi, a deeply spiritual artist. After a heart-wrenching spiral of rejection and loss, the heroine, in the concluding shot of the film, bows her head, with total reverence and will, in the precincts of the temple. It is acquiescence and devotion. It is what the French spiritual writer Jean Pierre de Caussade meant by "self-abandonment to divine providence." It spans all the traditions, and all experience. And when this beautiful movie is over, you want to be like her. —*Paul F. M. Zahl*

# The Final Four

I have moved up to 14,521st place in *The New York Times* NCAA basketball tournament bracket. I was in the 35,000 range at one point, so 14,521 is an improvement. If North Carolina wins the national championship, I could move within 10,000 of first place, I suppose.

In other words, I should keep my day job. I won't make a living handicapping college basketball. Or horses, or stocks, or anything that depends on mastering the orneriness of two-legged or four-legged critters.

Even so, I found myself watching a semifinal game and muttering at the players for errant passes, airball shots, and clumsy hands. Not that I could do any better. But it's fun to care, if only briefly, about the outcome of a game.

Segue now to God. Our Creator has the same problem with trying to resolve the orneriness of humankind. Free-willed creatures insist on living freely, even to the point of self-destruction. God can nudge, God can call, but in the end, believers are as likely to be recalcitrant fools as anyone, and non-believers, well, aren't they often a surprise with their generosity and grace?

I don't picture God as a mildly engaged spectator, but as deeply engaged, deeply troubled when we go astray, deeply gladdened when we find our way home. Our errant choices and clumsy efforts must evoke sighs in the heavenly realm.

And so God bids us turn to prayer. For prayer—if you can stand a seasonal basketball analogy—is like a time-out, a moment when we step off the court and catch our breath, accept some guidance, maybe confess a failing. In that time-out, our "coach" urges us to play better. That's what we so often need: not to win, not to star, but to play better, try harder, give more, trust more.

—*Thomas L. Ehrich*

# Stay

*Thou dost keep in perfect peace*
*those whose minds are stayed on thee.*
—Isaiah 26:3

I'm pedaling furiously, the muscles in my legs on fire. Utterly absorbed in moving the bike forward, I hear a shout from behind, sharp as a pistol crack: "Stay!"

One summer years ago, I enrolled with my young sons in a "developmental cycling" program near our home. Least developed of all the cyclists, I was regularly lapped on the track. The command "Stay!" meant that one of my speedier classmates was about to pass me, so I was not to change lanes. If I did, a collision might ensue. Therefore: "Stay!" Stay on course.

I couldn't diminish the pumping of my legs by so much as a sweat bead; if I slowed down much I'd topple over on the steeply banked track. It was imperative to push ahead, but without deviating an inch from the straight and narrow way.

The implied command in the verse from Isaiah is analogous. Stay. Yes, you must (as the hymn says) stretch every nerve and press with vigor on. But even as you do so, heed the divine counsel: Stay.

Stay. Keep your intention and your orientation fixed on God, even as you move with hectic speed. As you run this day's race, let your mind stay on the eternal stillness, the wellspring of inner peace and constancy.
—*Bruce Birdsey*

*O God of peace, you have taught us that in returning and rest we shall be saved, in quietness and in confidence shall be our strength: By the might of your Spirit, lift us, we pray, to your presence, where we may be still and know that you are God.*
—The Book of Common Prayer, "For Quiet Confidence"

# *Pruning and fertilizing the soul*

*They are like trees planted by streams of water,*
*bearing fruit in due season,*
*with leaves that do not wither;*
*everything they do shall prosper.* —Psalm 1:3

It's not that easy. Even I, the most casual of gardeners, know that trees, even when well-situated, need consistent tending. Like the human soul, gardens are not static, but constantly changing. Noxious, hard-to-root-out plants can spring up overnight and strangle the good greenery; walk away for a week, and you don't know what you'll find (poison ivy, in my recent experience).

To restore a long-neglected yard, I have hired a sort of spiritual director for turf, Tony the Lawn Guy. Like any good counselor, Tony observed the situation before suggesting possible improvements. Despite its dire state, Tony believed the lawn could be salvaged. He began by clearing the thatch, and punching a multitude of holes across the length and breadth of the yard. Next, he cast vast quantities of grass seed over it. Then he set up a system of hoses and sprinklers on a timer, to water it twice a day. For about a week, nothing much was evident except mud. Then one day I leaned over and saw them: tiny, spring-green blades of grass, spiking up from the holes. A few days after that, the new grass was up, confident. We're not done yet, of course. The price of a handsome lawn is eternal vigilance, plus fertilizer.

So it is with us. The gardens of our souls need to be watered with prayer, weeded with repentance, and tended with grace on a daily basis. The longer we put off doing those things that ought to be done, the more we're going to need the pruning sheers and the spiritual equivalent of Roundup. But while we're alive, it is never too late for God's love to make a difference. —*Sarah Bryan Miller*

# *Nine pianos*

How would our church ever integrate? The moment had passed in the late '60s as the neighborhood changed, and we found ourselves a lily-white church amid people of color. The pastor at that time had been ready to retire and did not have energy for a project of that magnitude.

I had been called as associate pastor with the specific charge to integrate the congregation. What to do? This church had an educational wing with nine classrooms, each housing a piano. Since the college conservatory was just up the street, our congregation also had a slew of retired music teachers, mostly piano teachers.

I went to the board. "I have this wild idea. We have all these pianos and all these teachers…" They agreed to an experiment, and pretty soon we had nine volunteers, each agreeing to give six free half-hour piano lessons every Wednesday afternoon.

Up and down the streets of the neighborhood we went. "Hello, we are offering free piano lessons at the church on the corner. Would you have any children that might be interested?" And so it began.

Within a month we had fifty-four piano students playing scales on Wednesday afternoons. Then we added a 6:00 p.m. dinner for them and their families.

The children began to come to Sunday school, then church. We started an "Adopt a Grandparent" program so our folks could help guide inexperienced children in worship. We began two Scout troops. The church became a polling place for voting.

Gradually, parents joined their children. There were plenty of hiccups along the way, but the church finally accomplished what had needed to happen years earlier.

It's amazing what can happen with nine pianos, 126 willing hands, and a little imagination. —*Gregory A. Russell*

# Release to the captives

*He has sent me to proclaim release to the captives*
*and recovery of sight to the blind,*
*and to let the oppressed go free.*
—Luke 4:18

Many years ago, I worked as a chaplain in a prison. I led a weekly Bible study and gradually made friends with many of the prisoners. They were truly a captive audience, full of questions and very interested in the scriptures.

Later we moved to a new city and I was no longer able to serve at the prison. That was fifteen years ago.

Not long ago, I was volunteering at a local soup kitchen in the city where we now live. One of the guests coming through the serving line stopped and stared at me for some time. It took me a moment, but I recognized him from the prison. He had recently been paroled and was trying to get his life in order. We had a good reunion, and he shared that he was still reading the scriptures. He was full of hope for the future and I offered encouragement.

I haven't seen him again, but I pray for him and his new life, and I give thanks to God that he is free. —*Jason Leo*

# *Good Friday, one week early*

One week before Good Friday and what do you know—I see Jesus carrying his cross as I'm on my way to work this morning. I slow to 30 mph just to make sure. Yes, there he is, dragging his wooden cross. Only, it's not the Via Dolorosa; it's the interstate feeder road. And it's not a half-dressed man scourged and beaten; it's a guy in droopy cargo pants, t-shirt, and floppy fisherman's hat. And it's hardly a cross of the old rugged variety; this one comes with training wheels and a little platform near the base on which sits a box of belongings held tight by a bungee cord.

I consider stopping, but can't, swept along in the impatient stream of rush-hour traffic. For a moment or two, I see him in my rearview mirror, but then he is gone, blocked by traffic that carries me around a corner, out of sight, and on to work.

Minutes later, I park in my spot, and I ponder the man. I wonder where he came from. I wonder where he is going. I wonder if I go back over that way, would I find him?

And then an answer comes in the soulful question we often sing this time of year: "Were you there when they crucified my Lord?" And for the first time, I answer, yes. I was there. I was in the city the day it happened. I caught a glimpse of him there on the road. And I understood. He went on his way to giving his life, and as a result—without my having anything to do with it—I could go on my way to living mine.

This year, Good Friday came one week early. —*Jerald Hyche*

# *A new thing*

*Behold, I am doing a new thing.*
—Isaiah 43:19

Without change, we stagnate and die. But change can be terrifying while it's going on. It's all around us, constantly, in every aspect of our lives. There's a reorganization at work, a change in a parent's living situation, a child's choice to do something distressingly dramatic and damaging, the illness or death of someone precious to us. We move to a new house or rehab an old one while living in it, both recipes for stress. The news holds little but reports of change or the promise of it, and not much of it for the better.

Even God's "new things" don't always seem joy-filled while they are in process. Sometimes they're painful, and it's hard to tell if something is from God or has mere human origins; we have to test it. Some people are never reconciled to the changes.

God did a new thing in the person of Jesus Christ, and during the season of Lent we are reminded of how counterintuitive his career must have seemed. A Messiah who spends his time curing all who come to him, Jew and Gentile, instead of vanquishing the enemies of Israel? A rabbi who hangs out with lowlifes and mocks the religious establishment? The Son of God who allows himself to be handed over to the authorities and tortured to a horrible death? And yet this new thing which seemed to end in painful darkness instead brought us all into the light of God's grace. God is forever doing a new thing; let us, in the words of the prophet, declare God's praise.
—*Sarah Bryan Miller*

# *A story worth telling*

"It's an honor to be on this journey with her," he calmly stated. The man was not offering me the particulars of some delightful travelogue, but spoke as he sat beside his dying wife. I had been with him several times over the course of his wife's decline, and his countenance was always the same. As I walked out of the hospital room, I realized why he could look and talk that way: the man knew this was mainly his wife's passage. He was simply grateful to accompany her on the journey.

People have long wondered why Acts ends without a word about Paul's death. In fact, the only history book of the New Testament seems to conclude about midstride with Paul finally in Rome "proclaiming the kingdom of God and teaching about the Lord Jesus Christ with all boldness and without hindrance" (Acts 28:31). Luke, the talented author, is making one last point: Acts is not about Paul's death, nor Peter's. It is about Jesus Christ's journey into death and his resurrection from that death. After having read about the world's greatest apostle in most of the Book of Acts, you have to believe Paul would not have had it any other way.

Acts therefore ends as it began—an account propelled by the truth of Christ's crucifixion and resurrection. Without that fact, Luke really has no story to tell. Without that fact, our own story has hit a dead end as well. —*W. Patrick Gahan*

# *A confession*

For a long time I was convinced that everyone who approached me on streets or in other public places when I was wearing a clerical collar wanted money. This is not so.

Some years ago when my bishop and I were traveling to a meeting in North Carolina, we stopped at a large drug store. We were in different parts of the store when a man walked up to me, thrust out a card, and said, "Read it." I was certain it was the prelude to a request for money and I pointed to the bishop and said, "Ask the man in the purple shirt. He has the money."

The man ignored me, "Read it," he said. I began to turn away but he insisted, "Read it!" I gave up and looked at the card. It was an optical illusion that I couldn't at first make sense of, and then I saw it said, "JESUS." The man grinned and walked away.

Once when I was in a midtown shopping center waiting to meet someone, a man approached and greeted me. I returned his greeting, sure of what was coming. He had some slips of paper in his hand. "I've written a poem," he said, "and I'm giving them out." I took one and, resigned to what I was sure was coming next, asked what he wanted of me. "Oh, nothing. Just say a prayer for me." I told him I would, and he walked away.

I don't know where the poem is, long since lost in moving or mislaid in my files, but wherever its author is, he gets a prayer now and then.
—*Robert Horine*

# *Suffering vs. inflation*

One of the reasons our economy has had such a rocky road in recent years, such an up-and-down ride, is that America has overvalued itself.

I traveled and spoke in California during the heady days of the real estate boom there. Even then, outside Sacramento, you could see that everything was overpriced, overbuilt, and overloaned. There was no way those homes could be worth what the sellers were charging for them. Things were wildly overvalued.

The language of everyday life also became inflated. We were first enjoined to "Have a Nice Day," which soon became "Have a Great Day," which morphed into "Have an Awesome Day." The phrase-inflation of everyday American English was in painful contrast to the facts of actual home life for many people. No wonder prices tumbled! Everything tumbles when there is no accurate view of things.

The widespread suffering of both individuals and families, of which Jack Kerouac spoke at the beginning of *The Dharma Bums,* is real. It undermines inflated claims of human well-being. Let us be cautious when exposed to emotional inflation. Christian faith, in fact, deters us from inflated conceptions of reality. Reality involves suffering, change, and considerable disillusionment. "All is vanity," says the Teacher in the first chapter of Ecclesiastes. And Jesus is crucified for the sins of the world.

Then, too, the redemption, the divine grace expressed in that Man for Others, in his historic life and passion and Easter, can be properly valued and weighed. Given what we need to be saved *from*—the sorrow and self-involvement of human existence—the One we are saved *by* is all the more, well, precious. —*Paul F. M. Zahl*

# Feet, feet, feet

"Feet, feet, feet. How many different feet you meet?"

Perhaps you've read these wacky words and the ones that follow from Dr. Seuss' classic, *The Foot Book*: "feet in the morning, feet at night, left foot, left foot, left foot, right!"

Simple, crazy words, accompanied by simple, crazy drawings that have kept the attention of countless children over the years. But of course—in the typical genius of Dr. Seuss—*The Foot Book* communicates a critical concept without saying what it is, a concept integral to making our way through life. A concept that is a guiding truth for children to grasp and for adults to remember: opposites.

"Wet foot / Dry foot / Low foot / High foot."

"Slow feet / Quick feet / Trick feet / Sick feet."

"Feet, feet, feet. How many feet you meet!"

On Maundy Thursday, we meet Jesus' feet and the seemingly opposite nature of his being. Not as the feet we fall to, but as the feet that carry him to us. No more parables. No more miracles. No more sermons. With deep humility and love, Jesus demonstrates the seemingly opposing nature of his dual identity.

The teacher who takes a seat in the student's desk.

The leader who goes to the back of the line.

The guest of honor who steps away from the lectern and starts busing tables.

The Son of God who suffers a sinner's execution.

Opposites all. Yet in Jesus, one in the same. In his paradoxical nature, Jesus provides us with the highest definition of God's Holy Word. What God did for us. And what we are called—indeed, what we are commanded—to do for each other, however opposite we may seem to be. —*Jerald Hyche*

# The life of all things

So many spent daffodils! Most of them are past their prime here, and the tulips have taken over. And even some of them are blowsy and over-the-hill, and the alliums are readying their assault. None of these glories lasts forever. The garden changes every day; its shocking spring beauty cannot last. One star must yield the stage to another. We take turns in our shining.

The bloom is a stage in the life of a plant. While it catches the human eye more than any other, it isn't the most important—there isn't a most important stage; they're all indispensable. After the petals have fallen to the ground, the leaves continue making sugar out of sunlight and chlorophyll. The roots draw in the rotted wealth of other spent lives, happy to absorb its recycled energy.

I can't keep up with all these faded blooms. I content myself with nipping off a few every time I pass. True, their successors will be prettier, but the real reason for helping them leave the scene is that the leaves and roots will continue to try to support them as long as they are there. They become a dead-end diversion from the work at hand: growth and preparation for the next season's life.

All of life is like that, to be lived in the present and in the future. We can remember the past, and we can love the ways it has nourished us, but we cannot live in it. We must do what we are doing now and prepare for what we will do. We can't afford to divert our energy to support things whose season has gone.

That something comes to an end doesn't mean it wasn't worthwhile. Human things are not eternal; they come and they go. They change from current reality to blessed memory. We need never lose them if we accept this, the life of all things.

—*Barbara Cawthorne Crafton*

# Who is your Helen Louise?

In the book *All I Really Need to Know I Learned in Kindergarten*, Robert Fulghum whimsically but seriously encouraged "seasoned citizens" to rediscover the wisdom that they had first learned in the sandbox at school. "Share everything. Play fair....Clean up your own mess....Say you're sorry when you hurt somebody....When you go out into the world, watch out for traffic, hold hands, and stick together." He challenged his readers to apply these learnings to shape the adult realities of family life and work, nation and world.

I recently visited the congregation of my childhood. Many wonderful people in that faith community helped me grow as a Christian. But no one was more influential than my kindergarten teacher, Helen Louise. Diminutive in stature, she was a giant of a human being.

Helen Louise showed us how to make Advent wreaths. She gave us our first Bibles, our names embossed in gold on the black covers. She required us to memorize the Lord's Prayer. And she taught us to sing "Jesus Loves Me."

I've learned a lot since I left Helen Louise's class some forty-five years ago. I've absorbed ideas and lived experiences that I couldn't have imagined as a kindergartner. But what she taught me then shapes me still, not least of all the good (if incredible) news that "Jesus loves me, this I know." And loves you, too. And everybody.

Helen Louise died at the age of fifty-four. She's buried in the parish memorial garden, along with my father and others who are now numbered among the communion of saints. But she continues to live through me, and through many others whose lives she touched. I give thanks to God, and to her, even as I continue to process what she taught me in kindergarten.

Is there a Helen Louise in *your* life?

—*Charles F. Brumbaugh*

# *Yearning to rise*

The rain broke and sunshine appeared. I immediately thought: let's walk the three miles to 43rd Street and Sixth Avenue for a rehearsal performance of *A Prairie Home Companion*. Stop halfway for supper. Make the entire trip in two hours. Should be doable. A perfect way to spend a crisp day in Manhattan.

An hour later, the clouds returned and rain threatened. Now what? The dream had seemed so enticing. Does the dream depend on weather?

No, the dream has deeper substance. Be outdoors, walk with my wife, explore this amazing city, get deliciously tired. That dream still matters.

Our yearning for God is like this. Sometimes the dream is so near the surface that we can hardly breathe. Other times we keep a lid on, so as not to embarrass ourselves. But the dream is still real. Our hearts ache for God.

I say "our" even though I don't know you, because I believe we all yearn for God. God has placed a yearning deep inside us, and it just bursts forth. Theologians of sin like to describe the human condition as "fallen." I think it would be better to describe us as "yearning to rise." We ache for connection with God. We try other ways to approximate that oneness, some noble and some unsavory, but only God can satisfy the dream.

Cling to your dream, I say. Rise as close to God as you dare, then catch your breath, and rise some more. If you walk downtown from 96th Street, you eventually pass 43rd Street and 4th Street and Wall Street, and you run out of island. But we can never walk beyond God's desire for us. —*Thomas L. Ehrich*

# Stay with us

*Lord Jesus, stay with us, for evening is at hand and the day is past*
—The Book of Common Prayer,
Collect for the Presence of Christ

It's never easy to say good-bye. Years ago, preparing to end our visit, my wife and I were in the car, turning around in the driveway, saying good-bye to our eldest daughter and her family who then lived on the west coast. As we drove away, we turned to see our daughter, her face contorted by grief, crying her eyes out. Neither one of us spoke during the twenty-minute drive to the airport, not a word, until we sat side by side, ready to board the plane.

"What was that all about?"

"One of our good-byes will be the last. We never know."

"Right, but who wants to be reminded?"

The fact is we all need to be reminded, which is why at the end of every day Evening Prayer directs us to pray, "The evening is at hand, and the day is past." We place a period at the conclusion of one experience, one day, then give thanks and ready ourselves for the next day, knowing that the day just past could be our last. One such day will be just that—our last. It's inevitable. We may not welcome it; tears are inevitable. Still, we give thanks to God for all we have been given through God's grace and mercy. —*Edward S. Gleason*

# Cosmonauts of inner space

During the space race of the early 1960s, the Scottish novelist Alexander Trocchi once called writers "cosmonauts of inner space." Anyone who reads a lot instantly understands what Trocchi means by this phrase. The interior life, much more than the planet or even outer space, is the unexplored area where most of our inquiring energy is (or should be) directed.

Novelist John Cheever was a faithful and regular church-goer, an old-style "eight o'clock Episcopalian." In his *Journals* Cheever regularly records what is going on inside him as he attends church. Here, as he reflects on Easter, is a brief example:

> And that this [Easter] message should have been revealed to us and that we should cherish it seems to be our finest triumph. Here in the chancel we glimpse some vision of transcendent love, some willing triumph over death and all of its lewd guises.

One of the precious and beautiful things about church-going is the way it habituates us toward introspection. To be sure, we go to church to be with others and to praise God as part of a community of faith. But we also go to church because the habitual act of doing so allows us the mental and temporal space to examine our interior lives, to become (if only during the musical offerings and the prayers) "cosmonauts of inner space."

The rhythms and demands of contemporary life make it difficult for us to attend to our inner worlds. That is tragic, because God is at work as much in us as in the wider world. If we never attend to our own inner life, we will never appreciate the wonder of ourselves or the generous mystery of God. —*Gary Hall*

# *It's everyone*

While I was delivering my sermon from atop one of those old colonial wineglass pulpits one Sunday, my mind took a left turn. I had been in this parish long enough to know most of the folks, and it suddenly struck me that everyone I could see had either been through a crisis, was in the middle of a crisis, or would probably experience a crisis soon. I thought: "My God, it's everyone!"

The fantasy in life is that for most people things go along just fine, but that once in awhile something goes wrong and there is a crisis for the few unfortunate among us.

Actually, crises can touch anyone, as was so aptly portrayed in the 1980 film *Ordinary People,* in which one son of an affluent suburban family dies in a boating accident, leading to the dissolution of the whole family. The mother (Mary Tyler Moore) cries out that she just wanted an ordinary life—i.e., everything going smoothly—and cannot deal with this "change of plan." The point of the film is that theirs is an ordinary life. A cross to bear is, in fact, the norm.

Being a Christian does not make us less apt to get hit by a bus. Rather, being a Christian is about what we bring to the table as a resource, what sustains us and gets us through when the bus shows up.

It goes right to the heart of our faith, the cross, where the worst that life can dish out is met by the overwhelming power of love and life that will not be defeated. For when we take up our cross, it is the Lord who shoulders it with us, to comfort and guide our hearts.
—*Leonard Freeman*

# *Be good to you*

I have a clergy colleague who is bright and articulate. I respect his judgment and enjoy his company. He is a good listener in a group and makes his point without being obnoxious. He gets you laughing and then slips something serious in. He's just a really nice guy. I know I could go to him if I ever needed someone to talk to.

When he says goodbye to you, his standard farewell is, "Be good to you." Not, "Be good," but "Be good *to you*." I had never heard anyone say that before, let alone heard anyone say it to me, so I asked him about it, and this is what he said:

"Folks get pretty busy running around taking care of everybody and everything. Preachers do this. Moms do this especially. Lots of us are taking care of aging parents or kids or both. You spend a lot of time trying to be good to everybody else, but you need to remember to be good to yourself as well. After all, Jesus said, 'Love your neighbor as you love yourself.' I figure he was as serious about that as he was about anything else. So be good to other folks, yes. But don't forget to be good to you, too."

I had never looked at it quite like that, but I think he's on to something. So, be good to you. —*Gregory A. Russell*

# *Easter and remembering*

Easter people remember their first flush of love with Jesus. I am a diehard romantic. After thirty-three years of marriage with Kay, I still see in her that quiet, dark-haired girl who rode horses bareback from sunup to sundown, who did graceful handsprings in her front yard, and who has made my heart do backflips ever since I was twelve years old. Remembering is important in a vibrant romance, not so much to hold us back in a web of nostalgia, but to catapult us into an even more vigorous future.

The first thing the resurrected Jesus says to his mother and Mary Magdalene (after telling them not to be afraid) is to tell his "brothers to go to Galilee; there they will see me" (Matthew 28:10). Jesus wants his eleven remaining disciples to return to where they first met him. In Galilee they will remember and rekindle the love that began there along the shore of the lake and among the fertile hills scattered above it. In my own faith life, such remembrance would center in the boarding school where the monks, athletic coaches, and priests formed me and later at college where leaders in Campus Crusade for Christ and the Navigators first opened the Word for me.

Where did Christ first bring you to life? Remembering is the engine of an Easter faith. After all, we're the ones who say every week:

> *We remember his death,*
> *We proclaim his resurrection,*
> *We await his coming in glory.*

> —The Book of Common Prayer,
> The Holy Eucharist: Rite Two

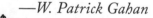
—*W. Patrick Gahan*

# *Partners in all things*

*You are my refuge and my stronghold,*
*my God in whom I put my trust.*
—Psalm 91

Here's my question to pray on today: why do so many of us think being a Christian is going to mean we will have an easier life, when we wear tiny crosses around our necks, the very expression of sacrifice made by our Lord?

We do, though. "Why did God allow this to happen?" someone asks after a terrible diagnosis, as if there must be a moral reason for his cancer, a reason related to his own failure, or as if his illness were in violation of an agreement.

It would be a cruel thing indeed, if we were to think we had an agreement with God that nothing would ever go wrong in our lives. Our fall would be mighty: things go wrong in every life. About most of them, we have little choice.

But we do have a choice as to how we will survive them, or even how we will approach them when it is clear that we will not survive. Will we insist on solitary misery, or allow God to be our partner in our suffering as he is in our joy? —*Barbara Cawthorne Crafton*

# *Who am I really?*
# *Do I amount to anything?*

Most of us have fantasized about our origins. Beethoven, born into a family where depressed, alcoholic adults regularly beat their children, convinced himself that he was actually descended from nobility. John James Audubon thought he was the lost Dauphin of France. He clung to this, rather than acknowledge he was a Créole, the bastard child of a French sea captain and his Haitian mistress. And as for me? Growing up working-class in suburban London, I felt sure that my mother would tell me, at the right time, that I was the bastard son of a Russian prince, or at least the abandoned child of gypsies. How about you?

Our longings can get us into trouble and make us look ridiculous, but they also tell us something important about ourselves. Journalist Russell Baker writes of his longing for success, gnawing at him when he was a young man: "My mother had taught that if I worked hard I could amount to something, could make something of myself. She had been proved right, yet I was vaguely dissatisfied...I felt success *ought* to make life more satisfying, *ought* to bring peace of mind, a maturity, a serenity toward life, which I did not feel."

The truth is that we are deeper and lovelier than we know, and we have to sit still sometimes and allow the awesome fact of being here at all to surprise us with significance. Laughter helps, too. Woody Allen helps us laugh about ourselves: "If God would only speak to me— just once. If he would only cough. If I could just see a miracle. If I could see a burning bush or the seas part. Or my Uncle Sasha pick up the check." —*Alan Jones*

# *Tell me a story*

"Tell me a story," our four-year-old said from the back seat of the car.

"Ask your mother," I temporized. It was late, and I was tired. We were driving home after dinner at a friend's house. Still a long way to go.

"Will you tell me a story, Mom?" he asked.

"I'll tell you about Rumpelstiltskin," she said.

It had been years since I heard the story in full; all I remembered was how it ended. I had forgotten the impossible task given the miller's daughter by a greedy king; the queer little man who appeared, offering help; the dreadful promise he forced her to make; the song he sang as he danced around his fire in the woods:

> Today I bake, tomorrow brew,
> The third I'll have the young queen's child!
> It's glad I am that no one knew
> That Rumpelstiltskin I am styled!

And then the *denouement*, with great rejoicing that all has come right in the end.

It's only a mild exaggeration to say I was spellbound and hardly noticed the tedious drive back to our home. The story had been a gift, as of wings, to speed our journey.

The gospel of Jesus Christ is first and foremost a story. The earliest preaching was the *story* of this person, not a theological doctrine about him.

What happened in his story is the pattern of what happens, and will happen, in our own. That's why we listen to it breathlessly. And when we hear it again after a long time, or hear it told with a fresh accent, or our ears catch some previously unheard note in the telling, it speeds our journey. —*Bruce Birdsey*

# *Book lurking somewhere*

For years I have thought about rifling through my old sermon files to see whether there is a book lurking there somewhere. But I have to admit that it's also been years since I wrote out my sermons word for word. I am always a little shamefaced to admit that I preach just from notes, and sometimes even without them. I tend to be at a loss about how to respond to requests for printed copies of a sermon, or even worse, requests for a tape. It usually means I have to go home and reconstruct what I said, which sometimes varies considerably from the notes I'd prepared in advance. It's what my wife calls chewing your cabbage twice. I'm daunted by that character in Marilynne Robinson's novel *Gilead,* old Reverend Ames, who estimates that in a lifetime of preaching to people week after week in the same little country church, he has accumulated thousands of sermon manuscripts, now stowed away in crates in the attic.

Nonetheless, now that I no longer preach regularly, I've decided it's time to take a second look. There won't be any systematic theology emerging from this material. If there is a book submerged in this stuff, it won't be the book I imagined when—earnest and naïve—I started preaching two decades ago, writing out every paragraph, reading the manuscript aloud word for word. Thank God that obsessive behavior didn't last. My surviving notes provide less a well-worked out theology or a consistent scriptural hermeneutic (a word I would try never to use in a sermon), than an oddly inadvertent and sometimes comic record of my life as a parish priest, and of the congregations that have patiently put up with me. I like to think that someone, somewhere, might find such a record useful.

There is a book, or at least a tale worth telling, lurking in the notes of every life. Have you identified yours? Have you written or told it? *—Roger Ferlo*

# *Popcorn prayers*

This spring I'll be the spiritual director on a retreat for about one hundred and fifty teenagers. The kids are spontaneous and fun and faithful. They lead prayers, often called "popcorn prayers," where they pray before a peer gives a talk, sitting in a circle around the speaker, laying their hands on that person and saying whatever comes to mind. They usually pray for strength and bravery and for open hearts so that the talk will be well-received.

The adults on the team have asked me to give a half-hour talk on prayer. They want the kids to learn more about the art of prayer, to pray with more depth. They have asked that I talk about things like adoration, confession, and gratitude. Fine. I can do that.

But I think God must like those popcorn prayers. I think he wants to know what's in our hearts, unrestrained—whether anger or confession or requests. Usually it's the latter. The kids tend to focus on the requests. Maybe we all do. And that's okay. God doesn't want us merely to check off a list while praying.

I'll tell the kids that every single thing ever said in prayer still rings loud and clear across the universe. If a grandmother or mother or father has prayed for a child, that prayer is still in motion, still making a difference. God hears it all, because he doesn't work on linear time as we do.

I will urge the kids to retain their spontaneity and to keep talking to God as a friend. They like friends at that age. Most important, I will tell them never to stop praying. "Pray without ceasing," says Saint Paul. Keep those prayers popping up, just like popcorn.

—*Lindsay Hardin Freeman*

# *The truth that is hard to see*

*Before our white brothers arrived to make us civilized men, we didn't have any kind of prison. Because of this, we had no delinquents. Without a prison, there can be no delinquents. We had no locks nor keys, and therefore among us there were no thieves. When someone was so poor that he couldn't afford a horse, a tent, or a blanket, he would receive it as a gift. We were too uncivilized to give great importance to private property. We didn't know any kind of money and consequently, the value of a human being was not determined by his wealth. We had no written laws laid down, no lawyers, no politicians, therefore we were not able to cheat and swindle one another. We were really in bad shape before the white men arrived, and I don't know how to explain how we were able to manage without these fundamental things that (so they tell us) are so necessary for a civilized society.*

—John (Fire) Lame Deer,
Lakota Sioux (1903-1976)

John Lame Deer had a point. In the midst of material prosperity, the truth is hard to see because everyone wants a piece of the pie. Yet, when material times get hard, people seem more open to a truth other than the dominant view which says, well, that those who dominate ultimately win. Bo Lozoff, of the Human Kindness Foundation, says all problems can be summed up in a single sentence: "Human life is very deep, and our modern dominant lifestyle is not." —*Bo Cox*

# 'Tis a gift...

Being "low church," as I am, does not mean you aren't religious. It doesn't mean you don't revere, hopefully to your toes, the God of Abraham, Isaac, and Jacob.

But being "low church" *does* mean that you treasure simplicity. You like your trees and your clouds to come through clear windows. You'd prefer less rather than more. You like value without artifice. It doesn't mean you prefer ugliness to beauty. You favor classic, with straight lines and fine materials.

There is simplicity in what you are about. You want the core element to get out and not be covered over with, say, a ritual that becomes conscious of itself, or a trillion acolytes who are more worried about where they're supposed to stand than why they're supposed to stand at all. The reason you do what you do is everything, and you don't want the trappings to get in the way of it.

My favorite writer is William Hale White. Under the pseudonym "Mark Rutherford," William Hale White wrote novels about small towns in the English Midlands in the mid-nineteenth century and about small-town Christianity in that place. He wrote with impeccable diagnosis and wide compassion. But he also wrote as simply as Isaac Watts. In his day, few people read William Hale White. He is still read by few. But André Gide loved him, calling him "the most Protestant of English writers." D. H. Lawrence couldn't get enough of him. I regard the novels of "Mark Rutherford" as the best things I own.

Let's not dismiss simplicity. Let's not dismiss "low church." Ask, rather: Is the word of grace getting through? What can we do to help it break the sound barrier of present social deafness?
—*Paul F. M. Zahl*

# The church for the rest of us

I once attended a church that claimed to be the church for the best of us. It said so right on the front of the bulletin, beneath the church's name and address: "The Church for the Best of Us." Of course this was a play on words. On the one hand, this was the church where the best people in town worshiped. But on the other hand, it was a church that brought out the best in people. After worshiping there for a year, I realized the latter meaning was lost on many of the parishioners.

In twenty-five years of parish ministry, I found that many of the most interesting people didn't fit in very well. Artists, the badly broken, the skeptics who kept searching—these were the people who challenged me and made me think. Increasingly I heard, "We love God but not the church." I spent twenty-five years trying to convince people they couldn't do that. It is a package deal.

In the early days of computers there was a saying, "Do not fold, staple, spindle, or mutilate." The punch cards going through the computer had to be perfect; no ripples, damages, or irregularities of any kind.

Now, as I sit with those who have fallen through the cracks of Christendom, I wonder whether there is a place in the kingdom for those of us who don't fit into the right angles of institutional church. Can you love God and be a little iffy about the church? Can there be redemption beyond institution? Is there a church for the *rest* of us? It wouldn't be a big church, and it wouldn't be for everybody, just an irregular sort of thing for those of us who are folded, stapled, spindled, mutilated, and who know it. —*David L. James*

# *The good earth*

Many people enjoy gardening and planting flowers, vegetables, trees, and grass. I even enjoy weeding, getting the offending plant—roots and all—and moving it out of the area. It reacquaints me with the soil, the deep, chocolatey richness of it. We liked digging in it as kids. Some of us still do. Handling the earth and the stuff that grows in it soothes us and gives us peace. Earth brings us back to reality, to where we got our start.

I can believe we were made out of soil, that thin layer covering much of this planet in which things grow. Whether symbolically or in reality, soil is the magic, blessed stuff from whence we were taken, from which miraculous plants and trees grow, wherein a dried-up seed stretches upward into new green growth. Soil is itself comprised of flesh, fur, and feces, as T. S. Eliot says.

How fitting that we return to the soil at our earthly end, that our flesh and bones finally disintegrate back into original components. But the story does not end there. An incomprehensible metamorphosis will occur for each of us, just as Jesus showed with his own body in resurrection. Our flesh and soul will reunite, earth and spirit become one; our dry bones will live, as Ezekiel predicted, in the new heaven and new earth that John foresees in Revelation and where once again we will be in the garden with the tree of life.

We began in a garden; we end in a garden; we begin again in a garden, and the gardener is our Lord, Jesus Christ. When Magdalene asked him in her confused and wondering state, "Are you the gardener?" perhaps she was not far from the truth. —*Carol McCrae*

# *P-R-A-Y-E-R*

Prayer takes many forms and formularies. No one is better than the other as long as prayer is sincere. One way to approach prayer can be found in the word itself.

Praise. Begin by acknowledging God's holiness, God's providence, God's steadfast love, God's glory. Praise helps us see that. As Sister Joan Chittister puts it, "Life is punctuated by God, awash in God, encircled by God."

Reverence. Reverence naturally follows praise. It is dwelling for the moment in the holiness and mystery of God, letting God soak in. As the late Urban T. Holmes once said, "Christianity is better seen as a marinade than a glaze."

Amendment. Amendment bids us take honest stock of ourselves and the life we are living, asking God for forgiveness and help to turn to God and God's will for us.

Yearning. Listen. Listen to your heart, to what are you longing for. Listen to the cries of a wounded and wanting creation. Listen to discern what God is yearning for.

Employment. Prayer always calls us to action. It asks that we let God use us in whatever ways God desires, in and through our daily lives.

Requests. Prayer concludes with lifting up to God the cares and concerns of our hearts and minds and lives, praying for ourselves and for others, entrusting all to God. —*James L. Burns*

# Save us from ourselves

*O God, the King eternal...*
*drive far from us all wrong desires.*
—The Book of Common Prayer,
A Collect for the Renewal of Life

Most people spend all their days dreaming only about wrong desires. Don't drive them away—draw them ever closer! The tenth commandment speaks of the man who longed for his neighbor's ox and ass and coveted his wife. Today's equivalent might be the neighbor's large, fenced estate and his BMW, operated as if the driver were the only person on the road, while both biblical and contemporary man covet the gorgeous wife, who is undressed in the imagination with practiced eye.

Yet here we read words from *The Book of Common Prayer* beseeching God to "drive far from us all wrong desires." Why fly in the face of natural desire? The reasons are manifold.

It's a waste of time to wish for what will derail, delude, and deter us. We have more important things to do, like seeking God while he still may be found. For just as the hairs on our head are counted, so our moments on this earth are numbered. If lust and greed are all that matters, what's the point? The answer is that there is no point if all we amount to is lust and greed. Life then would be meaningless.

There is time enough and more to our days if we are freed from all wrong desires. Then we are freed to fulfill our purpose as loving, giving, productive persons whose days will improve the world and the lives of those around us. —*Edward S. Gleason*

# *Help*

Walking uptown on Broadway at 65th Street, I stopped at a red light, looked around a parked car, and saw a taxicab speeding west to make the light. I sensed a blur to my right, a woman about to walk into the intersection, and instinctively reached out to stop her. I immediately apologized, for touching a pedestrian is a no-no here, especially a man touching a woman. She looked up from her cell phone, smiled, and said, "Thanks! You saved my life!"

That instinct to help could have created a mess. She could have gotten angry. My hand could have accidently touched more than her sleeve. She could have screamed. But we both got lucky.

Not to make too much of a small moment, but I think this instinct to help provides a glimpse into Jesus. Biblical scholars like to chart his every step, as if he followed a carefully planned itinerary. In fact, he seemed to go here and there, teaching whoever would listen, feeding the hungry when need arose, healing the sick who were brought to him, and exercising this instinct to do the right thing. Without hesitation, he stopped when the blind beggar cried out, protected the woman about to be stoned, called Zacchaeus out of his tree, and went with his captors to a certain death.

This is our connection with Jesus: we, too, have that God-given instinct to do right. Watch a parent protect her child. Watch strangers stop their journeys to help a wounded person. Watch busy people build houses for the poor. Watch neighbors carry food to a newly widowed woman. Even though we often stifle that instinct, it still bursts forth, and it is our truest self.

Helping can get us in trouble, as it got Jesus in trouble. But the instinct won't die. —*Thomas L. Ehrich*

# *Empty out your tombs*

Did you know that it is still Eastertide, and will be until the Day of Pentecost in May or early June? This is the season in which to renew your life and remove the remains of old experiences which keep you stuck. Easter Day, the Day of Resurrection, is the beginning of the season, not the end.

Most of us tend the tombs of our lives very carefully. I have one of those funny jars which says "Ashes of old lovers." It could just as well read "Ashes of old expectations, old lost opportunities, old mistakes, old guilts and regrets, old undeserved wounds, old angers, and old sorrows."

Real losses require real grief, and feeling that grief during Eastertide can be a useful way toward healing. As for all the other "Old Stuff," you may be continuing to nurture and magnify happenings in your life which are over and done with and need have no place in your present. Life is not fair, people misunderstand each other, and hurts occur. Let them go. We all have bad and sad things in our history. We would like to take scissors and cut them out of our story. Since we can't do that, we stash them away in our tombs, and give them the power to make us unhappy.

Jesus is our model. He was misunderstood, even by his disciples. He was despised and betrayed. We would expect him, in our modern way of thinking, to be depressed. Instead, although he was sometimes angry, he didn't carry all that baggage around with him. He emptied out his tombs before he was ever placed in one. We can do likewise and find resurrected energy for the place where we live, the today of our lives. —*Lee Krug*

# *At the Jabbok*

No matter how often we reverently speak of "the God of Abraham, Isaac, and Jacob," nothing can change the fact that Jacob was a scoundrel. Indeed, his name in Hebrew may mean "crookedness." His story is told in delicious detail in Genesis 25:19-34; 27:1-29. After years of wiggling through ethical and moral fences, he found himself at night by a creek called the Jabbok. In the morning he had to face his brother whom he had cheated long ago. All he knew was that his brother Esau was accompanied by four hundred men, a scant source of comfort.

Genesis 32 tells a mysterious story of Jacob spending his night on the Jabbok wrestling—with what? Conscience, God, angel, demon, all four? Who knows?

But at the end his adversary blesses him with a new name, Israel. The word literally means "strives with God."

It is a wonderful story, but it becomes a *powerful* story for me when I consider what happened with that name.

Jacob kept on being called Jacob until his dying day.

But when the people of God were considering a name for themselves and for us, they chose to call themselves the people of Israel—the people who strive, wrestle, struggle with God. Some probably wanted to use a more positive term.

Islam, for example, means "submission," a very fine thing to be before God. I am sure others opted for "obedient" or "faithful" or "sincere," but the decision went to the name Israel.

I struggle with God a lot. Perhaps you do too. When it bothers me, as it often does, I remember the Jabbok and I remember that wrestling with God is what the people of God do. It does not make my struggles easier, but I like knowing that they are expected.
—*Francis H. Wade*

# *The Lord is my shepherd*

There are two texts that most Christians can recite from memory: the Lord's Prayer and the Twenty-Third Psalm. The visually impaired members of the group of elderly ladies I lead in Morning Prayer each week can say them both clearly, with no need for the book. And in both cases, contemporary language versions need not apply. In the case of Psalm 23, the King James Version is the English translation as far as most people are concerned. It finally made it into the American *Book of Common Prayer* in 1979 as an alternative: the Coverdale translation of the Psalms, used before that, is not quite the same.

We lose something by saying the Lord's Prayer in its sixteenth-century form, because the meaning of "trespass" used there is now obsolete. "Save us from the time of trial" is a better translation as well as more appropriate than "lead us not into temptation" for the loving God we worship.

But I think the King James loyalists are right in hanging onto "The Lord is my shepherd; I shall not want." Coverdale lacks its particular poetic cadences, and the modern translation—"You spread a table before me in the presence of those who trouble me"—is downright clunky.

The poetry helps to convey its message of comfort. It's a message we need right now, with the financial markets collapsing and the entire economy threatened as a result, with wars continuing and human suffering hitting close to home.

"Yea, though I walk through the valley of the shadow of death, I will fear no evil; for thou art with me; thy rod and thy staff, they comfort me." Walk in faith, through every crisis, and know that God is with us. —*Sarah Bryan Miller*

# Children

In my forty-plus years as a priest, some of the strongest statements about life and faith have come from children.

At the end of a Sunday service, the deacon dismissed us: "Let us go forth in the Name of Christ," and as the congregation responded, "Thanks be to God," a child's voice overrode their words asking, "Where are we going?"

A girl, just old enough to answer for herself at baptism, answered the question, "Do you desire to be baptized?" not with the proper "I do," but with a "Yes!" that filled the nave and the hearts of us all.

Many strange and wonderful things happen without words. Once I was visiting a family that had an autistic child. I had been talking with the parents for only a few minutes when the boy walked across the floor, climbed up on my lap, and stayed there until I left. His mother said he had never done such a thing. Another afternoon I was visiting in a rehabilitation hospital when I was asked by parents I didn't know to pray for their wheelchair-bound child, victim of a gunshot wound to the head. I laid my hands on the boy and said a prayer. He responded, his parents said for the first time.

On Christmas Eve a tiny girl in a red dress escaped her parents and walked the length of the aisle to the chancel steps where the deacon was about to read the opening of the Gospel of Saint John: "In the beginning was the Word..." She stood below him looking up as if she were taking in every word. When he finished she turned and went back to her parents.

What do they know that we forget? I'm pretty sure it's something important. —*Robert Horine*

# Step one: disillusionment

Step One in the Christian Way through life is disillusionment with the world. This doesn't come by itself. And it doesn't come naturally. Disillusionment results from painful experience, from being check-mated. It comes by way of the Big Hurt.

A successful clergyman in his mid-forties was telling me all about the growth of his parish. It was a wonder to behold. Attendance was soaring, giving was good, and he had surrounded himself with a cadre of students and seminarians that was almost unique. "Any curve balls?" I asked. He thought about it a minute—he had to search his mind—and said, "Well, there was a little resistance at the start from some of the old-timers."

I was sad for my friend, and worried for him. As sure as he is a human being, the Big Hurt is coming. As sure as he lives in this world, some impasse or disappointment or attack or intrusion is looming. I won't be the one to convince him of this, won't even try.

Poet e. e. cummings wrote that Jesus hadn't convinced us of the futility of war. Plato hadn't either, nor had Confucius. But an enemy bullet through the head, well, that could "convince" us.

Step One to wisdom comes in the form of disillusionment. It happens when things you counted on come apart. She leaves you. They hate you. He ambushes you. Your doctor reports... The stock market doesn't rebound. A lawyer comes after you. Different forms of the same thing.

The first step toward being saved, in life and by God, is the disillusionment that life brings. It is a good thing—though I wish it were not so. —*Paul F. M. Zahl*

# *Back off!*

*If I speak in the tongues of mortals and of angels,*
*but do not have love,*
*I am a noisy gong or a clanging cymbal.*
—1 Corinthians 13:1

My mother-in-law became very ill, and my wife went to take care of her. She was gone for over a month, and I temporarily joined the ranks of single parents. I did not enjoy it, but did become proud of my organizational skills and ability to balance my job, multiple schedules, and housework.

One morning my ten-year-old son was dragging, and my voice became loud and impatient. His eyes immediately welled up with tears. My fourteen-year-old daughter grabbed me by the arm and led me to another room. She scolded me as if she were my parent. "He is really homesick for Mom, and you need to back off and show him some love!" I was humbled and speechless.

Saint Paul reminds us that we can have all things and be all things, but without love we are nothing. Jesus has put the love of God into our hearts, and that love is to be shared, no matter what. —*Jason Leo*

# *Listen and live*

*Inebriate of air am I, And debauchee of dew,*
*Reeling, through endless summer days, From inns of molten blue.*

So wrote Emily Dickinson in an ecstatic celebration of life. On this beautiful May afternoon her song resonates in my soul. The sky is powder blue behind a diaphanous film of white clouds. Birds chant jubilantly; a warm breeze dances through the pines. God's creation is very good!

It's impossible, of course, to live every moment in such a state of unfettered wonder. After all, there are places to go, people to see, problems to solve, tasks to accomplish. *Do, do, do!* Sometimes the daily adrenaline rush is exhilarating. But too often it's simply exhausting and mind-numbing.

There's another way: *Be, be, be.* This is the teaching of Thich Naht Hanh, Buddhist monk and peace activist. He encourages us to "listen deeply" and "live mindfully."

Jesus practiced deep listening and mindful living. Yes, he traveled to and fro, teaching and healing while fencing with the authorities. And yet he regularly withdrew to a place apart to be still, to pray, to *be*.

To live in this way is to trust that God will keep the world spinning even if we rest from putting our shoulder to the wheel. The yearning to live such a balanced, faithful life is expressed beautifully by another poet, Denise Levertov, in "The Avowal":

*As swimmers dare/to lie face to the sky/and water bears them,/as hawks rest upon air/and air sustains them,/so I would learn to attain/freefall, and float/into Creator Spirit's deep embrace,/knowing no effort earns/that all surrounding grace.*

May we all find ways to rest and play. In the stillness, God will rekindle our amazement in the miracle of our life.
—*Charles F. Brumbaugh*

# *I believe in the resurrection of the body*

"The Pat you know on the earth is the Pat you will know in heaven" is how I often explain the line in the Apostles' Creed about resurrection of the body. About the time we leave our robust thirties and begin our march toward middle age, we become less excited about the mere resuscitation of our present bodies after death. It seems our physical bodies are "out of warranty." When we profess our belief in the resurrection of the body, we are asserting that the real person we are on earth will also be known eternally in heaven.

Jesus himself is the best example of this. In his post-resurrection appearance on the road to Emmaus (Luke 24:13-35), Jesus is not immediately recognized, even though he must have been well-known to the two disciples there. It is not until he breaks the bread for their supper and reveals the meaning of scripture to them that they realize who he is. Once Jesus does those things that disclose his real self, they recognize him. Again in John 21, the resurrected Jesus is only recognized by the disciples after he directs them to a bonanza cache of fish, a reprise of an act he had performed three years earlier when they first met (Luke 5:1-11). The real and most enduring qualities of Jesus have not only been retained, but accentuated, in the miracle of the resurrection. What has transpired in Jesus will also take place in all of us who believe in him. After all, we contend that Jesus is the "first fruits" of those who have died; thus, we will "be made alive in Christ" (1 Corinthians 15:20-22).

If the resurrection of the body will highlight our real, most authentic selves, why wait? Let's pull off our hollow masks and really live. —*W. Patrick Gahan*

# *Telling our stories*

It is wisely noted that when something goes without saying, it is likely to go—without saying. In other words, the things we do not talk about, even if they are obvious things, have a tendency to slip away from us so quietly we do not know exactly when they were lost. It happens in relationships, when people stop saying that they love one another. It happens in faith, without what Desmond Tutu calls the "habitual recollection" of corporate worship. It happens in nations and churches, where the founding story is not told and retold. It underlines for us the importance of saying our Truth as a way of keeping our Truth. That may be part of the reason Saint Paul said "Woe to me if I do not proclaim the gospel" (1 Corinthians 9:16).

Recognizing that if we don't speak the gospel we will lose it gives us a slightly different look at the importance of evangelism. That word has been stolen and much abused by its captors. Evangelism literally means "story telling," but it has been corrupted to imply "sales pitch." Evangelism is not me talking you into seeing as I do. Evangelism is me sharing my story as faithfully as I can. What you do in response becomes your story and yours to tell. An evangelist, as T. S. Eliot wrote in *The Rock*, must "Take no thought for the harvest, but only of proper sowing."

We must seek first the kingdom of God, seek to live into the gospel truth so we have a story we can tell of the Living God. Then evangelism must follow, not so much because you need to hear my story but because I need to tell it. If I do not tell my story, I am in more than a little danger of losing my story, because that which goes without saying tends to go—without saying. —*Francis H. Wade*

# *Resurrection victory*

When we read the great stories of the early church, the theme of the resurrection is always about victory. It's about the triumph of life over death; the triumph of justice over oppression; the triumph of flourishing over diminishment. That's why the early Christians loved the stories of Jonah and the whale, Daniel's rescue from the lions' den, the three young men and the fiery furnace, and above all the deliverance of Israel from slavery in Egypt. They saw these as resurrection stories that gave them hope in what was often a cruel and difficult world.

So ask yourself some strange questions: What whale has swallowed you? What savage beast terrifies you? What burning ordeal awaits you? What prison suffocates you? Remember, our faith is not an *argument*. It's a love affair. As people of faith, we are captivated by a joy and secure in a victory that will not accept the cruelty and indifference of the world. The victory makes us one human family. We are well-connected. The victory makes us subversives, committed to fight and undermine all that would hurt and diminish human flourishing.

Let's recover this sense of victory—particularly today, in the face of so much injustice, violence, and violation. The early church understood that the victory had to be utterly human—even if it were beyond our powers (only God could win it). They came to see that the glory of God is a human being fully alive. Our prayer is, "O God, make us truly alive!" —*Alan Jones*

# The ideal mother

My ideal mother has her feet firmly on the ground as her imagination orbits the universe. She encircles her children with love and talks with them about the meaning of life. She sets boundaries for them, but is not rigid. She allows them to fail without always rescuing them. She is not judgmental. She is receptive to differences of opinion. She encourages her children to look at options, however foreign to her they may seem. She listens, and doesn't overtalk or moralize. She owns up to her own mistakes, and her children find their values by observing her. She has an infectious sense of humor, but is not ashamed to cry or stand in the midst of their tears.

Children grow up. Some wander or purposefully go off to find their own destinies. A wise mother lets them go while holding them within the circle of her concern. They have their own journeys. She does not try to live her life through them. But she always keeps in touch. She cares not that they be successful, but what kind of people they become. Are they passionate about something? Are they compassionate with others? Do they meet adversity with hope? Do they believe in a holy spirit available to them?

There are many styles of mothering. No one person can consistently embody the above description. Not every mother is a good one. Before any woman became a mother, she was first a daughter, and she has been marked for better or worse by that experience. For those who cannot celebrate and rejoice in mothers, it is important to connect to the nurturing spirit of God, and come to realize that God has both male and female qualities. —*Lee Krug*

# *Where are the lines?*

I always tried to have something interesting each Sunday to share with the children who came forward for a few moments with me prior to the sermon. This particular Sunday I had brought a big poster of the earth. Called "Earthrise," it is a photograph taken from the surface of the moon. We all saw it. We all remember it. It's magnificent.

You can see the outline of the North American and South American continents in perfect detail. All the rivers are there, and you can see the snow on the Rocky Mountains and the Andes. It is a huge poster, square and nearly as big as I am tall. The kids helped me roll it out and hold it in place so we all could see. It took all of them to pull that off.

"What is this," I asked?

"Earth," came the chorus of young voices—except for Garrett.

Four-year-old Garrett looked at the poster intently, then got up and moved closer. He studied it some more. It was clear he was thinking about it; something was puzzling him. You could almost hear the gears whirring. And then he swept his hand over North America and asked, "Where are the lines?"

"Lines? What lines?" I asked.

"You know," he said, "the lines between the countries."

"Oh, Garrett," I said, "you're thinking of a map." He obviously had seen only a map or a globe before this. "There aren't any lines," I continued. "This is the way the earth really looks."

And in the indignant voice that only a four-year-old can muster, he said, "You mean we just made those up?"

Yes, Garrett, we just made them up. Jesus was right. A little child *shall* lead them. Class is dismissed. —*Gregory A. Russell*

# Golf, Tiger, and me

*Be perfect, therefore,*
*as your heavenly Father is perfect.*
—Matthew 5:48

I play golf—badly, most of the time. Imagine that I were commanded: "Be as perfect a golfer as Tiger Woods." I'd say, "Oh sure!" and go on playing my mediocre game. Or I might really take the command to heart and decide I must measure up to this exacting—nay, impossible—standard. I'd then become anxiously perfectionistic and get depressed about the wretched state of my game. Neither way would I improve.

But say some wise Golf Deity, some Lord of the Links, took pity on me and explained a basic principle. "Look, Bruce. You and Tiger are both golfers. He's much better at it than you. But the same Essence of Golf that underlies his swing underlies yours. You're both tapping into the fundamental energy that makes golf happen. This Zen of Golf is as available to you as it is to Tiger."

Such words would be less command than invitation, and that is what we get from Jesus: an invitation to step into a force field that's over-around-below-within our individual selves. "Love one another, as I have loved you" means "love one another with the same love I've loved you with." The divine love in which Christ lives and moves and has his being is available to us. Turning to him, putting one's whole trust in his grace, is the key. We place ourselves in that force field and allow it to draw forth our answering love.

Living in this energy and essence makes possible the moral life, the keeping of the commandments, the obedience to *Thou shalt* and *Thou shalt not.* Jesus' promise is that divine love—its energy and its essence—dwells within us in that abiding presence we call the Holy Spirit. —*Bruce Birdsey*

# Noises

In moving from a twelfth-floor apartment overlooking a busy intersection to a third-floor unit facing into a courtyard, we have exchanged street noise for children at play.

Before, we heard every siren going to danger, every trash truck rumbling down Columbus Avenue, every motorcyclist feeling his oats, and sometimes in the early morning after taxis had given up, the voices of people shouting at each other. I treasured every sound, because they were all so human, so urban.

Now I awaken to utter stillness, and I love it. Mine is the only light on at 4:00 a.m. I have this courtyard vista to myself. Later the children come out to play, as New York apartment dwellers define play, and I love their noise, too. It's the sound of life.

In recent years, the only sounds I found grating were the leaf blowers in our former suburban cul de sac. I enjoyed the children, backyard parties, occasional cars and trucks, even the lawn mowers and chain saws. But the leaf blowers struck me as ugly, perhaps because they were an unnecessary tool to replace the wonderful rhythms of raking and sweeping. I never understood why someone would prefer a deafening noise to the pleasure of raking.

Noises, like everything else about life, strike each of us differently. Some of us cannot endure the shouts of children; some loathe the silence. Whatever our limits, we need to know that we are surrounded by people who see the basics of life differently. That's just who we are.

Faith, it seems to me, enables us to tolerate those differences. Without needing to stifle the other, or to declare our own superior taste, we can choose to get along. God gives us the patience we need.
—*Thomas L. Ehrich*

# Mid-life blessings: God is so good

"Kit's doing fine," the vet said. "You can come and get him this afternoon." Well, good. I doubt if "fine" is exactly how Kitten would describe how he's doing, but nobody's asking him.

We've had enough searching conversations with cat savants to lower our expectations about what this surgery will mean in terms of moderating his behavior. He might still jump on Ben—he walks across the bed toward him on his hind legs, his front paws swinging wildly, like a pair of fists. Even to me, it's a frightening sight, and I outweigh Kitten by a fair amount.

You'll notice that I still call him "Kitten." I intend to keep doing so, because I think it's so cute. I expect still to call him "Kitten" when he's the size of the coffee table, which I reckon will be soon—that cat can eat. My husband uses "Kit," which he thinks is more manly. This is rather like the armed truces that develop between parents, in which the dad wants to cut off his little boy's beautiful curls and the mom can't stand the thought of it.

We use the cats as surrogate children. We found each other late in life, my husband and I; being parents already, we did not have children together. This was before parents were as ancient as they are now— if we had been more aware of current trends, we might be the parents of a teenager today. Just thinking about all the things we are missing makes me want to take a nap.

The cats have now completed their education. It looks like their teeth won't need straightening. They never did idealize us, so we won't have that walk through the valley of the shadow of dumbness one has with human teenagers, who simply cannot believe that anyone could be as dim as their parents are. The cats will not get pregnant or marry Philistines. They will never learn to drive.

God is *so* good. —*Barbara Cawthorne Crafton*

# The rusty rain barrel

I know a woman named Monica who works in the impoverished Eastern Cape of South Africa. One of her colleagues, a Xhosa woman being trained as a nurse, had been living in a tiny hut in a squatters' settlement, dividing her time between work at the clinic (several kilometers away) and caring for her disabled brother at home. A storm had destroyed her ramshackle hut, and Monica had organized a work group to build a more stable mud-brick house, fashioning the bricks from the ground on which the house would stand. They had put out a large rain barrel to collect the water necessary for their brick-making, but supplemented it in the dry spells—which come all too often to the Eastern Cape— with water carried on their backs and shoulders from a distant well.

I treasure two photographs of the site. One is of the still unfinished house, a view through one of its rough-hewn windows of the setting sun and the harshly beautiful hills beyond the settlement. But it's the other, more pedestrian, photo that I cherish most. It's a shot of the rusty rain barrel, full to the brim with water. You can see Monica's outstretched hand extended toward it, pointing toward the water, in a joyous, gorgeous gesture of triumph and compassion. I would have liked to have taken that barrel home with me, to place it near the door of my church instead of the font we already had. For me that rain barrel is what any baptismal font should look like: the work of many hands, a source of living water, a wellspring of liberation and homecoming, destined for building up and not for tearing down—a fountain from which Jesus would gladly have drunk his fill. —*Roger Ferlo*

# *Lead us*

*Lord, we pray that your grace*
*may always precede and follow us…*
—The Book of Common Prayer,
Collect for Proper 23

God's grace, like most good things that change the world, is invisible. We become aware of it only when it touches and changes us and makes us know that God is ever-present in our lives. The grace that precedes and follows us comes in many forms and all kinds of persons, even in the unexpected presence of a young schoolboy who cares for his teacher.

The month was May, the sun was bright, the academic year was drawing to a close, and for no good reason I was feeling sorry for myself. Sitting in my office, preparing for a late afternoon class, I heard a knock on the door, and Ned Hallowell entered.

"Rev," he said, "I seem to have left my copy of *Cry, the Beloved Country* here. Mind if I look around for it?" He'd done no such thing, I knew, but why not humor him? Ned pretended to look, then said, "Guess it's not here. Mind if I sit for a few minutes?"

He did. We talked of the year coming to a close, what it had meant, how good it had been, what had been accomplished. It was one of those conversations that puts everything in perspective. Ned left, I finished my work, and whistled as I left the office and walked to class. The world had been changed.

That evening at supper, my wife asked, "Did Ned Hallowell find you this afternoon? He walked by as I was working in the garden, and I told him you were over in your office feeling sorry for yourself. He said he would stop by and say hello." —*Edward S. Gleason*

# The sheep and the goats

*When the Son of Man comes in his glory…*
*he will separate people one from another*
*as a shepherd separates the sheep from the goats.*
—Matthew 25:31-32

This is not happy news for the goats, who "go away into eternal punishment." So the question becomes, "How can we avoid goathood?" Fortunately, Jesus gives us a checklist for being designated a sheep: feed the hungry, give drink to the thirsty, welcome the stranger, clothe the naked, care for the sick, visit the prisoner—for when we do something for those in need, we are doing it for Christ himself.

Interestingly, he doesn't mention beliefs—but the system is faith-based because Jesus is asking us to be selfless, to make real sacrifices for those outside our families, our circle of friends, our parish, our city, our nation. And it is not in human nature to do any of that unless we really believe in Christ's message. Jesus didn't say, "Feed the hungry when you have extra groceries; give them something to drink when you've got water to spare; welcome strangers if it's not going to strain the budget." This is a command without qualifications, to love our neighbors as ourselves even if we might have to do without as a result. This is a command to stand with the sheep even when it means giving up some of our own comforts and surrendering some of our warm woolly coats when a sharp cold wind is blowing.

We sheep and goats are separated not by the finer points of theology, but by how well we listen to Christ, by how well we obey his commands, both in good times and in bad. And we decide, through our faith in and obedience to God, which way we will go.
—*Sarah Bryan Miller*

# *Robin's tale*

It was a fat, healthy baby robin the kids found, holding it cupped in their hands, its mother screaming. How could we get it back up the tree? It was getting dark. We put it in a box that was open on top and took it inside. Eagerly, the baby ate the pet store mealy worms we dangled from tweezers. In the morning, we set the box outside for air, keeping watch for cats and squirrels. Amazingly, the mother perched on the edge of the box, feeding her baby. We alternated feedings, she during the day, we at night.

One morning, the baby was screeching. The mother, poised on the edge of the box, had put a wriggling worm down into the bottom. Finally, the baby got the message: "Ya gotta bend your head and pick up the worm. Mom's not gonna do it for ya." Humbly, I learned to ignore the baby's screeches and temper tantrums. If that bird was going to survive, it had to learn to eat off the ground and catch its own food.

Feeding her baby out of the box, the mother enticed it to hop up and fly out. Later, she taught it to fly to a low bush, a small tree, and the tall oak branches. At last, it flew out of the treetops into the sky, free, wild, and adventurous in a way we earthbound creatures never could be. My spirit soared upward with the bird.

The mother bird taught me to parent God's way: do what's needed, but teach the little one to do for itself. All our little ones need to learn to feed themselves and to fly. We have to be strong enough to let them screech until they learn to do it for themselves. —*Carol McCrae*

# *Without a wedding garment*

Jesus once told a story about a king who gave a wedding banquet (Matthew 22). Those on the original guest list spurned the invitation and suffered consequences. One meaning seems clear: God invites us into glorious relationship, yet many spurn the invitation and suffer loss because of it. But Jesus goes on. When the original guest list fails to show, the king invites a ragtag group to come and fill the hall. It is a point Jesus makes many times. God favors those the world does not favor: tax collectors and prostitutes will enter the kingdom ahead of preening piety. But Jesus goes on. The king spies a man without proper attire, binds him hand and foot, and has him thrown not only out—but down to what the parable hauntingly calls "outer darkness."

What does that mean? That God has a bad day every once in a while, like when Jesus told that woman with a sick child that he wouldn't give his good bread to dogs? Or that the unrighteous don't get a free ride but must conform to God's standards? Whatever it means, it stands as a clear reminder that people like you and me cannot figure out the ways of God. If we believe that God is good and just only because we are able to recognize goodness and justice in God's actions, we are presuming to stand in judgment of God, which is a dangerous thing to do.

I don't always, or even often, understand God's actions. I don't know why I live so well and others so sadly. I don't know why goodness and justice appear so random. I don't know why some people get caught without a wedding garment and others don't. All I know is that God is good and just, whether I can see it or not. —*Francis H. Wade*

# Did Jesus laugh?

A regular feature in *Reader's Digest* used to be "Laughter, the Best Medicine." It's a cliché; it's even trademarked. But it's true.

Last night my wife and I watched *The Office* on TV. Its sly, pointed portrayal of human frailty (and, by extension, ours too) was instantly recognizable. We laughed and laughed.

We needed the laughs. This has been a difficult season, as we've worried over the declining health of loved ones. But our laughter left us feeling cleansed, newly euphoric, and resilient.

Laughter is rarely mentioned in Holy Scripture, and most biblical references to it are not positive (e.g. Mark 5:40). Still, I wonder: did Jesus laugh? The gospels don't report it. But some say that Jesus' acerbic encounter with the Syrophoenician woman (Mark 7:24-30) was actually a playful exchange. Others suggest his use of rabbinic hyperbole was delivered with a nudge and a wink: "It is easier for a camel to go through the eye of a needle than for someone who is rich to enter the kingdom of God" (Mark 10:23-27).

I like to picture Jesus laughing. Perhaps as the disciples solemnly sailed on the Sea of Galilee, Jesus suddenly broke the silence with something like, "Hey, did you hear the one about the Pharisee, the centurion, and the prostitute?" Amidst their hopes and joys, Jesus and the twelve lived with a heaviness that only laughter could relieve. Imagine all thirteen of them rolling about the boat laughing, tears running down their cheeks, suddenly refreshed and able once again to go forward.

Laughter is a gift we can give and receive, a blessing that fans out in ever-widening circles. God wants us to know the healing rinse of laughter. Why else would Jesus say, "Blessed are you who weep now, for you will laugh" (Luke 6:21)?

—*Charles F. Brumbaugh*

# *What's different*

"What's different about being a Christian in the workplace? In the business world? At home? At school?" In preparation for a sermon, I took an informal survey, calling people whose cell phone numbers I had, even catching one parishioner on the golf course.

Gratitude, said one. "I slipped off a ladder while painting and rode it down two stories, where I landed on a hard driveway. But I could still move. I got off that ladder and said, 'Thank you, Jesus!'"

Honesty, said several others. "You give your word, you shake hands, and that's it. There's no question that you'll follow through."

Witnessing, said another. "It's not always easy to do in the work setting, but there are ways. Wear a cross, or keep one on your desk. Talk about how much fun church is; about what a positive thing it is in your own life. Offer to say a prayer with your coworker if the occasion calls for it."

Going the extra step, taking that risk you might not otherwise take, said yet another, telling this story: One day he walked into work and said "How're you doing?" to a coworker. "Not so well," said the man, and then told of his child who lay critically ill in the hospital. "Come on, I'll go there with you," said our parishioner. "I've been there. We lost our son as a baby."

It was the man who had lost the child that I caught golfing. He put his clubs down and talked for twenty minutes, embodying what being a Christian is about: gratitude, honesty, witnessing, and going that extra step. He provided a base from his own experience to help another bear his cross. —*Lindsay Hardin Freeman*

# Om mani padme hum

I shall not try to sum up in a few English sentences, or even several paragraphs, what this Tibetan Buddhist mantra means. It is a look at the condition of human suffering.

Some people believe suffering is unnecessary. Whatever your philosophical, spiritual, or religious approach, everyone believes to some degree that nobody *wants* to suffer.

Perhaps the way we approach suffering depends on where we think it comes from. Do we see suffering as an external thing, subject to conditions outside us, or do we see it as internal, something that may have to do with external conditions but is more about our *responses* to those conditions?

The first approach leads to a certain irresponsibility and lack of accountability—it is someone else's fault. The second acknowledges that nothing, no thing, can determine our response to the world outside of us except us.

Impersonal, you say? What about God? No matter what, life and death have a rhythm and purpose. Compassion for others and turning away from self is the way to navigate this maze with the greatest of ease—and less dis-ease is a good thing. To believe that is pretty heady—and very God-conscious.

In fact, I would go so far as to say all the great spiritual leaders and teachers of history have understood this: maybe none better than the Carpenter from Nazareth. If only we could follow his example and his essence, and not the often-divisive dogmas developed in his wake.
—*Bo Cox*

# *Social networking*

I don't resist new technology. If anything, I am what is called an "early adopter."

But I have been slow to venture into social networking tools such as Twitter, Facebook, and LinkedIn. I opened accounts right away, but it is only today that I created a Facebook group to help my "On a Journey" readers dialogue with each other, and in the process I added "friends" to my Facebook account.

I had the usual objections—too much information, too self-obsessive, open to all the world—but I think I was actually just unsure of my ability to master the medium. Egged on by a reader, I took the plunge today. I am happy to report that Facebook is reasonably intuitive and easy to use.

Is it for you? That's for you to say. But I encourage you to explore, not just dismiss it before trying.

In an odd sort of way, social networking reminds me of Christian evangelism. Users tend to be advocates; they are eager to share and to convert their friends. The medium itself has odd insider language—"tweets," "follow," "friend" (used as a verb) and "wall"—which should chasten all church people about insider language.

The point is to get people together. It's about connecting. In that, social networking is both analogous to Christian community and a useful adjunct to it. The heart of Christian community isn't getting people into a single room for worship; it's helping people find each other in many ways, including Sunday worship. —*Thomas L. Ehrich*

# I don't do this all the time

Christian living includes some odd moments. Somewhere back in the rock and roll seventies I spent a day with a heavy metal band: Black Sabbath, Ozzy Osbourne and friends in their first incarnation. As media reviewer for *The Episcopalian* magazine, I was covering them because, of all things, they were doing a benefit concert for an Episcopal church in New Jersey. They were getting paid, but anything above a certain gate amount went to the church's youth work. And it was a sold-out event.

I'd been interviewing them. They were good Christian boys, Ozzy assured me, showing me a large metal cross his dad had made for him to wear to ward off evil influences.

The four of them and I, huddled in a tiny room offstage, were waiting for the opening act to close. It did, and then the sound system went crazy—buzzes, hums, crackles, all the squeals and electronic interference you could think of, as if the powers of hell were objecting to what was to come and trying to interfere.

I remember it clearly. We were all getting a little antsy and amused when Geezer Butler, the bass player, turned to me and said, "Hey, Father, maybe you should try a prayer." I shrugged and then started in "Dear Lord." The sound system suddenly snapped into normal mode. All was quiet and ready to go.

I looked at the band as if to say "I do this all the time," and they went out to play. Actually, I don't do this all the time. But sometimes the Lord seems to have a sense of humor. And who are we to complain? —*Leonard Freeman*

# Receiving the Spirit

On the day of Pentecost, the disciples found themselves filled with the Holy Spirit and suddenly, miraculously, able to speak in other languages to spread the good news of "God's deeds of power." Uneducated Galileans, they preached that morning in all the tongues of the Roman Empire.

In our time we have a different sort of seemingly miraculous ability to communicate with others. With e-mail, mobile phones, landlines, and broadcasts, both words and images can reach people around the globe in seconds.

Others can reach us, too. In fact, the signal-to-noise ratio—the percentage of real news over junk, of valuable ideas versus spam—is severely tilted in favor of the spam and junk. Most of what comes over our televisions and radios or flows into our online mailboxes is useless; some of it is downright bad.

In the Gospel of John, Jesus speaks of the Spirit of truth. The world, he warns us, cannot receive the Spirit. The world has its own concerns. In our time and place those tend to be superficial in the extreme, arriving in a torrent of images, sounds, and verbiage that never slows down.

As Christians, we're supposed to have the Spirit abiding in us; we're supposed to be paying attention. Being human, though, too often we don't listen. As a friend of mine put it, "We leave the Bird outside the building, beating its wings against the window," and make important decisions in our own lives and that of the church without prayerful consideration.

Take a moment to turn off the broadcasts, to log off the computer, to walk away from the phone, to find a quiet moment with God, to listen to the Spirit. The peace that Jesus promised is there, if we'll pay attention. —*Sarah Bryan Miller*

# Selling a church

I was staring down the barrel of a new decade of my life and wondering if it would be my last when I decided to visit my boyhood home. Like the dragonflies in Brazil that return each fall to the lake where they were born to touch down once more before dying, I set off for a farm town in Illinois.

A lot had changed in sixty years. I remember farmers coming to town on Saturdays in horse-drawn wagons. As I walked down a street toward the home I grew up in, I passed a church I had never been in because it was not on the approved list of my fundamentalist parents. A big red sign on the lawn said "Sale." Not "Flower Sale" or "Tag Sale," just "Sale."

I asked a man on the porch what kind of sale it was. He said a church sale. I said you can't sell a church. He said, "Sure we can. Take a look. The silver is gone, a restaurant wanted the pews, and someone bought the baptismal font for a planter, but there's lots of good things still left."

So I ambled in, and sure enough there were price tags on chancel furniture and semi-matched china from the kitchen, and a big stack of hymnals were marked, "Free for the taking."

I had a boyhood friend whose family attended this church. They seemed normal enough and my memory was that his church was more interesting than mine. I asked the man who seemed to have an official role why this church had died. He shrugged his shoulders and said, "Times changed, and we didn't. We thought the pendulum would swing back to the church that stays the same. But people haven't been buying what we were selling for years, so now we're selling what people will buy." —*David L. James*

# *Free to stop*

You might say that rest is the last thing that God created.

After God made everything, we are told in Genesis, God rested. It's hard to believe that Almighty God needed to kick back, stretch out, and take a nap to recover from all that work, but perhaps God just might have suspected that these wonderful but potentially flawed creatures which had just been created—human beings—might one day begin believing that they were as powerful and creative as God, not to mention just as invincible. And they might even begin to try to outdo God in using their power and creativity. Improbable, of course, but possible. And so the last thing God created was the freedom to stop, be still, rest, and reflect on the limits of being and the nature of a right relationship between creature and Creator.

Two threads weave themselves through all of God's creation: love and freedom. God loves us enough to endow us with freedom. We are always free—free to reject God's love, free to diminish and misuse God's gifts, free to pretend that we are gods and that the world cannot survive without us, free to believe that our value and worth are found only in our accomplishments. We are free to ignore the meaning and purpose of Sabbath rest, but we do so at our peril. —*James L. Burns*

# *If you understood it, it would not be God*

I often do or say things that surprise and confuse me. These words and actions seem to come from some part of me that I do not know, that I am not in control of. Socrates admonished us to "Know yourself." How can we do that?

When writing his spiritual autobiography, *Confessions*, Augustine posed this hard question to God (and also to himself): "Is there any room in me for you?" He was really asking if God's inscrutability to him had some relation to his own inscrutability to himself.

In one of his sermons, Augustine addressed this question head on: "Since it is God we are speaking of, you do not understand it. If you could understand it, it would not be God." God is a deep mystery, unfathomable to us limited humans. And because we are creatures made in God's image, we incarnate the depth of that divine mystery, at least in part. So Augustine's question, "Is there any room in me for you?" means both that most of the time we crowd God out of our heads and that even when we don't, something about God and ourselves will remain deeply unknowable.

We can only know ourselves, then, by seeking to know God. And we can only seek to know God if we pay attention when God speaks to us through scripture, other people, and prayer. But the truth is that we will never quite entirely know ourselves because we will never quite entirely know God. All things shall be revealed, but, as Augustine knew, our hearts will continue restless until they rest in God. —*Gary Hall*

# *Just as I am*

Consider how we are measured. As children, relentlessly by classroom, aptitude, and standardized tests. Later, it's by athletic ability. Adults have performance reviews. We are measured sexually by consumer advertising, socially and physically against movie stars. From birth to death, we are measured by tribunals, pollsters, peers, politicians, the census bureau, tailors, and tax collectors. Good grief!

And consider, too, the Beatitudes and how *they* measure.

Do other people also grow tired of all the measuring and being found forever wanting? Never bright enough, athletic enough, quick enough, or tall enough? Years ago there was even a toothpaste that promised to give your mouth sex appeal.

We might take comfort in the company of imperfect saints: Zacchaeus and his small stature, Peter and his bumbling love, John the Baptist and his dirty clothes, David and his lethal nonsense, Jonah and his pouting, Moses and his murderous temper, Sarah and her old age snicker, Jacob and his theft of his brother's birthright, Paul and his tendency to scold and lecture. A different standard is at work here, a Christ-like measure: forgiven, redeemed, and glorified for the sake of Jesus. God so loved the world as to send Jesus, ample demonstration of the true measure of love for you and me—just as we are.

The next time you find yourself being measured and found wanting, remember that the proof is in the marvelous measure of God. Then go out and reflect that wonder for the sake of your neighbor who is also weighed down from being measured a day late and a dollar short. —*Richard L. Shimpfky*

# *Ground floor, please*

The Southern rock band the Allman Brothers released a studio album in 1994 that includes the stirring number, "Back Where It All Begins." I like that title, for it could just as well be a primer on the Christian view of human existence.

We should always try to go *back to where it all begins*. And where is that? It begins with love. Christ is the heart of God, and he brings to sinners the love that everybody needs. This love, like the love that babies need, creates the ground floor of personality. For us, this love is the archaeology of *being*.

There are other archaeologies. The English writer Nigel Kneale wrote a phenomenally successful television show for the BBC in the 1950s, which placed the blame for human "original sin" on the Martians whose spacecraft had landed in London millions of years ago. Or there is the Buddhist idea of "dependent arising," by which we are all a mix of fluid factors that jell into a single personality for a brief life span. And there are other theories of our human beginnings.

I will always opt for love to explain things. You see this in people with *un*-loved foundations from childhood—they're insecure. You see it in people who had good loving at the start—they're more confident. The key is prior love, which we had no agency in procuring. This is the love that came to earth in Bethlehem of Judea. —*Paul F. M. Zahl*

# *Perfect imperfection*

Washington, D.C., is one of my family's favorite cities. We lived inside the beltway for three years when our three daughters were school age, and we spent many a weekend dashing down to the Mall, making our way through the museums, the monuments, and the masses of other Americans relishing the stately beauty of their nation's capital.

No visit was complete to me, however, without a good, close look at the Washington Monument, that gleaming, white obelisk that honors our first president, punctuates the city's skyline—and stands as a stark reminder of the paradoxical power of imperfection.

At 555 feet, 5⅛ inches, the tower of marble, granite, and sandstone is a tribute to exact engineering and exquisite beauty. But a good, close look reveals a blemish about 150 feet up, where the stones abruptly turn a slightly lighter shade of sand—a watermark left by a flood of troubled times in United States history when construction was halted for years in the wake of political unrest, unfunded budgets, and the Civil War.

Some might say the monument, therefore, is flawed, but I disagree. It is in the structure's imperfection that we find perfection: a monument that not only honors history, but embodies the past— its pain and its glory—in a way that is historic, authentic, and, to me, perfectly imperfect.

This is what Jesus means when he calls us to be perfect. Not flawless, but perfect in the way we stand as living monuments to honor God. From a distance, we can luminously reflect his divine light into the world. Anyone who gets a close look, though, will see faults and failures, scars that are the perfect expressions of pain suffered, wounds healed, and life lived. —*Jerald Hyche*

# Church building

Another Manhattan church plans to close its worship space to public use on weekdays, following an assault on a custodian. I understand, and I think the pastor made the right call for the time being. Staff must be able to feel secure. The next phase needs to be studied.

My hope for the next phase is that members will step up and stand vigil. If there is any justification for a large worship space and associated tax benefits, it is that the space serves the city. Not just church members on Sunday, but the entire community throughout the week, with sacred space available for drop-in use, concerts, homeless sheltering, and civic meetings.

So let the members take turns providing a security-minded presence during weekdays. If half a dozen were on site and visible when the church is open, it might deter crime. It would also give members an updated perspective on what it means to be a church in the twenty-first century in a large urban area.

The key here is to be overt about giving something away. People tend to be protective of what they have, even church people. To live faithfully in God's economy, however, we need to accept ancient biblical principles such as gleaning, caring for widows and orphans, feeding the hungry, sheltering the homeless, and tending to the needs of the fallen stranger. This is basic gospel.

Like anything to do with the gospel, it only becomes real when we live it out. The gospel isn't a compilation of good intentions. It is love in action. It is the Word heard, read, marked, inwardly digested, and made a cornerstone of each believer's daily existence.

If we can't find a way to make our church buildings safe and available, then we have no business keeping them in operation.
—*Thomas L. Ehrich*

# *A little faith*

Well, it finally had happened—we were heading to Ohio. Jane, with her newly minted Ph.D., was going to teach at Hiram College, and I was going to…to…what *was* I going to do?

I had talked to the Ohio regional minister who said, "All our pulpits near Hiram are filled. Realistically, it's going to be a while before we can get a match for you that's within reasonable driving distance. Maybe you should consider an interim with a sister denomination."

Hmmm. Not exactly what I had hoped to hear. Here was Jane, finished with the rigors of student life and headed to her terrific new job, and here I was, having just left a wonderful church, and now at loose ends. As we sat in my parents' living room, out it all poured—all of my predictable, middle-aged male angst. "I am happy for her, but I just don't know what I'm going to do!" And so on and so forth.

My stepmother, a good Church of God woman, drank it all in. She patiently let me wallow until she could no longer stand it and then said, "Oh, for God's sake, you're a minister! You ought to have a little faith!"

There it was, a hug and a kick in the slats at the same time. I needed both. Mom was right. We all, not just the ordained, should have a little faith. —*Gregory A. Russell*

# *We're already praying*

"I have trouble sleeping at night," she said. "It helps when I take my medication and turn the fan on. And sometimes," she confided, with a trace of an embarrassed laugh, "I imagine that God is out there in the dark beyond the window." In her mid-seventies, though a confirmed agnostic, there is still something within her that both acknowledges and yearns for the Other.

I wasn't surprised. As Saint Augustine confessed to God: "Our hearts are restless until they find their peace in you." Human beings seem to be hard-wired with a desire for God. This hunger is both a divine gift and the beginning of prayer.

"Lord, teach us to pray!" his disciples implored, eager to taste the intimacy with God that Jesus enjoyed. Jesus responded with what we've come to call the Lord's Prayer. It's simple, beautiful, all-encompassing. But there are many kinds of prayers and many ways to pray.

We're already praying. Whenever we provide for another's needs, we're in conversation with the Giver of all good things. Whenever we notice the miracle of a green leaf, we're in communion with the Author of life. Whenever we cry out in anguish, we're in dialogue with the One who willingly suffered with us.

On some level, the human/divine conversation is always going on. As Saint Paul assured his friends in Rome: "We do not know how to pray as we ought, but that very Spirit intercedes with sighs too deep for words" (Romans 8:26). Even in our subconscious and in our dreams, it seems our minds and hearts are chattering to God, and God is chattering back!

We can learn much about the practice of prayer. But perhaps the place to start is to pay closer attention to the dialogue already in process. —*Charles F. Brumbaugh*

# *The Trinity*

To know God is to know reality, to know what life is really all about, and so to have the necessary information for making good decisions.

I used to think this was complicated, but it's not. The Trinity says in essence that we experience God in three different ways, but it is all the same God. One God in three Persons.

• God the Father is God in creation, nature, and the natural sciences: that Absolutely Other who is eternal and greater than us.

• God the Son is God known through the human story, embodied in Jesus the Christ but also seen in our stories: history, psychology, the humanities.

• God the Holy Spirit is God within us: experienced, moving, guiding our lives through intuition, inner truth, and spirituality.

Each piece on its own provides only a part of the picture.

Creation and nature, the sciences on their own, can seem to present a world cruel and heartless, survival of the fittest, "nature red in tooth and claw," as the poet Tennyson described it.

Left on our own to forge our human story, we can forget the greater One and forget our tendency to sin. Atheistic Communism and Nazism, on paper, were great visions of what humans could accomplish. In reality, they were horrific frauds.

The Spirit, on its own, can seem to support a self-indulgent narcissism, a "me first" attitude. The word "religion," as opposed to spirituality, means a discipline, something more than just me. It may be inconvenient, but necessary for the health of our souls.

It is only when the witness of these three come together— Father, Son, and Holy Spirit (or nature, story, and inner self)— that we know we have come into the holy presence of reality and truth. —*Leonard Freeman*

# *I don't like roller coasters*

It is every parent's nightmare: the good kid studies all night at the university library and then as she heads home is struck by a drunken driver and critically injured. And Laura is an exceptionally good kid: bright, hard-working, talented, blessed with a lovely voice. She has been a mainstay of choirs and summer Royal School of Church Music camps. Her parents play those recordings for her now, taking shifts at the intensive care unit where she has spent the last two weeks in a coma. She is their only child.

ICU waiting rooms are places where tired people hold grim vigils, where every face turns to view and assess a newcomer: doctor? relative? priest? friend of the family? I have been in ICUs before, usually as part of clinical pastoral education. This is different. This is not a stranger hooked up to the drips and the monitors; this is not someone who has had a long life. This is Laura, just on the cusp of adulthood and so full of promise.

"It's a roller coaster," her mother says. Improvements take them emotionally up, but new problems plunge them back down again, around sharp curves, lurching unexpectedly. "I don't like roller coasters."

I try to pray "Thy will be done." I don't really mean it; I just want to see Laura restored to normalcy. I try to say my mother's standard prayer for healing, leaving it up to God to decide what form that healing should take, but it turns into, "Give us a miracle, Lord."

Laura is wrapped in prayer like a baby in swaddling clothes, carried by love like an infant safely asleep in her mother's arms. Hundreds of people around the world, in an impressive variety of faiths and traditions, are carrying her and her parents in their supplications. "Lord, have mercy." —*Sarah Bryan Miller*

# *Climbing Everest*

Laura was in her coma for weeks, fighting off pneumonia and various infections. Now that she has emerged, her parents face a new set of problems, from her jaw's painful tendency to dislocate when she yawns (resulting in several trips to the emergency room) to Laura's own dawning realization of, and unhappiness about, her condition. Her father, who is accustomed to working nights, stays in her room in the rehab hospital to hold her when she tries to escape from her bed. Does she know what she's doing? "Oh, yes," he replies.

For all the problems and all the uncertainty about the future, Laura's parents find and appreciate new miracles every day: important doctors agreeing to see and treat Laura, her increasing ability to use her once-paralyzed right arm, the moment when they realize that she can read the get-well cards.

To follow Laura's progress is to appreciate the importance of scale. Tasks she once did without thinking must now be relearned; the simple becomes complicated. Nothing comes easily, and the frustration level is high. Yet compared to her situation just a month ago, she has made giant strides. Then we didn't know if she would live; now we don't know the extent to which she can recover. But hundreds of us are praying for her and trusting in God for her welfare.

Her mother keeps a journal; her father is keeping a photographic record. The photo of her lying so still in the ICU while a friend plays his viola for her contrasts with one of her smiling and stretching with both arms. Laura is doing the equivalent of climbing Mount Everest. The faith of those who love her helps to provide the oxygen in this thin air. —*Sarah Bryan Miller*

# *Curves and surprises*

Laura continues to progress in a way that her doctors and therapists call miraculous. Less than two months after the accident she walked out of rehab using only a cane; she now commutes to therapy three days a week.

Five months on, her feeding tube is finally out. Her neurologist has tweaked the delicate balance of her meds. The surgeon says his work to repair and replace the delicate bones in her left ear is healing well; her hearing should be restored soon.

The prayers and other help continue. Laura's voice teacher visits and works with her on the building blocks of sound. Her appetite is still minimal; her aunt comes in regularly from Tennessee and cooks tempting meals for her. Her friends from church and the university have not forgotten her.

Laura and her incredible progress were the cover story of the hospital's widely distributed magazine; her father's photographs illustrated her journey, from a picture of her lying still in the ICU to one standing upright and working on a treadmill, a big smile on her face.

The future isn't entirely clear, though. Whether Laura will speak or sing again is still unknown; whether she'll be able to finish her education and fulfill her plans to work with autistic children is up in the air.

The road that she and her parents must follow is full of curves and surprises. Whatever happens, it is a journey undertaken in faith. Says Laura's mother, "We trust that if God wants her to sing for him again, it will be so." —*Sarah Bryan Miller*

# Miss Ollie

After I had served a year as a university chaplain, I was called to be rector of St. Stephen's Church, a small parish in Covington, Kentucky, across the Ohio River from Cincinnati. The bishop had sent me off with his prayers and the charge that I should go to that congregation and "just love them." When I arrived, Miss Ollie was already an established character among characters. Years before I came, she had somehow acquired the bishop's chair from a church that was closing in Cincinnati and brought it many miles by streetcars to place it in St. Stephen's chancel. The loving was easy.

The neighborhood was half Roman Catholic and half Protestant. When there was intermarriage, the couple often came to the Episcopal Church. This was a good thing, for our congregation was elderly. One year I had twelve burials from a Sunday attendance of about a hundred.

We also drew people who were curious about our beliefs and practices. Many of them joined us. One was a young man named Rick. We had a number of conversations, and I invited him to attend a service. He did, and I asked him to stand with me afterward and meet the members. When it came Miss Ollie's turn, she showed her delight and as a token of welcome reached into her bag and gave Rick a grapefruit. He knew he had found his church home.

Rick's parents and a family of friends eventually joined him at St. Stephen's. Rick became a priest and many years later at a home-coming event he gave due credit to Miss Ollie and the grapefruit.
—*Robert Horine*

# *A prayer answered*

*Ask, and it will be given you;*
*search, and you will find;*
*knock, and the door will be opened for you.*
—Matthew 7:7

I was standing in the parking lot of a church camp, welcoming parents and campers on opening day. A priest from an inner city congregation arrived with a van full of kids. All the kids went immediately to registration except one. He stood next to me in the parking lot and carefully surveyed the scene. He stared for a long time.

"Can we swim in that pool?" he asked.

"Absolutely," I responded.

"Do we sleep in those cabins?" he asked.

"Yes."

"Can we fish in that pond?"

"You bet."

I saw a tear coming down his cheek. He looked up at me and said with an enormous smile, "Mister, I have been praying to the Lord all my life for a place like this."

It is a blessing to be part of a church that has the occasional and amazing opportunity to answer someone's prayer. —*Jason Leo*

# *Wisdom*

*Almighty God, the fountain of all wisdom,*
*you know our necessities before we ask...*
—The Book of Common Prayer,
The Collect for Proper 11

When Mother Teresa was asked what she said when she prayed, she replied, "I don't say anything. I listen."

"And what does God say?" was the next question.

"God doesn't say anything. God listens."

What are we to say when we pray? What words should we use? This question is often asked by those who will go on to say: "I'm not articulate or wise, not when speaking with God. I don't have anything to say."

What should we say? Perhaps we should say nothing. This is more than a suggestion. It could be a rule that applies not only to those moments when we are speechless, but all the time. If we do not have anything to say, be quiet and listen, just listen.

God knows our necessities before we ask. There is nothing we actually have to say. Listen. Let God pray with us and for us.

The one quality missing from our lives more than any other is silence. It is the most precious commodity we need to find; it is what we need most. It is totally absent from most of our lives.

When was the last time you experienced complete, absolute silence? It is elusive and difficult to find. So set your mind to the task right now. Seek and find silence today. When you do, let God speak. God knows your necessities before you ask. —*Edward S. Gleason*

# *Unseen but real*

*Harvey* is Mary Ellen Chace's popular play, written in the late 1940s, concerning a certain Mr. Elwood P. Dowd who was befriended by a six-foot-tall rabbit named Harvey. Her play became an even greater success when it was made into a movie starring Jimmy Stewart and Josephine Hull.

*Harvey* is a hoot, with mistaken identities, small-town characters, a little romance, and a lot of heart. It is also *the* play about grace. Elwood P. Dowd is such a forgiving and compassionate character, with such a dear, light touch, that the audience loves him from the first time he enters until the final curtain. If Tolstoy and Dostoyevsky descry grace in narrative terms, and Victor Hugo in poetic terms, Mary Ellen Chace gets it in *absurd* terms. The rabbit "Harvey" does not exist formally—or does he? But he is the unseen god of grace to Elwood P. Dowd, who then becomes the visible bearer of grace to everyone in town.

The unreality and actual futility of human existence was caught by T. S. Eliot in the 1920s. But the unseen *reality* of love and hope was captured twenty years later by Mary Ellen Chace. Or to put it in New Testament terms, "Those who do not love a brother or sister whom they have seen, cannot love God whom they have not seen" (1 John 4:20).
—*Paul F. M. Zahl*

# God spelled backwards

Dog is God spelled backwards. After my release from prison, my wife and I found a puppy in the ditch. He was a little red ball of fur and looked like a small Teddy bear.

Dookie grew into a big, red Chow and Rottweiler mix. We played for hours in the backyard and spent lots of Saturday mornings with him in our bed splayed between my outstretched legs, head on my stomach, sleeping peacefully, whimpering and twitching at his dreams while I stroked his head and told him it would be okay.

One day we were sitting in the swing on the front porch, Dookie curled with his head in my lap. Gratitude swelled inside me as I ran my hand through his ruff. I was grateful that we had found him and been able to give him a loving home. I thanked God for the chance and the grace to act as benefactor.

Then Dookie raised his head and looked into my soul as if to say with his eyes, "You know you've got that backwards, don't you?" Then I remembered coming home scared or mad or overwhelmed, to be met at the door by that wagging stub of a tail and the encompassing love of those eyes. I thought about how my chest could be as tight as a drum, but all my stress would dissipate when Dookie settled up against me and sighed. I remembered all the times I had been impatient or irritable and he would lick my hand as if to say, "Let me wash that away."

Tears now streaming down my face, I lifted his face in my hands and kissed him on his cold, wet, black nose. —*Bo Cox*

# Connecting

A walking city like New York has many virtues. But some of them disappear on a day of heavy rain, like today. As I watched a young woman walk resolutely along without the least bit of rain gear, I admired her spunk and sympathized with her. I was doing the same.

Shared experience, even if negative, is one of life's great joys. Tough times connect us in a way that prosperity doesn't. When a child's antic catches several adult eyes, we exchange smiles as if we had just seen to the heart of life.

The genius of Christian faith isn't right opinion or perfect rules. It's the sharing of life, as heart touches heart in the experience of being human together before God. That's why the church kitchen is often the heartbeat of a congregation. It's why worship leaders need to laugh together and pray together first, so that they have something to offer the congregation.

Jesus created circles in which that radical sharing could take place. I have no patience with Christians' tendency to exclude, to declare some unwelcome, to set rules on who is acceptable before God. Jesus set no such rules. Neither should we. Jesus welcomed all, even the least desirable. So should we.

And when they were together, the disciples ate, touched, prayed, talked, learned—and, yes, made fools of themselves. So should we.

We aren't called to rule the world. We are called to connect and to extend our connecting to others. —*Thomas L. Ehrich*

# *Doing love*

I spied the bag on the floor and noticed it was packed with a velvety gray blanket and a variety of treats. The bag stood out against the cold institutional surroundings of the hospital room. My friend was being attended by his wife and buoyed up by an intravenous morphine drip. The night would likely be short for him, but long for his wife sitting vigil in the hard, plastic-covered hospital chair. The bag was for her. A member of the parish remembered how cold and hungry she had become on long nights of keeping watch over her own husband. So the bag spoke volumes of love without speaking a single word.

The author of 1 John believed love talk should be replaced by acts of love. "Little children, let us love, not in word or speech, but in truth and action" (1 John 3:18). Christian love cannot remain cerebral. Action is necessary. The incarnation of Christ, God taking on human flesh, is the divine witness to the content of true love. In much the same way that Jesus Christ walked among us, love must be seen, touched, and experienced.

Some disagreed with John's description of love. They saw love as the highest ideal or thought. These people, perhaps forerunners of what would become a much stronger Gnostic movement in the early church, contended that God would not disgrace himself by becoming a lowly human. In that scenario, Christ becomes an ideal and not a person, and love is diminished in the process. John considered such a departure from the authentic nature of Christ's love to be the "spirit of the antichrist" (4:3).

Tempting as it may be to over-spiritualize our Christian faith, we should resist such attempts and instead love in word and deed.
—*W. Patrick Gahan*

# Saint Anthony

*Tony, Tony, turn around.*
*Something's lost and must be found.*

I first heard this verse when I worked in Boston, in my twenties. Our office secretary was Roman Catholic, and if you were Catholic in Boston, you knew the saints. Whenever she lost something she prayed to Saint Anthony. And the item was found, usually right away. Soon I began saying those words when I lost things. And I found them. Or maybe it wasn't me finding them. It could have been Saint Anthony.

Thirty years later, I write a lot on computers and I am surprised to find that Saint Anthony even knows how computers work. He finds things in the archives, in the files. The guy knows his stuff. Really. Perhaps he has been taking continuing education classes in heaven, because he was a fourth-century hermit. In the desert. In the caves. Saint Anthony was an ascetic, living without much in terms of material things. His mind was clear.

It still seems clear. I have come to believe in Saint Anthony. I have come to believe that others in heaven know their stuff, too. Like Michael, one of four archangels mentioned in the Bible. Michael is a big, strong angel, and I envision him putting his arms around cars and planes, keeping family members safe.

There are no egos in the Communion of Saints. Everyone works for God. I like to think of both saints and angels responding to prayers, delivering messages, helping the Holy Spirit. Sometimes I picture prayers being said, lifted up like incense, as the psalm goes, and then upon reaching heaven, being quickly handed off to the best angel or saint for the job. —*Lindsay Hardin Freeman*

# *Good enough*

I'm downloading a new security program on my computer this morning. It will protect me from notifications of secret lovers who are dying to meet me and invitations to try medicines to increase the size of an organ I do not possess. You can download these things in the comfort of your own home, but it still takes time, and you can't always work alongside it. When I began, I had almost two hours to write an eMo, a meditation to post on my website—the perfect amount of time. After all the restarts and updates, though, I now have forty-five minutes until I must be on the train.

Ah, well. That old saying about any job worth doing is worth doing well doesn't always apply. Many things worth doing don't have to be perfect. If you lack time to do a perfect job, do a good-enough job, a best-you-can-in-the-time-you-have job. Sometimes good enough is just going to have to be good enough. You can't do better than the best you can do in the time you have.

I look at my old books and articles—a word here would be better left out, I see, and here is a sentence that could have been structured differently, to its advantage. They're all tissues of error, really; not one of them is perfect. But they got done and they got out there, and no reader has yet died from their imperfections.

Get it as done as you can and get it out there. If you have the luxury of time, savor it—there is no greater gift. But if you do not, don't think that you cannot create. Some people turn the gift of time into a curse: they tinker and tweak for years, and their work never sees the light of day. They die with it all still in a drawer, frightened of the world's reception of an imperfect work. But most work is imperfect, and the world barely notices.
—*Barbara Cawthorne Crafton*

# *Fear*

Fear has its uses. It makes us cautious. It heightens our awareness of danger. It keeps us from rushing, in a foolhardy way, into perils we had best avoid.

But many of the problems of modern life stem from an excess of fear rather than a deficit. That is not to say that there aren't real dangers out there. But it is to say that we can spend so much of our mental and emotional energy focused on things that frighten us that we lose the ability to act on behalf of others and ourselves.

The writer Edward Hoagland once noted this in his diary: "My father, dying, sailed his little boat more boldly in Long Island Sound." Aware of the certainty of his impending death, Hoagland's father felt free to sail boldly. With nothing now to fear, he was free to take risks that expressed themselves in greater creativity.

One of the great gifts of the Christian life is that those who follow Jesus also have nothing to fear. That is true in part because, oriented to the cross, we know that, like Jesus, we shall die. But we know something else, too. Oriented as we are toward Easter, we know that death will not have the last word about us. As death is robbed of its power, we too have nothing to fear. We are free to live courageous and creative lives on behalf of others, knowing that all will be well.

Edward Hoagland's father expressed his creative freedom rather late in life. He "sailed his little boat more boldly in Long Island Sound." That is how he gave shape to what it means to live without fear. How will you? —*Gary Hall*

# *Nourishing or noshing?*

Jesus calls himself the bread of life. When we receive Communion, the priest says, "The Body of Christ, the bread of heaven." Christ enters into us to meet our deepest need.

Food of all kinds fills our day. Usually, whether it involves food or mental intake, we are noshing. We grab a donut, eat a candy bar, snack on chips. Then it's late at night and we nibble on leftovers.

We live on sound bites. A new bishop is to be interviewed on TV, and it turns out to be a three-minute session. We go to our doctors and feel we are in a factory production line, with a maximum of ten minutes. We place a phone call and are put on hold while being fed whatever loop of promotions they want to inflict on us. Daily life is a series of bits and pieces. Not much is there to nourish us.

So much information and so many opinions are flooding us every day. It all accumulates. It's too much—something has got to give! And so I may nosh on food, on dumb TV programs, on trivia, anything to divert myself from the awareness that I'm overwhelmed. On good days my awareness of Christ inside me enables me to attend to what matters: to take time to chew a real piece of bread, to read a book, to have phone conversations with far-flung children and grandchildren, to e-mail a friend, to devote more than a passing glance to the news of the day, to observe times of silence.

My family thrives on words. But when I am eating bread, I cannot speak. "I am the bread of life." "Yes," I say to myself, "hush up and be fed." —*Lee Krug*

# *Rewriting history*

Have you noticed your resistance to new information or perspectives? It's called "cognitive dissonance." That's when new information is inconsistent with your concept of yourself as an honest, intelligent, and well-meaning person. What happens when the story you've been telling yourself about yourself no longer rings true? When you wake up to the fact that you've begun to believe your own publicity? It's excruciating. I conveniently forget facts that suggest I have behaved stupidly or badly, and I go on the hunt for new information that will confirm my good view of myself. It's interesting that in the legal system there's a resistance to trusting DNA testing. Even if it proves the suspect innocent, some prosecutors still cannot admit or even believe that they were wrong.

It can work in the opposite direction, too. Some of us refuse to believe the good news about ourselves. When I taught in the theological college in Lincoln, England, several years ago, I was told the story of a daughter of the dean of the cathedral in the late seventeenth century. A strong Calvinist, she was utterly convinced that she was damned, and nothing could persuade her otherwise. She was so convinced that while standing on the stone floor of the deanery kitchen, she picked up a glass pitcher and said, "I am as surely damned as this pitcher will break when I hurl it onto the floor!" She threw it down and it didn't break! And her whole picture of herself had to be abandoned. This was cognitive dissonance in a positive direction. It is said that she later fell in love and had a wonderful family. She experienced a revolution in imagination. —*Alan Jones*

# *You are my daddy*

I had a theology lesson from my daughter one day. She was about three and a half, still sleeping in a crib but definitely old enough to reason. As I put her to bed, she stood at the rail in her bunny pajamas, looked up at me and said: "God keeps us safe. You are my daddy; you keep me safe. You are God!"

I stuttered for a moment, then replied from somewhere in my parental unconscious, "Well, no, I'm not...but it's kind of like we have a line-of-action going. God keeps your mommy and me safe, and we keep you safe..."

Afterwards, it struck me that this was not bad theology. That really is the way it works. Human beings are among the few animals that don't come out of the womb ready, or at least to some extent able, to take care of themselves. I remember helping in the birth of a calf, pulling it out of its mother's womb. It whumped to the ground, stood up, and looked around at me to be fed. I pointed it toward the mother and moved off.

We humans don't work that way. We need lots of keeping safe, lots of nurturing, just to begin to think about taking care of ourselves. So God gives us each other to do the job, not only physically but also to convey some of the most important lessons of life: that we are valuable, that we are loved, that the larger world wants us to be here and to grow in healthy directions.

When we do that for one another, we are taking our place in the line of divine action—"God keeps us safe, and we keep you safe."
—*Leonard Freeman*

# *Tattoo*

When I was seventeen years old, every boy I knew wanted a tattoo. Not the little press-on/wash-off kind you can buy today, but real tattoos that didn't come off. You couldn't get a tattoo in our town, or a drink for that matter. Too many Baptists. But you could go over to the seedy part of St. Louis and get both.

When I told my parents, they said a tattoo would be a sin, a desecration of the body, and a permanent mark I would later regret. One Saturday night a carload of boys headed off to St. Louis. There was lots of nervous laughter as we talked about how it really didn't hurt like people said it would, and what design, and how big a tattoo we would get.

We parked the car in front of the largest tattoo parlor. The display window contained photos of snakes on shoulders, messages of eternal devotion, and flags on arms. I wondered what it would be like to have one of those designs on my body for the rest of my life. I'm told that at great expense and discomfort, a tattoo can be partially eradicated but once you got it, you got it.

One boy in our group announced he was just looking, another said he had to check with his girlfriend, and we all breathed a sigh of relief that we wouldn't have to go through with it. But what sent a cold chill through me that hot night was a picture of a man's bicep with the words "Jesus Saves" over a purple cross. Something about those words in that setting turned my stomach.

Suddenly, I didn't want to be there because I had been tattooed before. I had been marked with the sign of the cross by a Methodist bishop at my baptism when I was three weeks old, and once you got it, you got it. —*David L. James*

# *This little light*

Rider conduct on the New York City subway is governed by a tacit code. *Thou shalt avoid eye contact with thy fellow passengers. Thou shalt not speak. Thou shalt act as though no living being is near thee.* Having just arrived in the city, my wife and I observed the rules without question. For twenty minutes, the only sound was the cacophony of steel wheels on steel tracks.

Then three middle-aged men, shabbily clothed, entered at an uptown station. As the train pulled out, one of them hummed a musical pitch, and they broke into "This little light of mine, I'm gonna let it shine." Their beautifully harmonizing voices were a magical incantation, calling us stone statues into life. We shifted our posture to turn toward them; we exchanged smiling glances.

They were businessmen, of course—street performers. Their song finished, they held out a cup to receive change or a dollar bill, then moved on down the train. But their light had indeed penetrated the underground grayness, dispelling the chill of the car. In the warmed space the buskers left behind, people even chanced a remark or two.

A couple of hours later, Brenda and I were seeing for the first time our month-old granddaughter. So *little*, I thought as I held her. But big enough to shine a compelling brightness and warmth. Some part of my sixty-year-old self, long stony, softened.

It takes only a little light. —*Bruce Birdsey*

# *Memorialized and missed*

I spend a lot of time in my seminary chapel reading memorial plaques. The fact that I do this says less about the quality of seminary worship than the quality of my attention span. But then, the plaques in this old space are really splendid things. The building dates from the 1880s, and its architecture reflects the quaintly Gothic tastes of an otherwise staunchly evangelical set of founders. To be fair, the plaques are not the first thing you see when you walk in. They were intended to be relatively inconspicuous. But still, once you've settled into the daily round of prayer and praise and scripture reading, morning, noon and evening, day in and day out, when your mind begins to drift a little, you start to notice the plaques.

Near where I tend to sit, there is an eloquent memorial to W. Cosby Bell, "Professor of Theology in this Seminary":

> A Man Who Loved the
> Mountain Streams, the
> Hearts of Men, the
> Christ of God.
> A Thinker who Sensed the
> Wonder of Life and
> Interpreted its Fulness to a
> Bewildered Age.

You seldom hear the word apologetics any more (or you mistake it for apology, which my fellow Episcopalians find themselves spending all too much time doing). But W. Cosby Bell must have been an eloquent apologist for the hope that was in him. Our bewildered churches could use a W. Cosby Bell in these contentious days.
—*Roger Ferlo*

# The wound of enlightenment

When you become disillusioned—and it sometimes happens in an instant—you are ripe for enlightenment. Generally we think Eastern or Asian when we hear that term. Enlightenment is supposed to be something that happens to you under the Bodhi Tree.

But enlightenment is just *life* coming at you, with its full dismantling impact. Paul was afterwards touched to the core by his own part in the stoning of Stephen. He was the "wretched man that I am" of his own later letter to the Romans (7:24). On the road to Damascus he had become ripe for enlightenment. "Saul, Saul, why do you persecute me?" Paul pitched from his horse, was blinded for days, and then Ananias conferred that sacrament of enlightenment. Paul's scales fell off.

Human deconstruction is what happens when everything goes south. It is what happens when what you thought was trustworthy and real is revealed to be moth-eaten and crumbling. "How could I have been so wrong about so much? I had better bark up a new tree, maybe the right tree this time."

God speaks—which is another word for enlightenment—when the "world" with its "vain pomp and glory" (1928 Prayer Book) comes crashing down around you. But it is as if God cannot, or does not, speak until the wound is fresh. When the walls of your protective Jerichos are blown down—Hurricane Katrina? Hurricane Ike? Lehman Brothers?—the restoring voice of Glory will be heard, right where you live, even among the ruins of the former things. —*Paul F. M. Zahl*

# *Making the team*

There was a time long, long ago—before organized leagues and uniforms and parents who watched—when a ragtag clump of kids would gather on the side of a vacant lot or field and play the game. The hoots and the hype, the teasing taunts, the smack-mouth talk would quiet, and the self-appointed captains would take over the excruciating process of choosing players.

"I'll take Tommy," says one. "I'll take Jimmy," says the other. Slowly, one by one, the best are chosen first, the average are recruited as needed, and the least quite often never have a chance. It was a hard rule learned early and repeated in subsequent arenas of life—school, clubs, business, and the board room. There are winners, and there are losers. And never the two shall meet.

Unless, of course, you are talking about Jesus, the divinely appointed captain who betrayed the usual logic for recruiting his team. "I'll take Peter," he says, despite the fisherman's blundering faith. "I'll take James and John," he says, ignoring their tempers. "I'll take Thomas," overlooking his skeptical eye. "I'll take Judas," accepting his own tragic fate. And all the others nobody else would have chosen to be anything close to a decent team of disciples, much less a dream team.

But that's the way it was—and is. Jesus knows that what we're lacking in talent we make up in our inability to be faithful. And yet he sees us not as sinners but superstars, with our greatness rooted not in our abilities, but in his call to us.

Jesus chooses us. If we are still and we listen, we can see him. He looks us in the eye, gives us the nod, and utters the words we so want to hear: "I'll take you." —*Jerald Hyche*

# *Jonah and John*

Jonah and John the Baptist were angry men, righteously angry at those who avoided God's well-marked path and abused God's well-chosen people, and angry with despair at people whose greed and sloth were a stain on every form of hope. Those people were spinach on the teeth of God's beautiful smile—they had to go. Jonah and John were not only convinced of that fact, they relished it. Jonah's sights were set on the people of Nineveh, whose wickedness was known to God. "Forty days more and Nineveh will be overthrown!" promised Jonah. John focused on his neighbors, calling them "a brood of vipers" and warning that the Messiah would come with axe, fire, and sifter to straighten them out.

I can understand their frustration even if my sense of good manners keeps me from hurling prophetic curses. I take God's Word seriously while many do not, or at least they take it very differently. I am appalled by much of the behavior our society seems to enjoy and encourage. I know people who would have no personality at all if it were not for greed and sloth. They make me angry, and I find myself standing with Jonah, John, and the author of Psalm 139 who said "Do I not hate those, O LORD, who hate you?...hate them with a perfect hatred."

Fortunately our righteous little group does not seem to include Jesus. When John the Baptist sent messengers to ask whether his cousin was going to start smiting people hip and thigh, Jesus said he was more interested in healing than hurting. When Jonah got through with threats, he found God genuinely "concerned" about the Ninevites. The psalmist sometimes seemed to say, "I hate your enemies—why can't you do the same?" But Jesus said, "Love your enemies...so you may be children of your Father in heaven" (Matthew 5:44-45).

—*Francis H. Wade*

# *Heart's desire*

Angry and hurt, I cried. My application for an academic position at a university had been rejected once again. I had left college teaching tenured and successful. For the past seven years I had been trying in vain to get back in. The last time I interviewed, I was selected out of a thousand applicants, until the department realized that they could staff more cheaply with part-time instructors rather than hire a full-time person with benefits.

I railed against God. Heaven was shut and deaf to my cries. My career was ended; my plans smashed. It was then that I was reborn. I turned my life and will over to God. In my misery, I went to see a clinical psychologist and then had a dream in which a cross, an anchor, and a glowing red heart appeared. The psychologist and I interpreted the dream to be about my new career possibilities: the cross (faith) was religious education, the anchor (hope) was alcohol and drug counseling, and the heart (love) was clinical psychology.

In my previous career, I had never asked God what he wanted me to do. In this new one, I asked every step of the way. For every test I took, I said, "God, if you want me to be a psychologist, let me pass this test. If you don't, give me the serenity to give up." I passed eighty-eight tests, a national written exam, and board orals, not to mention a year's hospital internship and three years' residency—all highly competitive, and I am not a competitive person.

I can see God's plan for me only in retrospect. Since I had asked him what he wanted me to do, he responded by firmly closing the door on my past career and giving me my real heart's desire. —*Carol McCrae*

# *Lines*

It seems to be human nature to draw lines, sharp lines that divide race from race, family from family, nation from nation. We are divided over possessions, lands, and ideas. Even within the different faiths that should unite people, dividing lines abound. Into this world of division God in Christ comes, knowing that his presence will not end divisions. What then are we to learn from his life among us? That division is never God's desire or purpose. Jesus continually crossed boundaries in search of outcasts and those who were cut off from God. He came, by his own admission, to destroy the divisions between a lost creation and God.

We draw lines, but God, who is Alpha and Omega, beginning and end, beholds "this fragile earth our island home" and fills it with his presence—the gift of incarnation. We may draw all the lines we like, believing that they are real and permanent, but God encircles our divisions with love. When we awaken to the presence of that love we will see that our lines serve no purpose whatever.

> *O come, Desire of nations, bind*
> *in one the hearts of all mankind;*
> *bid thou our sad divisions cease,*
> *and be thyself our King of Peace.*
> —HYMNAL 1982, #56

—*James L. Burns*

# The roof of the temple

I was a deacon, first year out of seminary, working at the cathedral in Boston. It was a beautiful June morning, with a blue sky and temperatures in the seventies. It seemed a perfect day. And I was excited. I was set to do my first baptism, an infant. I'd practiced the day before, holding my squirming cat.

But as I came over Beacon Hill, where I'd parked the car, to the cathedral, I saw police lights flashing and a white sheet with what looked like a body underneath.

A man had thrown himself off the top of the cathedral, just in time for the eight o'clockers to discover him. Or perhaps it was the sexton, now busy hosing the blood off the sidewalk, who found him.

No one knew him. Later, someone said he'd come to the soup kitchen downstairs occasionally. That was all we ever heard.

Death, self-induced. A baptism, new life. Completely opposite poles of life, but both wrapped ideologically around the building, both wrapped around the place where people come to know God, the church. Did the man choose to kill himself at a church because he was angry at God? Had he reached out earlier and we missed it? Had he been baptized himself? Was the roof of the cathedral reminiscent of the temple roof upon which Jesus stood, tempted by Satan? If so, Satan seemed to win this round.

I've never quite closed the book on that morning. But I hope the man *was* baptized. I believe that would have made finding his way home easier. And I hope that he, marked as Christ's own forever, is finally finding the peace he lacked in this life. —*Lindsay Hardin Freeman*

# Goodness has nothing to do with it

Think of the late Mae West who so famously said to the coat check girl who sighed "Goodness!" in admiration of the actress's huge diamond pendant: "My dear, goodness had nothing to do with it." Now hear the words of Hosea expressing the deepest longing of the Lord of hosts: "I desire steadfast love and not sacrifice, the knowledge of God rather than burnt offerings" (Hosea 6:6).

Hosea stood in judgment about eight hundred years before Jesus. Israel's unity from David's time had been shattered, and while the southern kingdom of Judah felt secure in her military might, the northern kingdom of Israel was close to anarchy. Hosea confronts the deplorable situation: "The LORD has an indictment against the inhabitants of the land. There is no faithfulness or loyalty, and no knowledge of God in the land. Swearing, lying, and murder, and stealing and adultery break out; bloodshed follows bloodshed" (Hosea 4:1-2).

Some say Hosea's lament was occasioned by the faithlessness of his wife, her transgression a sign of the state of the whole people; a people not unlike a young bull out of pasture in pursuit of the heifers, trampling the fences of restraint. A "spirit of whoredom" had led the people astray (Hosea 4:12).

Then, in the face of so great an apostasy, Hosea rushes to affirm the faithfulness and steadfast love of the Most High for his people: "How can I give you up? My heart recoils within me, my compassion grows warm and tender, and I will not destroy. I will love you, freely" (Hosea 11:8-9, paraphrased).

I think of Esau, grievously wronged by his brother, yet hugging Jacob's guilty neck. Here is encouragement to free us to hug our own guilty necks and serve the Lord's pleasure, knowing that our goodness has nothing to do with it!

—*Richard L. Shimpfky*

# Big, yellow steam shovel

The call came while I was on a trip with the neighbors: "Come quickly; your father's had emergency surgery."

That's how I took my first airplane ride, at the age of fourteen, from Washington, D.C., to Louisville, over the strip mines of West Virginia and eastern Kentucky, and over one of the largest steam shovels in the world. We had read about it in our *Weekly Readers* in Mrs. Smith's fifth grade class. As I looked out the plane's window, suddenly there it was—all twenty stories of it, taking huge bites from the earth, enough to fill six railroad cars at a time! In a flash it was gone from view.

With the exception of the steam shovel's intrusion, I spent the entire trip engaged in my childlike understanding of prayer: "Dear God, please don't let me be too late." I wasn't. When I got there, the surgery was over, but the outcome still was in doubt; my father had lapsed into a coma. Mother said, "You go in and talk to him. He'll fight for you."

Well, what do you say to a comatose man, even one who is your father? I told him that I was back from my trip, and that I loved him and hoped he would wake up soon…and, oh yes, about the big, yellow steam shovel.

And one day he just woke up. The doctors were doing a study on patients who had been in comas, and they quizzed him: "Mr. Russell, do you remember anything prior to or during your coma, anything at all?"

"No," came his reply, "nothing…except this silly dream about a big, yellow steam shovel."

You think that little things can't make a big difference? I know differently. —*Gregory A. Russell*

# *Worship for food*

Madison Square Garden used to be at Madison Square Park, at 26th and Fifth. Then it moved uptown to W. 33rd Street, atop Penn Station. Over time, the area around Madison Square Park declined and the homeless moved in. Now the neighborhood is gentrifying, as we say when people with money replace people without money and the homeless are rousted. They have nowhere to go, even though New York City is said to have enough vacant apartments to house every one of them.

Such is the talk when our church takes its turn leading worship and providing lunch for the homeless. Standing in a semicircle in a gravel area near the famous Shake Shack restaurant, at the southeast corner of the park, twenty of us sing, pray, and break bread. A seemingly disturbed man starts to preach his own gospel, but is persuaded to stop.

I like preaching in this venue. No time for frills, no patience for the bland. Being among people living on the edge tends to focus my thoughts. It's probably the closest I come to the way Jesus preached: out in the open, surrounded by need.

It's also important to realize that the homeless people attending this service are here primarily for the free bag lunches given out afterward. Worship is the price they pay for food. I like that perspective because I think it speaks to why we all come to God in worship. We'll tolerate liturgy, but it's food we want, whether literal food to assuage hunger or "living bread" to ease fear, loneliness, and worry.

I usually return home from this service feeling peaceful. I can't name my hunger as readily as a homeless person, but it's still real. God has fed me, too. —*Thomas L. Ehrich*

# Kinship

*You are dust, and to dust you shall return.*
—Genesis 3:19

It's been dry here lately in one of the remaining portions of the ancient Cross Timbers Forest, a mix of post oak, shin oak, red oak, hickory, eastern red cedar, greenbrier, and grapevine. It's a woodland so dense it caused Washington Irving to say, "I shall not easily forget the mortal toil and vexations of the flesh and spirit, that we underwent occasionally, in our wanderings through the Cross Timbers. It was like struggling through forests of cast iron." This density can result in pockets of darkness, even in broad daylight.

Occasionally I take a walk from my house and find myself surrounded by a mixture of this cast iron forest and its various shadows and dissecting blades of light. When it's dry, those rays of light have a depth that's a result of the dust in the air. They look as if you could reach out and wrap your fingers around them. This day, instead of trying to grasp them, I stepped forward and stood still, right in the middle of a grid of intersecting dust-and-light beams.

I stood there quietly, bathed in that heavenly and earthly collection—a collection of elements that are the basic components of all that is and ever shall be. Surrounded by minute particles of myself and the rest of Creation, I felt a tingle that went to my toes and into the sandy loam and red clay. From there it was absorbed by an outcrop of regal sandstone on the top of the ridge; rocks that had seen more than I will ever know. A stately centuries-old oak moved slightly, and a squirrel and a red-tailed hawk voiced a greeting. I was dizzy with kinship. —*Bo Cox*

# TRFs

I never liked the parable of the Prodigal Son, and I know why: it seems unfair. I'm a Terminally Responsible Firstborn. I identify with that older son, the obedient one. We firstborns have a tougher time of it. Our parents expect more of us. They hold us to a higher standard. Sometimes we respond by turning into nit-pickers and perfectionists.

It's easy to cherish resentment toward our prodigals for all the emotional energy they run through and all the second—and third, and fourth, and fifth—chances they claim. But Jesus is speaking directly to us TRFs in this parable. We may think we've earned what we have because we've behaved. We can be legalistic when it comes to who deserves what. We can be smug because we do what is expected of us.

We're annoyed when our rotten little brothers or their stand-ins go off and dissipate and behave badly. We're even more annoyed when they come to themselves, as the Prodigal does. At least when they are being bad, we can more easily overlook our own faults, build up our little virtues and make them seem bigger in comparison. And when our prodigal sibs repent and come home, we can go into massive snits when our parents forgive and celebrate them. It's not fair.

But grace is never fair, in human terms. Grace transcends our concepts of fairness. Grace is extended to all who will accept it. We are God's children—but we can't live into that without also accepting all of God's other children—even the most annoying ones.

If we accept God's grace, we must share it. We have to come inside and join the celebration. If we stand outside and sulk while they are feasting within, we are rejecting the greatest gift that God can offer. —*Sarah Bryan Miller*

# *Are you a judge?*

I was a newly ordained priest headed for a meeting with the bishop. I was dressed in my best clerical garb and a bit taken with my imagined importance.

He was a homeless man crossing the street opposite me. He was dressed in a dirty sweatshirt and tattered pants, and he honed in on me like a guided missile. He stopped me right in the middle of the street and, after eying me up and down, put his face uncomfortably close to mine. His breath betrayed that he hadn't had a solid breakfast. I was preparing to fend off a certain request for money and direct him to the nearest soup kitchen when he asked, "Are you a judge?"

"No," I replied, somewhat taken aback. With that he started laughing from head to toe.

"Neither am I," he said and walked off.

Truth be told, he was the truth teller and I was a liar. I had judged him from the moment I saw him. Truth be told, I think he might have been an angel with a message from God. —*James L. Burns*

# *Unexpected baptism*

Mother was reared in the Church of Christ in southern Indiana in the early twentieth century. Grandpa was an elder in the little church at Pekin. The families in that church took turns taking the preacher, who traveled there for Sunday worship services, home for dinner. Chicken was usually on the menu.

The Church of Christ practices immersion baptism after an age of accountability. Baptism is a very important decision, and the preachers wanted to be sure everyone knew just how crucial it was.

Following one particularly impassioned sermon on the importance of baptism and what would happen to you if you were not baptized, it was Grandpa's turn to invite the preacher home for Sunday dinner. It took awhile to get it all ready and everything on the table, and once that had been accomplished, it was time to round up the kids. My mother, who was about eight at the time, was nowhere to be found. They looked everywhere.

"Virginia! Virginia! Dinner's ready!" They called and called.

Finally, my mother came trudging up the hill from the spring house, behind which was a watering trough, with her two favorite old cats, one in each hand, clutched at the scruff of the neck. Both were sopping wet. Mother was still in her church clothes and patent leather Mary Jane shoes. She looked a fright. Although she had won, obviously there had been a tussle. She dropped her beloved pets at the preacher's feet and announced, "Here, I've baptized these two darned old cats, and if they go to hell now, it's not my fault!"

Is it worse to do the right thing for the wrong reason or the wrong thing for the right reason? —*Gregory A. Russell*

# *A life worth living*

To be born again means to receive a life we cannot give ourselves. This is a tough order for me. I am a control freak, at least in terms of my children. I so want their lives to be wonderful, hopeful, joyful, and characterized by smooth-sailing. Not only is that a bad wish for young people navigating their twenties, but it is also a ridiculous one. I cannot give my three adult children even a shadow of a life. For that matter, I cannot confer any real life even to myself. My vision for my children and for myself is clouded by—in a word—my sin. Yet I do know who can give us a full life, and so does Peter.

In the most beautiful Greek used in the New Testament, the author of 1 Peter states: "By God's great mercy he has given us a new birth into a living hope through the resurrection of Jesus Christ from the dead, and into an inheritance that is imperishable, undefiled, and unfading, kept in heaven for you, who are being protected by the power of God through faith for a salvation ready to be revealed in the last time" (1 Peter 1:4-5).

No matter how wealthy, resourceful, determined, or religious we become, we cannot give to ourselves or to anyone else a life truly worth living. The only way to receive such a life is to tame our desire for control and humble our sinful selves to Jesus Christ, who gave his life that we could be born again into a new, abundant life beyond anything we have imagined. —*W. Patrick Gahan*

# Daybreak

*Almighty and everlasting God,*
*who hast safely brought us*
*to the beginning of this day...*
—The Book of Common Prayer, A Collect for Grace

Here is a simple and disarming thought to remember when you first open your eyes tomorrow morning, consciousness dawns on you, and you realize that sleep has ended. Life, that most precious gift, has actually returned once again. It could be otherwise. One day will be your last. Well, not today. Not yet, anyway. When the end comes, will you notice? Will you pay attention? But right now, you still have the time and the opportunity, so, pay attention.

> *Sitting in the corner of the garden, she is statue still.*
> *Our headlights catch the reflection of the screech owl's eyes—*
> *Yellow brown marbles.*
> *No movement.*
> *We freeze, caught in the moment of surprise.*
> *Pay attention.*

This poem, written by my wife Anne, captured a singularly important moment in our lives and froze it, forever. We sat transfixed, knowing we were not merely staring into the eyes of a small screech owl, but into the face of God who created the owl.

It happens, you know, more often than you think. When it does, pay attention.

This is one of those moments when you wake up. Seize this moment as each and every day begins. You are awake, once again, to the ever-new possibility of life and breath and the discovery of the presence of God, who has safely brought you to the beginning of this new day. Pay attention. —*Edward S. Gleason*

# *Planted for others*

We had about an acre of land where I grew up. All over that land were flowers and bushes, including a huge stand of lilacs, hundreds of feet long and maybe twenty feet wide—so immense that we created trails through the bushes. There was a catalpa tree that I liked to sit in. Lots of lilies of the valley and peonies, and a couple of apple trees. And we hadn't planted any of them.

By the time we lived there, those flowers and shrubs had been there for at least thirty years. They took care of themselves, with a little weeding. They were thriving. I took them for granted, but knew deep down that someone had planted them, that someone had loved them, that they made my life better because I could walk in the yard surrounded by such beauty.

Someone before me had cared. Someone before me had taken the time to put together something lovely. I was lucky enough to see the plants in their prime, which the one who had planted them probably never did. Little violets came first in the spring, then irises, then tulips, lilacs, and peonies. Flowers, especially those sweet-smelling lilacs, blessed the inside as well as the outside of our house, spilling from vases. I knew summer was getting on when the tiger lilies came into their bright orange glory.

Someone had made that possible. Someone had planted seeds and transplanted seedlings so they could stand the test of time. Someone had watered them and weeded them. Someone had rooted them deep and left something strong and good and right and beautiful for me.

God bless those who plant the seeds. —*Lindsay Hardin Freeman*

# The orange t-shirt

*In the same way, let your light shine before others,*
*so that they may see your good works and give glory*
*to your Father in heaven.*
—Matthew 5:16

Every Sunday, an eighty-year-old blind woman sits in the front row of our church. She arrives early in her wheelchair. She is our self-appointed matriarch. Most Sundays she is surrounded by children and teenagers and obviously enjoys her superstar status. She is exceptionally open and expressive about her love for everyone. The fact that she is blind and in a wheelchair in no way inhibits her.

One weekend we hosted a regional youth event, and more than a hundred teenagers from the area spent the weekend at our church. They worshiped with us on Sunday, and before they entered the nave I told them they would be sitting with our matriarch and that she would greet them with a whole lot of love. During worship they surrounded her, and I could see her smile from across the room. Before the dismissal, they presented her with a t-shirt commemorating the weekend. It was neon orange, so bright that it looked as though it had electricity running through it.

The following week I visited her at her nursing home. She was holding court in the dining hall, surrounded by friends and staff. She was telling them about her church—and wearing her new shirt.
—*Jason Leo*

# *Angels' eyes*

We parents sometimes see our children as if through an oblong blur. We look at them and see a continuum of ages—4, 6, 11, 17, 24. It is as if they are all of those ages at the same time in our heads and hearts. Which is why the marriage service makes such a point of separating newlywed persons out from their parents, so that we can see them with new eyes—with angels' eyes, I like to say, as the persons they have now become.

"For this reason a man shall leave his mother and his father," we read aloud. And dad steps up, only to be told to go back and sit down after giving away his daughter.

I recall the day I came to know my daughter genuinely as a young woman. We were in a grocery store in New York City and the aisles were very tight, so much so that you had to leave your cart at the end of an aisle, go and get what you wanted, and then return with your groceries. In the tightness and hustle of the crowded store I lost sight of my daughter for a moment, and turned to ask a woman next to me: "Have you seen a short person?" Then I realized the woman *was* my daughter. Out of the corner of my eye, beyond my usual field of vision, I had seen her anew, for the first time as the woman she truly was.

Seeing with angels' eyes. Some of the great truths of our lives can come to us out of the corners of our vision. In moments of grace we are given glimpses of reality unblocked by the preconceptions of our conscious minds. —*Leonard Freeman*

# *Night walk*

On summer nights before I go up to bed, I go out the back door, walk around to the front of the house, and stand for a few minutes. Our street is a cul-de-sac, and at that hour I seldom see a car or a pedestrian. There are the night sounds of insects and the low hum of city traffic, but otherwise all is quiet.

People who come to live on this street of modest houses usually stay for a long time. We have been here a quarter of a century and are nowhere near being the senior residents. It's a good place. Often when someone hears where we live they say, "Oh, yes!" or "I love that street."

One night I did see a figure standing a few doors away. I knew her and her situation: a teenager who used to live across from us with her father and younger sister. She was looking at the place where she had last known happiness. When she saw me, she approached and came inside to talk. On this street we know each other and in time of need can count on neighbors. There are inevitable troubles—goodbyes, disagreements, family squabbles, divorce, and what I can only describe as occasional lunacies. But the inherent kindness of our common life transcends all the hard stuff.

It's hard for me to put into words why I do these late night outings. Part of it may be that, like a kid, I want to put off going to bed. But mostly, I believe I go out and stand in the quiet darkness to breathe a soul-full of ambient grace. —*Robert Horine*

# Christianity is a verb

"It was the best of times, it was the worst of times…it was the epoch of belief,…the epoch of incredulity…the spring of hope,…the winter of despair." Charles Dickens's description of Revolutionary France in *A Tale of Two Cities* is applicable to every age including our own and the era of Benedict of Nursia, whose feast we celebrate today. Benedict was born at the end of the fifth century and died in the middle of the sixth, when the Roman Empire was in the final spasms of its long, sad death.

Benedict, like his Eastern contemporaries whom we know as the Desert Fathers and Mothers, turned away from the crumbling world around him and staked a claim in the kingdom of God. At Monte Cassino in Italy, he wrote his famous rule which became a guide for western monasticism and many contemporary Christians.

Benedict realized that Christianity is a verb: something people do. The beating heart of Christianity is belonging believers living in community, working together on the mission Jesus proclaimed. Benedict's Rule knows that we have to *do* community or the community will not survive.

Do you know why we are called "followers of Jesus"? It is because Jesus is going somewhere. If Jesus were not moving on, into the future, if Jesus did not embody the verb-ness, the mission motif, of Christianity, we could be called *attached to* Jesus or *stacked next to* Jesus, perhaps *filed under* Jesus or *carved into* Jesus or *fixed on* Jesus or maybe *buried under* Jesus. But we are not called any of those things because Christianity is a *verb*, it is *mission*—a thing done in the best of times, the worst of times, epochs of belief, epochs of incredulity, in the spring of hope, and the winter of despair. —*Francis H. Wade*

# Dancing with the star

I arrived late to the ball, but now I am among the millions of Americans who drop everything on Monday nights to settle in front of the tube and watch *Dancing with the Stars*. No apologies. It's live, it's clean, it's fun—and unlike any other show I know, it surprisingly celebrates the symbiotic aspects of life with each other and with God.

Sure, there's all the glitzy glamour and reality-TV gimmickry of seeing celebrities out of their element, off-balance and under the rule of their professional dance partner. But these unlikely duos also demonstrate something more, like what happens when talent is paired with perseverance, skill is blended with hard work—and, at least sometimes, judgment is delivered with mercy.

The metaphor might be getting a little winded, but dancing with God certainly comes to mind. In a life of faith, we put ourselves in the arms of Christ, trusting him to teach us, to lead us, to catch us when we fall—and to make us look good.

Sure, there are steps to memorize and techniques to practice. But as the judges say on the show, getting a high score demands more than just knowing the moves; it takes that tricky step from head to heart—feeling the music, embracing the mood and "really going for it!" Have a blast doing the Lindy Hop. Relish the elegance of the Viennese Waltz. Dare to touch the scalding passion of the Argentine Tango.

And through whatever music life may bring, don't forget you are dancing with the star, the Master, the one who brought you, the one who loves you, the one who will hold you until the music ends, and, even then, will never let you go. —*Jerald Hyche*

# You are a born theologian

"The theologian soaked in the bath tub." So begins *Patterns of Grace* by Tom Faw Driver. How refreshing it is to be reminded that the work of theology is not confined inside the walls of academia or the church! Everyone, created in the image of God, is made with a natural impulse to "do theology," to think about God. We all share the yearning of Saint Anselm, the twelfth-century scholastic, whose motto was *fides quaerens intellectum*—"faith seeking understanding."

Our theology may take the shape of a massive, systematic, coherent whole, like the *Summa Theologica* of Thomas Aquinas. But more likely, it will take on a fluid, amorphous texture as we hammer out ideas with friends over a few beers or wrestle with nighttime fears and hopes upon our beds.

There are so many questions! I prayed fervently that my father be healed, but he died. Why wasn't he cured? Questions such as these can tie us into knots. They can also engender such passion, anxiety, and despair that they compel us to turn away from God and against one another.

But it need not be so. In 1903, Rainer Maria Rilke wrote this sage advice to a young poet:

> I would like to beg you, dear Sir, as well as I can, to have patience with everything unresolved in your heart and to try to love the questions themselves as if they were locked rooms or books written in a very foreign language…Live everything. Live the questions now. Perhaps then, someday far in the future, you will gradually, without even noticing it, live your way into the answer.

Live and love the questions. And, for God's sake, do not leave theology to the "experts"—can anyone truly be an expert in *mystery*? Just do it. You are, after all, a born theologian!
—*Charles F. Brumbaugh*

# *People watching*

On a walk up Broadway for a pastry, I came across several interesting people whose stories I imagined into rich detail.

No one spoke, of course, and I recognized not a soul. But imagination was enough for this outing. The two young men gliding out of an apartment building with eager glances to see who noticed—ah, now who were they? Freshly adorned for the downtown promenade, perhaps. The young woman bouncing along with an amused smile—a college student, I decided, still enthralled by Manhattan.

I know not to make too much of my imaginings. They're just guesses, and not necessarily charitable if I'm feeling irritable. Still, one joy of the city is being surrounded by such colorful characters.

As I ate my coconut pie and wrote in my journal, I decided that God must take delight in us. Yes, we let God down more often than not, and we can be so cruel toward each other. But we're colorful, we're different, we each have a spark of the divine, and God must be amused by us, even by our vanities. For I believe that God looks at us deeply, not requiring the filter of imagination, and sees the hope of what we can become.

That's why I don't place much stock in debates over whom God loathes. Why would God loathe any of us? Jesus forgave even notorious sinners and brought into his circle the despised and outcast. The standards that we impose so harshly on each other are merely our own projections onto God, and they aren't charitable.

Rather than dread God's judgment—and then apply to others what we dread for ourselves—we might emulate the naïve twenty-something who's still just happy to be here. —*Thomas L. Ehrich*

# *Getting even*

Most of us live by "naïve realism." I see the world the way it really *is*. *You* on the other hand, because you see things differently, are biased, stupid, or prejudiced. There are people who should know better who forget my birthday and don't even drop me a note at Christmas. They are self-centered and inconsiderate. On the other hand, if I forget, it is because I am swamped. When naïve realism infects religion it can get serious, even dangerous.

One aspect of the miracle of grace is that it heals our diseased imaginations. I find the key in the marvelous verses of 1 Peter 2:19-25: "When he was abused, he did not return abuse; when he suffered, he did not threaten; but he entrusted himself to the one who judges justly."

Crazy, isn't it? Living the life of faith means choosing not to live a life of getting even. This is why we call Jesus the Way. New Testament scholar Walter Wink puts it beautifully: "This is what may have happened: the very image of God was altered by the sheer force of Jesus' being. God would never be the same. Jesus had indelibly imprinted the divine; God had everlastingly entered the human. In Jesus, God took on humanity."

And here's the shock: something also happens to us when we follow Jesus. I'm talking about a change in consciousness. I have to give up my skewed view of the world and allow for a bigger reality which I can never fully know. The naïve realism of tit-for-tat gives way to the deeper realism of self-giving love. —*Alan Jones*

# *Understanding God*

*Do you not yet understand?*
—Mark 8:11-21

Jesus is perplexed and dismayed with his disciples. He has recently fed thousands of people with meager amounts of bread—on one occasion five loaves for five thousand and on another seven loaves for four thousand. And now, as they put out in a boat on the Sea of Galilee, the disciples anxiously complain that no one remembered to bring any bread aboard. "What part of God's abundance don't you understand?" Jesus asks.

Truth be told, I am too frequently in the boat with the disciples. I'm more focused on the problems at hand than the promises that await. I'm too worried about the cares and concerns of this life and too forgetful of God's loving providence that sustains me every minute. I'm too ready to pack my own spiritual survival kit, not trusting God's grace.

Jesus spent his entire ministry demonstrating God's love, God's healing, God's mercy, God's abundant passion for us.

Do you not yet understand? —*James L. Burns*

# Alone

*In the morning, while it was still very dark,*
*[Jesus] got up and went out to a deserted place,*
*and there he prayed.*
—Mark 1:35

A wise professor once suggested that time set aside for gazing out the window would be our best work. It would help us "see what really is." What if we really believed that?

Jesus was a busy man, yet he got up early and found respite. We too know about busyness. Our heads affirm it—"Idle hands are the devil's workshop," someone once told us. Is it rude, egotistical, or strange to prefer being alone? We hear internal messages that respite must be delayed until after all the letters have been responded to, promises kept, tasks done, errands run, obligations met, and demands satisfied. And yet we also know that never happens.

I run a couple of times weekly, and I often wonder why I do it. Am I running to or from something? It is a question of fitness but also a question of fear—fear of losing control, of a heart attack, of a stroke, and who knows what else. It's all part of my fear of being alone. What if, sitting there alone with my early morning coffee, all the faces, hopes, fears, and voices rushed in upon me with their awful questions?

Here are some questions for the lonely place: Where is God? Is God better seen or felt? And either way, is God outside ourselves or within? If within, where within? Where we ache, laugh, and finally die? What constitutes the true "nearness of God" in the time apart and in prayer?

Dawn breaks, and it is back to busyness, but perhaps we will also see more clearly what is, and who we truly are, and to whom we belong. *—Richard L. Shimpfky*

# *Jesus the biker*

A curious card from His Laboring Few Biker Ministry came across my desk. Emblazoned in red were the words "He would have ridden a Harley." Intrigued, I called the number and spoke for fifteen minutes with one Brother Tank.

His Laboring Few was founded in 1990 by Steve Ervin, once a member of the motorcycle gang Outlaw Bikers. "He was saved on February 13, 1987," Tank told me, then organized this ministry that passes out Bibles and tracts, along with food, at a hospitality tent during big bike events. "We witness and share Jesus during the day and hold church services at night."

I ventured the thought that many folks his ministry attracts would not be drawn to standard Episcopal, Methodist, Lutheran, or Presbyterian churches. He agreed. Suits and ties are not their style; they would feel unwelcome in traditional churches.

In one sense this is inevitable. Imagine the tables turned—that you're at a biker rally where you don't know the customs and the culture, the language and the way of life. Not fitting in, you might well interpret your uneasiness as a lack of welcome by them.

But in another sense, churches should be doing everything to remove barriers arising from such superficialities as dress, lifestyle, middle class culture, and the like. We should root out our unconsciously exclusionary signals as vigilantly as we keep the sanctuary clean.

The message on the card of His Laboring Few is a marvel of targeted evangelization: *Jesus the Biker.* The government didn't like him. The church thought he was weird. He was persecuted by hypocrites. He hung around people like you and me, not the goody-two-shoes Pharisees. Yes, if Jesus were here today, he would be next to you on his Harley telling you he loved you…enough to die for you. That is what we all have in common. —*Bruce Birdsey*

# *Who needs the bickering?*

A friend made a dig about the "pompous Mets." I smiled at his teasing. But then I had to admit: I don't know whether the baseball team is "pompous" or not. In fact, even though I read *The New York Times* daily, the Mets haven't taken on any personality for me. I hear their salaries are extravagant and their new ballpark is a throwback to Ebbets Field, where the former Brooklyn Dodgers did have a personality. Beyond that, nothing.

What does that mean? I love baseball, but two things happened, I think.

First, daily news about big league sports went from playful rivalries to tiresome, real-world bickering about money. Who needs more bickering about money?

Second, while living in North Carolina, I attended minor league games in Winston-Salem and Durham. I rediscovered the joy of this lazy summer venue, where you pay $4.00 to $6.00 for a ticket, sit close to the field, watch kids around you dream and teenagers preen, and catch the occasional superb play.

When old-timers reminisce fondly about "Dem Bums" or the "Gas-House Gang" or the "Yaz" mastering the "Green Monster," this is what they remember. Not salary squabbles, not hired-gun players who change uniforms every year, but the grace of a very difficult game that a few men manage to make look easy.

I think churches could learn from this. No one comes to church to hear about budgets, ordination battles, denominational politics, or capital campaigns. They come seeking God. They want to sit close and be touched. They want to know the personality of God, not the attitude of God's self-appointed partisans.

Who needs the bickering? —*Thomas L. Ehrich*

# Beauty and the Beast

In the folk tale "Beauty and the Beast," a disfigured, beastly looking man loves a beautiful princess. The story revolves around his futile attempts to court her. Eventually she agrees to a kiss, and he is instantly transformed into a handsome prince.

As a kid I liked this story because I was often ridiculed, laughed at, and put down by the other kids. In the second grade I was the shortest child in the class: "Hey, Shorty, how's the weather down there?" We moved a lot, so I was always the new kid on the block and sometimes wore hand-me-down clothes. My parents' piety, which forbade me riding my bike, playing ball on Sunday, playing cards, and attending a movie theater, didn't help. In the usual petty games of ridiculing other kids' appearance, the in-group vs. the out, I was always out.

But it was my family's civil rights activities and pacifism in the late 1940s and '50s, when it was neither popular nor safe, that really kept me on the fringes. I identified with the Beast. When we as a family suffered threats and intimidation, my father would say, "The most unlovable need the most love and are the least likely to get it because their behavior turns people away."

He taught us that anyone can love the beautiful, the charming, the loveable, but it takes a special kind of person to love the unlovable, to risk offering to the negative, the hostile, or the threatening a kind of love that comes from beyond ourselves, to create loveliness where it did not exist before.

He taught us to kiss and be kissed by the Beast. —*David L. James*

# *Prayers from a fresh, clear source*

Christians should never belittle George Harrison. Martin Scorsese is preparing a major film on the deceased former Beatle, focusing on Harrison's religion. Harrison was a passionate, if lovingly detached, believer. He believed first in Sri Krishna, then in Jesus. At the end of his life, he began to sign his letters with a cross—which simply means he was working hard at integrating East with West, or West with East.

What is touching to me is listening to George Harrison's album *All Things Must Pass* and hearing it through my present lens of experience and service. Way back in 1970, in Cambridge, Massachusetts, my wife Mary and I couldn't get enough of "My Sweet Lord." We didn't mind the "Hare Krishnas" and *heard* it all as Christian. We still hear it as Christian. That is because *All Things Must Pass* consists almost entirely of songs that are prayers.

In almost every track of this work of popular culture, Harrison is praying to God. He is lamenting, bearing witness, thanking, praising. How did he get by with it? I don't think people then were listening to what Harrison was really saying. "Hear me, Lord" comes through again and again and again. Humble he is, broken on the wheel of earth's sadness he is, weeping he is, softly he is.

If you want to hear a man praying to God, in "sighs too deep for words" (Romans 8:26), download *All Things Must Pass*. Or buy it. Or take it down from a dusty shelf with your other old records. Do this and it will be…well with your soul. —*Paul F. M. Zahl*

# Where two or three are gathered

*For where two or three are gathered in my name,*
*I am there among them.*
—Matthew 18:20

I often think of this verse on Thursday mornings, when I lead Morning Prayer at an assisted living residence. Gathering my little flock can be an uphill battle: forgetfulness is endemic, residents move slowly, people get sick, the staff is stretched thin, and client attendance at our prayer group is not a priority for visiting therapists and nurses.

The congregation varies from four to a dozen in number, and we never, ever, start on time. Those in walkers need extra minutes to make it to the activity room; those in wheelchairs need an aide to push them; someone always needs to go back to her apartment to fetch her reading glasses.

It's not church as I usually think of it. We have a priest just twice a year, for Christmas and Easter eucharists. There's no music and no homily, and a few of the women read along on the parts marked "Officiant." Sometimes we're preempted by a staff training session in the activity room and must hold our service in a noisy hall. Then I'm grateful for my ability to project, but it can be a struggle to make it feel like sacred space. Yet we are gathered in Christ's name, and that makes it church—even in the hallway—while we read and pray together.

This morning, as the northbound remnants of a hurricane drove rain against the windows and lashed the trees outside, I looked at the little circle of faces and thanked God for this brief respite from the storms of the world. With a heartfelt "Thanks be to God," we parted and went on to our other obligations and pastimes, knowing that, for a few minutes, Jesus had been among us.
—*Sarah Bryan Miller*

## *Not stuck*

My best friend in first and second grade was the youngest of four brothers, all of them handsome and bright. Their mother and father were both deaf and mute. Gary and his siblings had no language impairment, nor any other handicap, but no one could convince them that their parents' limitations had not been visited on them. Each brother felt stuck and acted out in the most desperate and destructive ways.

When spying a man who had been blind from birth, the disciples ask Jesus, "Who sinned—the man or his parents?" (John 9:2). Jesus surprises the twelve by stating that no family member's disobedience has caused the man's blindness. Rather, the man's calamity is an opportunity for God to act. Jesus then makes a muddy plaster with dirt and spittle, anoints the man with the concoction, and tells him to go wash it off in the Siloam waters. The blind man does so and comes back seeing. The man's neighbors are shocked at the healing, and the news of the miracle gets out to the Pharisees. Rather than rejoice with him, the Pharisees prefer the man to remain stuck in his old state of blindness.

Not our genetics, family history, neighborhood, social status, or economic standing can impact us the way Christ can. No one is stuck. Believe it. —*W. Patrick Gahan*

# Free in routine

I like to walk. There are hiking trails and bike paths all around where I live, and early on in my time here I settled on one or two set routines for how I (sometimes accompanied by my dogs) take in the scenery. My spouse opines that I am stuck in a rut. The dogs and I tend to think otherwise.

This disagreement about routines lies at the heart of the liturgical expression of Christian spirituality. Those of us who belong to churches that emphasize ritual find freedom in the reliability and familiarity of the ritual. This is not because we are rule-bound Pharisees. It is because there is something in the familiar structure and shape of a liturgy which allows us to relax into being present to what God and we are up to in this encounter. When I go to a church service with a lot of structural surprises in it, I am on my guard. When I take part in a liturgy where the action and shape are familiar, I can let down my defenses and be open to surprise.

In the poem "Corson's Inlet," A. R. Ammons noted how routines can be creative when he reflected on his daily walks on the same New Jersey beach. He put it this way: "Tomorrow a new walk is a new walk." Even the familiar is always becoming new.

There are times in all of our lives when we feel stuck. For some of us that "stuckness" may indicate a real need for a change. For others, though, the call may be into a deeper engagement in life's routines. Even the walk you took yesterday and today will be a new walk tomorrow. —*Gary Hall*

# Taste and see

Andrew discovered, when he was about eight, that he could sing. Choir practice in his little Kansas town became part of his life, and he learned that while practice might not make perfect, it sure made a difference in the kind of sound the choir made. Music became a doorway to a world which had hitherto been closed to him.

Later on in his life cooking became a passion, and Andrew learned that there are rules in this art, too. He once made parsley sauce for some fish by adding sugar to the chopped parsley. He had seen his English mother add a little sugar to the chopping board when she made mint sauce for the lamb. Why not add some to the parsley? It was a disaster. He learned that some things just do not go together: fish and sugar for one.

As Andrew grew older, he moved from the childhood fare of hot dogs and French fries to more exotic foods. He still talks about his first trip to London when he was eighteen, that first taste of scallops in a little bistro called Le Matelot in London's Chelsea. There weren't many scallops in Kansas. In fact, he had never before seen a scallop and had never heard of Coquilles Saint-Jacques. It was only later that Andrew learned that the name of this dish came from the image of Saint James and his symbol of the scallop shell. The dish now conjures up all sorts of images and resonances, from the food itself to the depictions of the saint in churches, to the great pilgrimage to Santiago de Compostela. Odd that a recipe could do that. But Andrew learned a great lesson about the world. It is full of resonance and presence. And it is to be *tasted*. —*Alan Jones*

# Take your demons to church

We like to say that the demons of Jesus' time were really psychiatric disorders, labeling them as schizophrenic, bipolar, personality disorder, and so forth. Yet is it not true that each of us has demons—memories and experiences that haunt us and keep us from fully embracing life?

Consider a couple whose wedding day was "ruined," in the wife's opinion, by her new husband drinking too much and telling off-color stories. The wedding was thirty years ago! The couple now has grown children, but she cannot let go of that memory. It still provokes numerous quarrels.

Our demons often inhabit our past. We are held hostage to our personal history. We have a story that we tell ourselves about us, and it is built on memories. We pour into today those recollections of sad, angry, guilty, fearful happenings from long ago. We see ourselves as victims and somebody else or "the system" as the perpetrator. Or we may visualize ourselves as the tormentors of others.

Why not take these memories to church and leave them there? There is no place else to leave them. Church for us may be a building or it may be a place inside us. No matter. Christ is a healer able to call forth these destroyers. Perhaps we are not crazy. We may simply need the power of God to create a path leading out from deep within us, on which the demons can walk into the light of day and then keep walking. Some are genuine tragedies, but we have magnified many from mere mistakes into crippling disasters. Be gentle with your past. You are God's child, and your heavenly Father wants you to enjoy a demon-free life. —*Lee Krug*

# Central Park

Among New York City's enduring mysteries is how Central Park has remained open, lovely, free, and safe all these years.

In a city where everything is monetized, even the air above buildings, commerce hasn't been able to get its hands on these 843 acres in the middle of the most expensive real estate in America. Other than a handful of small restaurants and pushcarts selling hot dogs, nuts, and water, the park is remarkably cut off from the mercantile world surrounding it.

Despite being used by an estimated twenty-five million visitors a year, the grass is sturdy and green, the trees look healthy, pathways are relatively free of trash, and the vistas that park planners intended 150 years ago are intact.

The answer, of course, isn't magic. It is a concerted effort by citizens and government to preserve this treasure for the entire city. A conservancy was formed to lead the effort. It strengthened police presence, expanded maintenance crews, enforced rules about acceptable use, and enabled all citizens to contribute small amounts.

This is how faith communities thrive, too. People work together to preserve human treasures like trust, mutual respect, openness, and fairness. A faith community's facilities require attention, too, but it is the human treasures that are most vulnerable to neglect.

Jesus didn't say anything about how a church ought to handle bricks-and-mortar or ecclesiastical power. But he did suggest how to nurture a healthy body of believers: love God and love each other.

When we do that, we present the world with a miracle even more astonishing than the survival of Central Park. After centuries of endless warfare, much of it in the name of religion, it is still possible for people to join hands and lives in a community that exists to serve others. —*Thomas L. Ehrich*

# The light

*We are all children of one God.*
—Geronimo

This morning, as I was walking my two dogs past the meadow, I looked to the east where the sun was rising.

We think of light as simply, well, light-colored. But that ranges from don't-look-at-me brightness, to golden strokes across clusters of bluestem and grama grasses, to translucent rays with sparkling silver dust particles dissecting the shadows beneath cedar boughs and at the edge of the oak and hickory. The spectrum is infinite.

In addition to being moved to tears at yet another aspect of the gift that has turned out to be my life, I had an eyebrow-raising moment. Without moving my feet one inch, I could describe that light in different ways. Were I standing at the foot of the Himalayas or the bank of the Nile or the edge of the Sahara, I would see even more variances of this same light, the light that comes from one source. Not only would I see additional hues and tones, but my language might change, depending on my origin. I might use different words to speak of this light that stops me in my tracks and soothes me. Not only might I use an unfamiliar tongue to describe the same light, but given my time in history, my reference points would change. In a flat, two-dimensional world, "up there" meant something different from what it means in a world of orbiting galaxies.

This morning, hair wild like Medusa, wearing sweats that didn't match, straddle-legged with arms dangling, and facing the east with my face turned up, I welcomed the light shining on me and knew that I am not apart, nor have I ever been, from those who see and describe this light differently than I do. —*Bo Cox*

# Martha

The other day I saw a book entitled *Having a Mary Heart in a Martha World*. Ah, yes, Mary and Martha of Bethany. Jesus' friends. Martha gets the bad rap again. Mary, the sister who sat at Jesus' feet and listened, wins again.

Martha has been the object of condescension throughout the years for not taking the time to reflect, for doing busywork and not listening. Jesus himself praised Mary for "choosing the better part," when Martha complained that her sister was not helping her in the kitchen.

But would Jesus have enjoyed coming to the little Bethany home had not Martha tended so carefully to the needs of her guests? No doubt Martha's food was plentiful and tasty, seasoned with fresh herbs. Linens were clean and fresh. Guests settled back for laughter and a relaxing good time.

Jesus wanted Martha to listen more, to see the big picture, to meditate on his word, the most important thing. Of course that makes sense. But maybe that word wouldn't have been so available had not Jesus felt at peace and nourished in that little house. Maybe his insights came because Martha had seen to it that he had a clean and undisturbed place to sleep, and a good meal in his stomach.

Legend has it that Martha went on to become a missionary after the resurrection, and traveled as far as what is now France, taming dragons with holy water in her quest to spread the word about Jesus. No one in the New Testament is better suited for such a mission, given Martha's single-mindedness, strength, and absolute conviction of faith after witnessing Jesus raise her brother, Lazarus, from the dead.

Back in Bethany, maybe the disciples could have pitched in a little more. —*Lindsay Hardin Freeman*

# Backs to the wind

I asked a friend if the tornado had affected the horses she raises on her farm. "Well, they all gather together," she said, "and they face each other, with their backsides facing out. They get through it that way."

That sounds like a good way to weather a storm: gather together within nuzzling distance of your sisters and brothers, and keep your backside to the wind. You're too small by yourself, but we're bigger if we all stick together.

Some of us go looking for company when the strong winds begin to blow, and some of us turn inward, not wanting anyone else around. This is a matter both of one's personality and of the moment. The same person can need different things at different times.

"The hospital was fine in every way," another friend said, "except that my roommate was the matriarch of an enormous family, and they were all there all the time. It was lovely to see, but it felt so good to get home to the quiet."

Most of my longing is for solitude. But that's because I see a lot of people for conversation at some depth, and need to regroup from it. I notice this need has become stronger as I've grown older.

But we're not all the same. "You know," a colleague told me, "I was surprised at the reaction of two of my older parishioners to a silent retreat. We always assume that silence is important in a retreat, but one of them said, 'I live alone. The last thing I need is more silence. I need to talk about things that matter.' So from now on, I'm providing an option for those who wish to talk."

Be alert to the signs of what people want and need. Stop and think about their lives, and then ask them if quiet or conversation would be better. A silent, compassionate friend or visitor can be an angel from heaven. So can one who offers a quiet talk.

—*Barbara Cawthorne Crafton*

# Working for Abraham

The patriarch Abraham was complex, widely involved, and multi-talented. His story is richly told in chapters 12 to 25 of Genesis. We learn that he was wealthy and capable of moral and physical courage as well as deceit and betrayal.

He had an abiding faith that often defied the logic of circumstances, and he was seldom on the losing side. Our view of Abraham tells us something of the life of Eliezer of Damascus, Abraham's manager, the man on the ground who looked after the details of Abraham, Inc. To gain such a position he must have been very talented, and to keep it he must have been very patient.

Eliezer's skills may have been God-given but we can only guess at the source of his patience. Abraham once complained to God that he was childless and "the heir of my house is Eliezer of Damascus" (Genesis 15:2). If Abraham thought Eliezer would inherit the business, there is a good chance Eliezer did, too.

Then Abraham and Sarah had a son they named Isaac and the rest, as they say, is history. But consider Eliezer who worked so hard under trying circumstances, expecting a certain reward only to be disappointed. I do not always understand Abraham, but I do understand Eliezer. We have all been Eliezer at one time or another. We expected to get the grade, the promotion, the relationship, to make the team, to get the job, to stay healthy, to be honored, but...

One of the tests of faith is what we do after "but..." To fold up is to admit that our work and our worth were really about the reward. To continue in spite of disappointment is priceless in the kingdom of God. No one knows what Eliezer did. We all know what we have done. —*Francis H. Wade*

# She struck out, but...

I didn't feel quite so foolish walking in a medium drizzle after I came to the North Meadow in Central Park and found two baseball games and one softball game going on. What better sign of hope than men, women, and children attempting a game that we never stop imagining ourselves playing well?

I watched one game for a while. It was what some call a "co-rec" league: men and women playing on the same team, with certain requirements for how many women need to be on the field. As in any sport, the players had different abilities, but no one ragged on a teammate for being a lesser light. All got to bat, and all were encouraged with shouts like "Great swing!" and "Next time, baby, you'll get it next time!"

I watched one young woman who clearly had never held a baseball bat before. Two outs, two runners on base—it wasn't a good time for her to be up. A young man tried to insist it was his turn. But she would have none of that. Nor would the coach of the other team. "I want to bat," she was saying. "Make her bat," said the other coach.

I watched the two teams working through this dilemma. Without a doubt, she would kill the rally, and probably feel badly about it. But fair was fair, and in softball, as in life, things tend to come around. Unfairness inspires more unfairness.

I imagine God watching us and asking, "Should I rescue them? Tilt the table, perhaps? Or take a longer view and realize that justice matters more than an immediate outcome, and honoring persons matters more than victory, and learning from failure matters more than the failure itself."

She struck out, of course, and killed the rally. But it's a long season, and there's always next year. —*Thomas L. Ehrich*

# *People*

*Treat all men alike. Give them all the same laws. Give them all an even chance to live and grow. All men were made by the same Great Spirit Chief. They are all brothers. The earth is the mother of all people, and all people should have equal rights upon it.*

—Hin-mah-too-yah-lat-kekt (Chief Joseph),
Nez Perce Leader (1840-1909)

Oral history tells of a time when Cochise began to see the end of the Apaches' fight with the settlers and the United States Army. He was so convinced the end was near that he sought out the chief blue coat and they talked of peace.

Cochise told the general his people were ragged and starving from running and he just wanted to find a place for them to live in peace. He pointed out his people had once lived in the Cañada Alamosa and he wondered if they could live there again. It is said that the general told him there were three hundred Mexicans living there, brand new American citizens and landowners, and they couldn't make them move.

Cochise reportedly saw no problem with this and told the general so. There was plenty of room, he said. Just put us farther down from them, make us citizens and landowners too, and we will take on your ways.

The general shook his head. "No, we can't do that."

Cochise wanted to know why.

"Because you can't become citizens and own land."

Why?

"Indians are not people. It is the law."

As we seek to walk in the sunlight and see the Master's thumbprint on all peoples, it will help to be honest about our history; how we came to be here now and also how others arrived where they are. Only then can we move on. —*Bo Cox*

# *I believe in the life everlasting*

"This is my idea of heaven," the young boy at the breakfast table said to Kay and me on our last day of Family Camp at the beach. He was not just talking about the waves, sand, sunshine, and recreation. The boy was overcome with the fellowship among the generations he had experienced there, the way his parents and siblings relaxed, the generous love shared all around, and the joy expressed every hour of the day. "This is my idea of heaven," he said. "I don't want it to end."

"Everlasting life" does not end. It only begins. The mistake Christians often make is to imagine eternal life as something reserved for us in the future on another shore. Paul declares that "our citizenship is in heaven" (Philippians 3:20), and Peter assures us that Christ has bequeathed us "an inheritance that is imperishable, undefiled, and unfading, kept in heaven" (1 Peter 1:4). Eternal life begins the moment we surrender completely to the lordship of Christ and give up the false gods we have picked up along the way.

As citizens of this new and wonderful commonwealth, our present lives are dramatically changed from the inside out. We permanently become the people so prized by that young boy at our breakfast table. Frederick Buechner succinctly states: "We think of eternal life, if we think of it at all, as what happens to us when life ends. We would do better to think of it as what happens when life begins."

Truer words have rarely been spoken. —*W. Patrick Gahan*

# God alone is judge

*Do not judge so that you may not be judged.*
—Matthew 7:1

The youth group in our parish is full of diverse and colorful characters. They are an energetic bunch. One young man seemed to have more energy than anyone else, but also appeared skeptical about the whole church thing. I often wondered if his parents were making him come. During discussions and worship, he said little and looked bored. I always wondered how long he would remain with the group. I confess that there were days when I hoped he would not come.

Each meeting on Sunday concludes with Evening Prayer in the sanctuary. It is a relatively large space, and as we are only a small gathering, it can feel a little intimidating.

One Sunday evening, I asked if anyone would like to lead Evening Prayer. There was complete silence and the kids all looked at their shoes. Suddenly our energetic skeptic said, "I'll do it." Before our collective shock could wear off, he had begun: "O God, make speed to save us." He led our worship with such reverence and dignity that when the words of the final prayer trailed off into the night, you could have heard a pin drop. It was a moment of grace for everyone present, and I was reminded that God alone is our judge, and what a true blessing that is. —*Jason Leo*

# Of summer snow and miracles

We had a wedding at a tiny chapel near Greve in Chianti the other day. Santa Maria della Neve was its name—Saint Mary of the Snow. It is named after a miracle involving the Virgin Mary, a sudden snowfall in Rome in the dog days of August, at the end of the fourth century. In Rome, the snow fell on just the spot where the Blessed Mother wanted the pope and a wealthy couple to build her a church, the present Santa Maria Maggiore.

People here in Tuscany, not to be outdone, say the snow fell here, too. *That's a miracle that bears repeating,* I thought, on this hot, dusty day: snow on the ground in summer; delighted children making snowballs of it and eating them; puzzled grapevines and olive trees frosted with it; farm animals stepping gingerly through it. I can see why people would remember that day for more than a thousand years, whether it happened or not.

It's hot here in Florence, but it's hot everywhere these days. My grandmother from Minnesota used to tell me stories of cold weather when it was hot: of the cat whose ears and tail fell off from frostbite, and how you could toss water from a basin up into the air and watch it come down like a shower of diamonds. Those are good stories to tell when you can't get away from the heat. Remembering what it is to be cold helps you feel differently about being hot.

Miracle stories—the Minnesota stories were miracle stories, too—help people get through hard times. Maybe all stories are really miracle stories. We can paint the world other than as it is, imagining away our cruel limitations. It helps us remember that this life is contained by a larger way of being, one in which things that break our hearts do not apply.

*It will not always be like this,* we think, as we imagine something better. —*Barbara Cawthorne Crafton*

# The meaning of life in a glass of water

Many people today wonder about the meaning of their lives. As our traditional beliefs and the institutions which sustained them are challenged from many quarters, we ask harder and deeper questions about life and its meaning. What is it to be human? What is the point of our strivings, our struggles, our sufferings?

Jesus does not spend a lot of time addressing these questions. He refuses to talk in large abstractions. Instead, he tells stories about women and men in hard circumstances, using images from the daily life of a Palestinian Jewish peasant. Jesus did not present a philosophical system. He gathered people around him, healed the sick, and proclaimed good news to the poor. Even before he went to the cross, his life was its own meaning.

The British critic and theorist Terry Eagleton recently published a book called *The Meaning of Life*. Surprisingly, his answer to the question of life's meaning turns on a reading of Matthew 25, the familiar passage where Jesus talks about what we have done for "the least of these." Eagleton concludes: "The key to the universe turns out to be not some shattering revelation, but something which a lot of decent people do anyway, with scarcely a thought." He adds, "Eternity lies not in a grain of sand but in a glass of water. The cosmos revolves on comforting the sick."

When I get to fussing and obsessing about life's purpose and meaning, the life and ministry of Jesus calls me back to all that I can really apprehend about life's big cosmic questions. What I think about big questions is not as important as how I respond to someone in pain. That awareness in itself is the meaning of life. —*Gary Hall*

# No secrets

*Almighty God, unto whom all hearts are open,*
*all desires known, and from whom no secrets are hid...*
—The Book of Common Prayer,
Holy Eucharist: Rite One

Our world is marked by secrets, secrets that define and destroy us. Afraid to mention "the elephant in the living room"—no matter what our elephant may be—we avoid speaking about what we know all too well.

The elephant couldn't be more evident, but we have become so accustomed to seeing mother passed out on the couch that she's become invisible. Only she isn't. Nor is Uncle Charlie. Remember him? After a series of affairs, he ran off with his best friend's wife. We hoped we'd never hear from him again, but he keeps popping up in conversation, along with all those other memories we wish we could forget.

Things such as the way Daddy smiled at my siblings when they came home but never offered me anything but the back of his hand. It bothers me that no one mentions the fact our first child was born six months after the wedding, but why should they? It's just that family secrets have a way of insinuating themselves into our lives, and then everything turns sour. It would be different if we could just face them, and then they wouldn't be secrets anymore.

There is one place—it may well be the only place—where we can face our secrets, live with them and grow through them. That place is the presence of God, from whom no secrets are hid. With God there is no dissembling, no hiding, no need to be a phony, for with God all hearts are open and all desires known. To be with God, to practice God's presence, means to be fully open, fully honest, fully known. No secrets. None. —*Edward S. Gleason*

# Nolan

As kids Nolan and I liked to play telephone pranks. We began with the old standbys like "Is your refrigerator running?" and "Do you have Prince Albert in the can?" Then Nolan hit on the idea of picking a number randomly and convincing the person who answered that you knew each other. His success rate was pretty low until he got an elderly man who really tried to remember, and they talked for some time. Nolan so enjoyed it that he called again and then again. What started as a prank became a little act of kindness.

Nolan was a good person. He belonged to a church with strict sabbath and dietary laws, and he was forbidden to read comic books, see movies, smoke, or drink Cokes. The kid culture we lived in made it hard for him to keep the rules. One day he was devout and the next day a backslider. As time went on, he did not seem to know what he wanted to be or where he belonged. We lost track of each other for many years, but I know he was married at least three times. He tried being a soldier, country musician, printer, taxi driver, process server, radio announcer, hospital orderly, and landlord of a mini-mall.

We met again during the last months of his life. I visited him regularly and we talked about old times and times to come. When we were kids, we had decided that at the moment of death you might be able to refuse to go. The theory was based on the well-known "fact" that in a falling elevator, if you jump up just as it hits bottom, you will be okay.

I was with Nolan the night he died. Near the end he rose up in bed and said in a strong voice, "I believe." I trust that it was an affirmation and not an attempt to jump up. That doesn't work.

—*Robert Horine*

# Conflict structure

The polarization of American society in recent times has been most upsetting. We all see it and feel it. It is reflected in the cable news networks, in political campaigning, in culture wars of every stripe, in litigation, and in blaming—it's everywhere.

It's also in the church, and not just in the Episcopal Church and the Anglican Communion. Polarization is rife among the Methodists and the Presbyterians and the Lutherans and the Southern Baptists, and in many other sectors. It has wrecked countless ministries and parishes, even entire dioceses. It certainly has wrecked me.

The problem is something that Christianity's critics refer to as our "conflict structure." They want to say that Christianity from the beginning had a sort of dualistic "we-they" approach to life, which infected the whole and which continues in a sort of me-versus-you mode of thinking and existing. I myself don't see this in the ministry of Jesus. I do see it in a whole lot of other places in our tradition.

Christ was the Prince of Peace, Emmanuel (God with us). He said he had come for sinners. To embrace the "other" as Christ did is not an ideological position. It was simply what he did, and the thing for which he got into hot water. I sure wish Christians would re-examine the conflict structure that affects much of our life. Our critics have something to say to us. They sure have gotten to me. When I look out upon the wreckage of the past few years in church life, I have to say something like, "OK! Uncle!" This kind of conflict cannot be right. O Lord, O Christ, where did we go wrong? Forgive us and renew us. —*Paul F. M. Zahl*

# *Pipes and paths*

Working on a kibbutz in Israel's Jezreel Valley in the 1960s, I decided one day to walk across the farm to a village in the middle of the fields, perhaps a mile or two off.

I found the terrain almost impassable. The richly irrigated soil was so moist that it quickly caked on my boots, three or four inches worth, so that walking was too tiring. It was like swimming out far from shore and finding myself too tired to swim back.

Looking up, I saw a way forward. Huge irrigation pipes, two feet across, crisscrossed the valley. By climbing onto them, I could walk along the tops.

I found I had two different tasks on this journey. Most of the time I had to keep my head down and focus on where I was walking, one step at a time, lest I lose my balance and fall off the pipe. But when I reached an intersection, the job was precisely to look up, get my bearings, and make a choice as to where to head next for the path to my goal. Then it was back to step-by-step.

The journey of life is often like that. We cannot always be looking ahead. Rather, we make choices, and our job then is to pay attention, stay focused, and make our way one foot after the other, lest we fall and get mired in the mud. But there come those intersection moments when our job is precisely to look up and ahead, get our perspective, and make the right turning for the journey of our life. The Lord asks of us, and presents to us, both opportunities.

Which part of the path are you on? What is your task right now?
—*Leonard Freeman*

# Beneath the mask

Ancient Greek drama was rich in story, myth, and theme. Those early dramatists used masks to represent character. The comedian George Burns coined a now-famous aphorism: "The most important thing in acting is honesty. If you can fake that, you've got it made."

This is a profound remark. A lot of life is acting as if something were true. We pretend a role in life and then live into it. The poet W. H. Auden pointed out that we all play roles (which isn't the same as being a hypocrite). The difference is between those who know that they are playing a role and those who don't.

Often we have to ask ourselves what role we are supposed to be playing in this particular little drama: parent? boss? spouse? Do I have a leading role in this play or am I simply a supporting actor? Many of us get into a fine mess because we have no sense of play (and "play" can be serious business), assuming roles and wearing costumes which are ludicrous, crass, or otherwise inappropriate. A father acting as if he were emperor or pope comes to mind—Nero at home and Caspar Milquetoast at work.

Many of us get to know the drama and cast of characters inside us through therapy. We pay someone to listen to our story, and he or she helps us identify the voices in the tape we play to ourselves. One of the most creative ways to help us understand the cast of characters inside us is to read the great stories of the Bible. These stories help us hear our own. —*Alan Jones*

# In the boat with Zebedee

One of the first things Jesus did in his public ministry was to select the core group who would be his disciples. He undoubtedly did it carefully, and those who accepted found themselves in the forefront of the greatest world-changing mission ever.

When the call was extended to the brothers James and John, they were with their father, Zebedee, in the family fishing business. Matthew is unusually complete in his description when he tells us that they were mending nets, tying the little pieces back together—a small, important, unglamorous, painstaking task. Jesus sweeps in with his dramatic invitation and the two boys are off into history, leaving "the boat and their father" (Matthew 4:21-22).

Zebedee is not heard from again in the gospel accounts. People who do small, important, unglamorous, painstaking tasks are seldom mentioned in the final report. But without them there would be no report to write. Who raised James and John to be the kind of people Jesus would call? Who gave the itinerant disciples a home base to return to? Whose boat did the disciples use when they saw Jesus walking on the water? Who provided the cash to buy the bread for the famous supper? It may not have been Zebedee in every case, but if not, it was someone very much like him. And very much like the altar guild for the early service, the church school teacher, the members of the property committee, the person who stuffs the bulletins or makes the coffee or remains attentive in a meeting that would bore a goldfish. Our church is full of Zebedees who make the gospel possible. I have sometimes been one, and I imagine you have too. —*Francis H. Wade*

# *When Friday falls on the thirteenth*

Friday the 13th. Not a good day to clean your mirrors (you might crack one), begin painting your house (best to avoid ladders), or visit the animal shelter (black cats in residence).

What is it with superstitions? Especially the double whammy of a number and a weekday?

Anthropologists speculate that the taboos around thirteen go back to the first human efforts at counting. To number things is to establish a kind of control over them. Using ten fingers and two feet, people got as far as twelve. Beyond lay the unknown, the uncanny, the uncontrollable—thirteen.

And Friday? The Norse god of chaos was Loki. The goddess of death was his daughter Hel (what English word does *that* lead to?). In time, Hel became confused with Freya, a goddess who rode in a chariot drawn by a pair of cats.

Freya eventually came to be regarded as a witch and Friday, her name day, as the prime time for witching. Witches were believed to meet in cemeteries, in the dark of the moon and in a group of twelve. Freya is said to have given them one of her cats, making the thirteenth member of the witches' sabbath.

Bad luck, death, chaos, witchcraft, hell—all of these "uncontrollables" frightened our ancestors. Do they still today? Yes indeed! Rational child of the Enlightenment that I am, I still observe this childhood admonition from my mother: don't tell a bad dream before breakfast or it will come true. That superstition embedded in my psyche governs what I say or don't say on certain mornings.

If it's control you're after, observe the taboos of superstition. If it's risky pilgrimage into the unknown and the uncontrollable, you are better off with faith. —*Bruce Birdsey*

# Saturday night knife and gun club

At a time in my life when I had no parish, no pulpit, no altar, I began to feel a need to do something priestly. So one Saturday night I put on my clerical collar and drove to the New York City hospital where my wife had spent five years in a losing battle with breast cancer. I entered the emergency room at 11:30 p.m., found a chair against a back wall, and settled in with my Prayer Book on my lap.

People came in with desperate looks on their faces, wanting information about a friend or loved one. Some sat slumped in chairs while others paced. As the clock ticked the hours, the noise level increased. Doors banged, people ran, doctors and nurses shouted, and people cried. By 1:00 a.m. the waiting room was full.

Some people looked at me out of the corner of their eye, looked away, and then back again, until they got up enough nerve to approach me, sit down, and ask for a prayer or a Bible verse. Some just wanted to talk. A nurse came to me and asked if I'd come into the emergency room to talk with the family of a young man who had just died. As we walked together, she said, "Welcome to the Saturday night knife and gun club."

Two policemen were just outside the curtain where a girlfriend and a mother stood over the body. I didn't preach, I didn't celebrate communion, I didn't have answers or explanations. I just stood with my arms over the shoulders of two sobbing women saying the Lord's Prayer, the Twenty-third Psalm, and parts of the burial office.

I left at 5:00 a.m. as the waiting room finally emptied out. This was the most meaningful Sunday morning service I had been to in a long time. —*David L. James*

# *Come*

I wanted her to come back to church. There she was, in the back pew, her normal seat, for three weeks in a row. We hadn't seen her for a while. When she came before, which wasn't often, she had remained an anonymous figure. Not many people knew her; she usually arrived a few minutes late, and didn't talk much afterwards.

But now things were different; anonymity was no longer an option. Her name and face had been plastered on the front page of the papers. She'd been busted. Turned in by an associate, she had no choice but to confess her participation in a multimillion dollar Ponzi scheme that threatened to leave hundreds of businesses in debt. Even worse, local charities and church-related organizations had lost money. Retirement accounts were gone. Philanthropic ventures across our community were ruined. Our parishioner had confessed all she knew and all she had done. Jail time would be a certainty; the only question was how many years.

And there she sat in the back row. She didn't come forward for communion. Neither did she the following week. The third week, she rose, made it halfway up the aisle, and then returned to her seat empty-handed.

Come up, I thought. Come up. Come to the altar. Receive the Body and Blood of Christ. Let Jesus embrace you. Let us embrace you. I wonder how many times Jesus thought that. How many people approached Jesus, or stood in the back of the crowd, and then turned away? Come up. Be forgiven. Start a new life. Be part of this family.

Jesus gives the invitation, over and over. He gave it then; he gives it now. We simply need to accept it. —*Lindsay Hardin Freeman*

# *Back to the valley*

I was just finishing my slow jog around our local high school track yesterday when the boys' football team began meandering out onto the turf. The freshmen were out on the field first, of course. Their faces gleamed with both the excitement and fear of what would come next. I remember my early practices as a freshman in high school and college. I would have liked to have lingered there in the glow of those sights, both on the football field and in my head, but I had to run off to tackle the tasks I now have before me.

Peter, James, and John got caught up in the sight before them, too. They took a strenuous walk up Mount Tabor and then a short siesta, only to awaken to see their rabbi Jesus transfigured into gleaming radiance (Luke 9:28-36). Intensifying the sight were the heroes Moses and Elijah radiating right there beside their leader. Caught up in the glory of the moment and the majesty of their past, the three disciples wanted to stay on the mountain a while longer in order to build a monument there. Jesus didn't offer an answer, but started walking back down into the valley to the people and their real work together.

Our memories of grace must propel our work today.
—*W. Patrick Gahan*

# A healthy balance

We stood in the chapel beholding the beautiful space, the sage-colored stone floor and soaring ceiling, the simple wicker chairs and intricately hand-crafted organ, the pleasing unity of altar, cross, and columbarium. I remarked, "I really like the large, clear windows." She said, "I prefer stained glass." I said, "But isn't it wonderful to see the outside world from within the church?" She responded, "I come to church to get away from the outside world."

Ah, the genius of the Anglican *via media*, middle way, revealed yet again. Sometimes a follower of Jesus is called to engage the clamoring world beyond our cozy walls. And sometimes that same disciple is called to come away, be still, and look within. It's always "both/and"—even for the contemplative and the social activist.

Our chapel's transparent windows help us connect with God's creation. Liturgy is enriched with a view of a glorious sunset or mesmerizing moon, and by glimpses of joggers, motorcyclists, and bus riders. These distractions remind us that worship is intertwined with the divine life that pulses through the world we see (and which, in turn, sees us) through the clear glass.

By contrast, the translucent stained glass windows in the larger worship space help us focus within, where we are immersed in the Word and sacrament, prayer, song, and fellowship of our faith community. Even Isaiah, an urban prophet engaged in the politics of his day, declared: "O God, you will keep in perfect peace those whose minds are fixed on you; for in returning and rest we shall be saved; in quietness and trust shall be our strength" (Isaiah 26:3, 30:15). Sometimes we need to withdraw from the world in order to engage it.

One day Jesus would fling himself into the maelstrom of conflict in the public square. The next day he'd withdraw into solitude or the quiet company of friends. Such is the healthy balance we seek. —*Charles F. Brumbaugh*

# *Really?*

I sometimes wonder whether I inhabit the same universe as the people I see on television. That is not because they behave like outer space aliens, but because so much of what passes for news is really a narrative we have agreed to tell ourselves in order to protect us from the facts. Norman Mailer once called *Time* magazine "the news as fiction." The various stories we tell ourselves about life, its experience and meaning, seem similarly invented.

I know from my experience in the church that life is a complex amalgam of suffering and joy, pain and pleasure, betrayal and faithfulness. People are complicated; I am complicated. Going to church regularly, I hear the outlines of this complex reality described in scripture readings, in sermons, in the liturgy itself. I talk there with people who are both up against it and doing well. When I am in church I feel, well, sane.

The British art critic John Berger put that experience of disconnection between private experience and public narrative this way: "Between the experience of living a normal life at this moment on the planet and the public narratives being offered to give a sense to that life, the empty space, the gap, is enormous."

It is only the gospel that finally gives us a narrative which explains our experience. Here is the reason regularly to reflect on the life and teachings of Jesus: they are a trustworthy guide to how things are. Jesus' experience is our experience. It is only his story which makes sense of our own. —*Gary Hall*

# God in a box

It's easy and safe to put God in a box. Some religions think they have cornered the market on God. Most often he is seen as male, white, straight, judgmental, and demanding, and if we do what he wants he will reward us with eternal life.

Some years ago our parish was stunned when Jesus was portrayed in the Palm Sunday pageant by a woman. God forbid! Now more of us are seeing the feminine aspects of God, who can be like both a father and a mother. We have multicultural renditions of Jesus showing him looking like various ethnic groups. Some have even speculated he was a husband and a father. The old pictures are reassuring and unchanging, but by limiting ourselves to them, we limit how we relate to God. In the Old Testament, God sometimes seems vengeful, full of bloodshed. Jesus came into the world to correct that error and reveal a God who loves everyone, a God who sorrows about the mistakes we make but will not bludgeon us into behaving better.

God lets us be. Why can't we let God be? We are made in the image of God, and we change. Could it be that God changes, too? Let God be whatever he or she chooses. Actually, God is what God is. We don't give permission, but recognition. God is never in a box. We just picture it that way.

For a start, view a God laughing as he created the world and us. Close up the empty box and see God dancing on top of it. —*Lee Krug*

# *Put in a good word for me*

On a hot and humid day I was taking the subway to a meeting downtown. Days like this make me wonder who actually thought up the clerical collar and why. As I stepped onto the train car, I noticed a woman eyeing me intensely. After a bit, she asked "Are you a priest?"

I was tempted to answer, "No, I just wear this collar for comfort," but I thought better and said "Yes."

She then asked, "Do you talk to God?"

I thought about saying "Why do you ask?" assuming she was troubled about something, but the car was crowded and noisy, and it didn't seem like a good place for a pastoral conversation. I paused for a moment, realizing that I was probably about to give her more of an answer than she was looking for, and simply said, "Yes, I pray."

"I'm sure you say your prayers," she replied, "but do you *talk* to God?"

"That's what I think prayer is most of the time," I answered.

"So you *talk* to him?" she persisted.

Now uncertain where the conversation was actually going, I simply said "Yes."

At that moment the train lurched to a halt. She grabbed my arm, leaned close to my ear, and said, "Well, then put in a good word for me." And with that she hopped out the door and was lost in the Grand Central Station crowd.

"Put in a good word for me." Isn't that what we all want? When you pray today, put in a good word for someone—a stranger, a loved one, an enemy, a friend, someone in trouble, someone you've lost touch with, yourself. The possibilities are endless. —*James L. Burns*

# *Keep going*

I think of God as one who nudges, and maybe today's nudge came from God. Maybe not. In any event, I found myself reviewing something I had posted on one of my websites.

I read, I cringed, and I mumbled to myself, "This isn't good enough." An hour later, I had rewritten the article. No one erupted in applause. Most of what we do isn't noticed. But I noticed, and I felt better for having made the piece better.

I believe that God goes through the same process: reviewing what God has made, deciding some of it could be better, and taking action. Sometimes people quote Genesis—"And God saw that it was good, and God rested"—and conclude that creation is a clock that God fashioned and wound once, and it goes on forever, untouched by divine hands. In fact, creation seems to be a never-ending act, in which God imagines what could be and sets about making it happen, despite human resistance and without taking away human freedom. God is never done with us.

Does anyone notice? Probably not as much as we would like. But I think we could notice what God is doing in our lives. As a writer, for example, I know that my skills were formed many years ago, but the content keeps changing, often getting deeper, because God is more a part of the quest. I see more, feel more. I take that as a nudge from God.

In our journey, I think God is the companion who keeps urging us to see more. To try a new road, perhaps, or try the same road with fresh seeing, or try the same seeing with fresh curiosity. Make more of it. Go deeper into it. Not because we are inadequate, but because God imagines more for us. —*Thomas L. Ehrich*

# Single-tasking

The hurricane crushed houses, tore off roofs, and toppled trees, including a towering oak and an assortment of lesser pines and hardwoods in my own back yard. And that is how I came to meet Bill the Tree Man, who cleaned out the clutter in my yard and in my soul.

He blew in from Minnesota in a beat-up pickup, riding the usual post-storm surge of fly-by-night roofers, questionable carpenters, and self-proclaimed tree surgeons. But Bill was different. His Detroit Lions cap shaded twinkling blue eyes. His easy smile framed good teeth. His t-shirt said something about Jesus, but he never did. Reeking hard work and good health, he offered a bid as fair as his Scandinavian skin.

Hanging and dangling high among the tangled carnage of trunks and tree limbs, Bill looked like a slow-moving Spiderman on casual Friday. I tied off a line for him on occasion, but mostly I was there to watch and learn. In almost a meditative state, he followed the simple steps of his work: Climb. Tie off. Climb. Tie off. Assess weight and character of limb to be cut. Estimate the fall. Unclip chainsaw from belt. Crank. Assess limb again. Cut. Watch fall. Kill saw. Clip saw on belt. Repeat.

I watched. I learned. I listened: "No multi-tasking up there," he said between bites of fruit and nuts on one of his regular breaks. "One thing at a time. It's the only way to stay alive."

Soon Bill was gone, but his work ethic lingers and reminds me of another man who lived that way. Who took a slow and steady approach to the tangled elements of life. Who devoted his undivided attention to the task, the situation, the person before him. So much so that some people, like Bill, wear t-shirts that bear his name. —*Jerald Hyche*

# *Hands*

Chief among the joys of being a bishop is that I see so many hands: young hands, full of vitality and strength, grace and beauty; old hands, full of care and beautiful with use; hands with calluses, like those of the carpenter Jesus; noble hands bent with arthritis; hands that have endured pain and survived great sadness; hands that have climbed mountains, written books, or made music; hands given in marriage, hands blessed at ordination; hands that defend the nation, wash dishes, raise children, serve meals; hands turned upward, reaching in faith for the gifts of God. All those hands hint of God's love.

The Bible often refers to hands: God's hand on Jacob's thigh, Jesus healing with his hands, Pilate washing his hands, and Jesus' hands torn by the nails and bleeding for you and me. Christians use their hands to love. My seminary professor said God had plunged a hand into the world and drawn it back bloody, a reminder of the cost of discipleship.

I covet for everyone the strange and magnificent discernment of God at the hands of others. I pray for everyone the experience of being God's hands in the life of others. For much too long people avoided hands-on involvement out of fear. I am reminded by my tennis-playing son that the best racquets are hand-made and that in this game, success is all in the serve.

May God find us and our hands newly at work in our shared calling: loosening the soil after a winter of frozen fear, breaking up the clods, separating and returning the soil to usefulness. May we be a blessing to all, even to the whole world, pulling and collecting weeds for the sake of the young shoots of the country's even now emerging new life. It is a hands-on opportunity. —*Richard L. Shimpfky*

# *Holiness needs no nametag*

I hate wearing nametags. Maybe that is why I am attracted to the unnamed people in scripture, like the anonymous woman who washes Jesus' feet in Mark's version of the story, or the unnamed young man who runs away naked to avoid being captured by the police who are arresting Jesus in the garden.

I think of Saint Bartholomew as part of their company. He didn't really have a name, at least not a name the gospel writer cared to record. Roughly translated, Bartholomew just means "son of Tolmai." No real claim to fame there, nothing to write on a nametag. Matthew, Mark, and Luke barely mention Bartholomew, and John seems never to have heard of him. As usual with such mysterious figures, legends have accrued, the most persistent being that he was flayed alive somewhere in Armenia, and that his body washed ashore on the Italian island of Lipari (a long way from landlocked Armenia), where a cathedral still stands in his honor. Colorful rumors, but not much to hang a sermon on.

The Prayer Book I use in church has a wonderful short prayer that pretty much sums up all we know about Bartholomew: that he had the grace to believe and the courage to preach. Even his courage is only an inference from the scarcest of scriptural data. This being the case, we are asked not to love and venerate Bartholomew (it's hard to love and venerate a relative cipher), but that we would "love what he believed and preach what he taught." The feast of Saint Bartholomew thus becomes a feast of holy anonymity.

I like that. In a day when many preachers swoop and preen before the cameras, a touch of holy anonymity would do all of us a world of good. —*Roger Ferlo*

# *Called to be God's own*

*Do not fear, for I have redeemed you;*
*I have called you by name, you are mine.*
—Isaiah 43:1

What does it mean to be called by God, to be God's own? When Jesus came up out of the water, we are told "a voice came from heaven, 'You are my Son, the Beloved; with you I am well pleased'" (Mark 1:11).

No heavenly voices were reported at my baptism (I am assured that I raised an unholy fuss throughout the whole affair), and there probably weren't any at yours, either. Yet despite the absence of exterior dramatics, we were all claimed by God, claimed as God's own, by that act. In our baptisms we are called as God's disciples, called to be witnesses to and practitioners of the Christian faith. Some are called to the ordained ministry; all are called to the ministry of the baptized.

As *The Book of Common Prayer* puts it, that means we are to "continue in the apostles' teaching and fellowship," to pray and participate in the eucharist, to "persevere in resisting evil," to repent whenever we sin, to "proclaim by word and example the Good News of God in Christ," and to "seek and serve Christ in all persons."

That's not always an easy set of tasks. Sometimes we have to drag ourselves to church when we'd rather sleep in; sometimes we have to squint a little to see Christ in the people we encounter. Sometimes we fall short. But we are God's own, and with God's help, we can live up to our callings. —*Sarah Bryan Miller*

# *One good thing*

My mother was a strong woman. Born and reared on a southern Indiana farm very early in the last century, her values and character were shaped by hard work and cooperation with the larger community. "You all just had to pull together for any of you to make it," she told me on more than one occasion.

She had a gentle disposition coupled with a real affection for the underdog, a trait she passed down to her son. Defying stereotype, she had little use for gossip. I never heard her say so much as an unkind word about anyone, and she always tried to find at least one thing to like about a person.

Someone once observed, "Virginia, you could find something good to say about the Devil himself." And Mother replied, "Well, you do have to admit he is an industrious soul."

One day the town reprobate died, and the community heaved a collective sigh of relief. Not long thereafter, Mother met an acquaintance in the grocery store, and that lady was talking about this fellow's recent death, enumerating his well-known failings in great detail. She didn't miss a single one of them.

I was with Mother that day, and I watched her search for that one good thing she could say about this fellow. You could see that the wheels were turning, and you could almost hear the gears grinding. Finally she said, "Yes, all that is true, but...but...he sure could whistle pretty."

There it was, that one good thing to which she could cling. She found something good to say. Thank you, Mama. You taught us better than you knew. —*Gregory A. Russell*

# *The cave of mystery*

Leonardo da Vinci wrote in his journal:

> Once as a child, I wandered in the hills above my home and came to the mouth of a huge cave before which I stopped for a moment, stupefied by such an unknown thing. I arched my back, rested my left hand on my knee, and with my right shaded my lowered eyes; several times I leaned to one side, then the other, to see if I could distinguish anything, but the great darkness within made this impossible. After a time there arose in me two things—fear and desire—fear of the dark and menacing cave; desire to see if it contained in its depths some marvelous thing.

How many of us really think of the journey of faith as a leap into the unknown?

I want my "cave" to be nicely furnished and well-lit. Some of us use the church as a way of *not* moving ahead into mystery. In fact, it becomes the means by which we refuse the journey. We shouldn't be surprised at our resistance. Our fear is understandable. But we're not alone. We are in good company, and the promise of some marvelous thing can be trusted.

Looking our fear in the eye can introduce us to the wonders of the cave. In Andrew O'Hagan's novel, *Be Near Me*, Mrs. Poole, the priest's housekeeper, has aggressive cancer. She wants the priest to be honest with her. It won't do for him simply to tell her that everything will be all right. She rebukes him: "It is not your job to understand. It is not your job to make things *smaller* than they are...I expect more than that from you. I expect you to help me prepare for death."

Perhaps that's what cripples our spirit—resisting the cave of mystery and making things smaller than they are.

—*Alan Jones*

# Despite our weakness

*Have compassion on our weakness,*
*and mercifully give us those*
*things which for our unworthiness we dare not,*
*and for our blindness cannot ask.*
—The Book of Common Prayer,
Collect for Proper 11

This is one of the most poignant, telling, and insightful statements buried in the pages of *The Book of Common Prayer*. Too seldom, and almost never out loud, do we say, "I'm sorry, but, you know, I'm not very good, and I'm not very bright." If we ever did say those profoundly accurate words, everyone within earshot would turn to look, aghast. How could that be? You spoke the very words each of them might have said, should have said. That's precisely the point. Our friends are not the only ones who listen. Such a statement gets God's attention, which is why the Prayer Book says it for us.

The key words are "unworthiness" and "blindness." To be unworthy is the same as not being very good. If that weren't enough, we are also blind, oblivious—another way of saying we are not very smart. Blind and unworthy. Help us. Speak for us; speak to us. Lift us, embrace us, love us, heal us. This is all we ask, and when we do, God hears. God answers. God responds.

How do we know this? It's happened before; it will happen again. Does it happen in precisely the way we hope and dream? Usually not. Why and how then does it happen? Because we are unworthy and blind. We have no idea what is best for us. But God does, and this is why we pray, "Give us those things which for our unworthiness we dare not, and for our blindness we cannot ask."
—*Edward S. Gleason*

# *On fire with faith*

Moses saw a burning bush that was miraculously not consumed but continued to burn. He turned aside to look and heard the voice of God calling him to an extraordinary task. It is certainly possible that the event took place just as described, but the way I connect my experience to that of Moses requires a little interpretation.

Fire is perhaps the oldest symbol for the presence of God. That is why our ancestors tended sacred fires and our acolytes light candles before a service. If fire represents God, then a fire that will not go out represents a presence of God that will not go away. The burning bush story becomes, for me, one of spiritual nagging, something that simply will not leave my mind or heart alone. Injustice can do this, as can opportunity. Most stories of a call to lay or ordained ministry include this sense of spiritual nagging, as do many stories of love and commitment. I have seen and felt many bushes burning in this way. Perhaps you have too.

One thing about these fiery firs is that they leave room for doubt. Moses certainly doubted and asked "Why me?" God promised him a sign: "When you have brought the people out of Egypt, you shall worship God on this mountain" (Exodus 3:12). That is all very good, but most of us want a sign that precedes rather than follows our commitment. Telling us what it will be like when we finish the job is scant comfort when we are afraid to begin the job in the first place. But God is like that, always asking us to proceed on faith and trust rather than the kind of confidence that comes from a secret peek behind the scenes or into the future. —*Francis H. Wade*

# *Present*

When I was a boy we lived next to a farmer's field at the edge of town, where I built forts in the hedgerows and played for hours watching the farm machines plow, plant, and harvest the crops.

One day as I was watching a mower behind a tractor, a pheasant flew out of the grass ahead of the mower. I screamed, "Stop! Stop!" because I knew the pheasant was trying to decoy the enemy from her young, but the tractor kept moving. After the farmer left I went to look and saw the brown feathers of the young birds mixed with the cut grass.

I went into the house crying "He killed the baby birds!" My father asked who had killed the birds and I told him about the tractor. Then I asked why God hadn't stopped him, why God let that happen. My father did two things in response. First, he said, "I don't know," which was no help at all. He was my dad, and he should know everything; besides, he was a minister. Second, he pulled me to him and held me, not talking. He just held me while I sobbed.

In my first class in pastoral care in seminary I began keeping a notebook of what I thought would be helpful words and responses to the difficult pastoral situations of illness, desertion, divorce, death. I thought the right words were the answer.

I've never opened that notebook in twenty-five years of parish ministry because I discovered I don't say much in painful times of crises. No platitudes, no clichés, no Hallmark Card theology. I'm just there to listen, to be a companion, to pray if they wish. But weeks and months later I've received cards from people thanking me for comforting things I never said, insights I never had, and advice I never gave.

It turned out that my first class in pastoral care at the kitchen table with my dad was the best. —*David L. James*

# *The trivial and the important*

It is raining in Manhattan. If the rain stops, we will walk up Broadway to the Garden of Eden grocery store and load up on fresh vegetables. If not, we will do leftovers another night.

Controlling nature in order to control schedules seems unimportant. Eating exactly what we want seems unimportant, too. In fact, as the current recession forces a reassessment of "necessities," it's fascinating how little truly matters, and how what does matter seems to matter intensely.

I suspect that this focusing, this separating of the trivial from the important, is a good part of what the Passion drama was all about. God didn't start loving when Jesus loved. Nor did God start sacrificing the day Jesus made his sacrifice. Relatively little about the Christ event was new. Nearly everything Jesus said had been said before; others had healed, chastised the corrupt, and broken bread.

What God did in Jesus was to focus the salvation drama in a single life, lived at a certain time with a clarity that was unmistakable. Other lives would follow, and the salvation drama would take many turns. This one moment, however, revealed God's highest purposes.

When we study that life and remember it, we need to avoid fixating on the trivial—exactly which night Jesus died, what kind of bread he broke, whether he called just twelve male disciples or others as well.

We need to reassess such institutional "necessities" and focus on what truly matters. Jesus showed us that the path to life is by way of death: death to self, death to worldly appetites, death to sin.
—*Thomas L. Ehrich*

# Peace that surpasses understanding

Four o'clock in the morning. Can't sleep. Hot, dry. Tossing, turning. So hot. Chemotherapy, taking its toll. So hot. They say chemo isn't poison flowing in your veins, but some of it is, rooting out any cancer cells that haven't been destroyed already. You try not to think of it as poison because that keeps the good vibes away, the good healing vibes that you need.

Cancer also brings loneliness, stark solitary times of walking through the valley of the shadow of death. As much as your loved ones support you, sometimes you are completely alone in that valley. Like that morning lying awake hours before sunrise, hotter than I had ever been, parched as in a desert, sweating, sick, worried, alone, even though my husband was right next to me, sleeping. Nothing to do but get through it. Again. Another endless moment, I thought.

But then, all of a sudden, I was no longer alone. I was in a boat, a small wooden boat. I think it was a fishing boat on a lake, a big, dark lake before sunrise. I was with Jesus. He was in the stern; I was in the bow. The air was perfectly still. The temperature had dropped about fifty degrees. I was cool, finally. Cool, in a matter of seconds. There was no conversation. No fish were jumping. But in that moment, I knew I was with Jesus, in his territory. The valley of the shadow of death had become a place of healing, of presence, of life, and of absolute trust.

From Philippians 4:7: "The peace of God, which surpasses all understanding, will keep your hearts and your minds in Christ Jesus." I understand now. Thank you, God. —*Lindsay Hardin Freeman*

# *The hours*

Years ago, I spent several days at a Benedictine Abbey. It was my first sustained exposure to praying the hours and to having my day structured not by meals or entertainment or work, but by prayer.

I returned only once. But something took hold, because lately I have been feeling a need to attempt at least a minor routine of prayer, using the four Daily Devotions in *The Book of Common Prayer*: morning, noon, early evening, and compline.

What comes of this remains to be seen. I don't see this as a "good intention" that will make me a "better person." I am not responding to a particular crisis, whose passing could end the exercise. I am just looking to structure my time differently, more with God in mind.

If you have found this section of the Prayer Book (pages 137-140), you know that each of the hours is marked by a psalm, a Bible reading, personal prayers, the Lord's Prayer, and a closing collect. To that, you can add whatever you want. I suspect I will add music, as well as longer Bible passages following the Daily Office Lectionary.

Who knows? Personal spirituality is wide open. Despite all the "shoulds" that accompany religion, personal devotions can be whatever we make them. The point isn't to do it a "correct" way, but to give the time to God.

I know that many people use the daily "On a Journey" meditations that I write. Others use *Forward Day by Day*. In previous periods like this, I have worked my way through a worthy book, one chapter each day.

I understand that monastic orders follow devotional traditions handed down for centuries. I honor the boundaries and clarity that such traditions provide. But I am eager now to design my own. —*Thomas L. Ehrich*

# *Finishing school*

In late September of 1984, my young son announced at the dinner table that he would be leaving school at the end of that school year. Trying to be a modern, active-listening parent, I asked calmly what had brought him to this conclusion. With a serious look, he said that by his calculations, he would have learned everything there was to know by the end of the third grade. He then started listing the subjects he would master in the next few months—addition, subtraction, reading, cursive writing, and geography.

The following April I was doing some continuing education at the Candler School of Theology at Emory University in Atlanta. During a break one day, I saw a student in the courtyard standing behind a folding table selling his books. Overhearing his conversations with other students, I learned he was graduating in three weeks. The books he was selling were books any seminary student at the time would have recognized—church history, homiletics, New Testament. They weren't new. Some had obviously been opened, perhaps read.

One prospective buyer who was thumbing through a book of New Testament maps asked, "Why are you selling your books?"

With a big smile he tapped his head with his forefinger and said, "Because I've got it all up here. Besides, I've got a church!"

Over the years I've often thought about that student and wondered what happened to him. Did he ever read another book or think a new thought? But more often I've wondered about the people in his charge and what did or did not happen to them.

Let us pray for the whole state of Christ's Church and the world. —*David L. James*

# *It's my wedding*

It was a classic wedding with the classic dynamics that sometimes make clergy shake their heads and reach for the Alka-Seltzer. Bride and groom were both adults, well into significant careers. But the mother of the bride was all over things like white on rice, as folks used to say. There was not a smidgen of wedding service or haute couture detail upon which she had not made her opinion known and her will supreme. This would be the perfect wedding by her standards, and hers alone, no matter what.

In my office, moments before the wedding was to begin, the best man turned to the groom and said, "Are you ready?" The groom nodded yes, and out of a small gym bag drew loud, garish, plaid bow ties and cummerbunds which they swapped into. As we walked out to the opening tones of the Trumpet Voluntary, I could see the mother-in-law's jaw drop from ten feet away. The message from the groom was clear: "This is my wedding, Madam, and this will be our life, thank you. You are not in control."

A priest/psychoanalyst friend explained to me early in my ministry that all parents subconsciously don't want their children to leave, even as their rational minds know it is in their children's best interests to find the right partner in life. It is what all the control issues at wedding rehearsals are about, he explained to me, and as a priest you're the one making the break specific.

Letting go is hard, but the marriage service makes clear that this is when we are to trust the Lord enough to turn loose of our dearest ones as they go out into life, out to the love of another. It is when our true faith shines through. —*Leonard Freeman*

# Dogs under the bed

Evelyn was one of the wisest people I've ever known. When her aged, beloved golden retriever died, she swore off dogs. "Not going to get another one. Too hard on me when they die." You know the drill.

But she started driving by the shelter on her way home from work, and the short story is that she named her new white German shepherd Angel. Angel had been abused. The shelter staff counseled patience and doggy bribes such as salami. It took Angel a week to come out of the garage into the back yard, but come out she finally did. She would chase a ball as far as you could throw it and as long as you were willing to play. She looked like a big white wolf as she loped across the yard.

Things went swimmingly until one day Evelyn absent-mindedly picked up a stick to throw instead of the customary ball. Angel took one look at the stick and hightailed it into the house. Obviously that had been the weapon of choice on the part of her previous owner.

Angel ran into the bedroom, hid under the exact center of Evelyn's king-sized bed, and refused to come out. Now this was one big dog; she had to weigh nearly as much as Evelyn.

"So, Evelyn," I asked, "how did you get Angel out from under the bed?"

And my wise and compassionate friend replied, "I didn't. I filled my pockets with dog biscuits and crawled in with her."

In one sense or another, we're all dogs hiding under the bed—all wounded, just in different ways. What we need most is someone imaginative and compassionate enough to love us in the midst of our woundedness.

Will somebody please pass the Milk Bones?

—*Gregory A. Russell*

# Discovering church

*On this rock I will build my church,*
*and the gates of hell will not*
*prevail against it.*
—Matthew 16:18

After Hurricane Katrina devastated the Gulf Coast, I found myself replacing a roof on a house in Mississippi. I worked with an elderly gentleman for most of the day. We worked well together and spoke very little. Now and then he would offer me roofing advice and remind me to drink a lot of water.

At the end of the day, he was writing our names on a volunteer list. When I told him my name, he looked at me and asked me where I was from. I discovered that he had been the leader of my church youth group when I was in the ninth grade. I had not seen him for close to twenty-five years. He was still active in the church and was in Mississippi with a group from his parish.

Jesus calls people into community, a wonderful and sacred mystery called church, a community that transcends time and space. He promised that the gates of hell would not prevail against it. I don't know what hell looks like, but it must look something like the Gulf Coast after that hurricane. Words cannot describe the devastation and destruction to buildings and property, the pain on the faces of the people who live there. I was often reduced to tears, but, in the middle of it all, I once again discovered the church, sharing the unfailing and eternal love of the Lord Jesus. —*Jason Leo*

# *Kindergarten*

When I became an editor for Forward Movement Publications in 1985, there was still a lot of cutting and pasting involved in preparing books and pamphlets for the printer. My co-worker Marge Bowden and I claimed that any messy work we produced was because neither of us had been to kindergarten to receive training in using scissors and paste. We formed our own organization, DOPE, which stood for Deprived of Preschool Education.

I guess I had also missed the correct cafeteria line behavior. Early in my first grade career, I was both talking and moving around when the kindergarten teacher yanked my arm and told me to be quiet and be still. The yank hurt my arm, and the whole thing hurt my feelings. She was mean. No one had ever treated me like that. I avoided her through all six years of elementary school. But I never forgot her.

Almost forty years later, working in a large parish, I was taking part in a healing service, laying on hands and praying with each of a dozen people kneeling at the communion rail. I moved from one person to another, and there she was. After all those years God had delivered her into my hands! Coincidence or divine humor? I bent and listened to her prayer request, and I laid my hands on her in the name of the Father and of the Son and of the Holy Spirit.

Some time later I asked for volunteers to visit patients in a psychiatric hospital. It was to be an indefinite commitment. She was the first to step forward and was still faithful in that ministry when I moved to another church. I never saw her again, but when I read her obituary it was with a tender thought. —*Robert Horine*

# Lifestyles of the poor and obscure

In the 1980s there was a television show called *Lifestyles of the Rich and Famous*, at the end of which the host would raise a toast to our "champagne wishes and caviar dreams." The program showed well-known and affluent people living in great (sometimes unbelievable) luxury. Thankfully, it is no longer on the air.

I always wondered what would have happened had someone proposed a show called *Lifestyles of the Poor and Obscure*. That program probably would have had few viewers. But for us followers of Jesus, it is they, not their "successful" counterparts, who are the objects of our special concern.

Penelope Fitzgerald wrote short, elegant novels about people who have, in life's terms, failed. When asked about that, she said:

> I am drawn to people who seem to have been born defeated or, even, profoundly lost. They are ready to assume the conditions the world imposes on them, but they don't manage to submit to them, despite their courage and their best efforts. They are not envious, simply compassless. When I write, it is to give these people a voice.

The central message of our culture is that unless you are rich, famous, notorious, or accomplished, you don't count for much. The gospel says something directly contrary to that: every human life means everything to God. And if it means everything to God, that life should mean everything to us.

The defeated, the lost, the compassless—these are the people who matter to God. When we are defeated, lost, compassless ourselves, it is then (and not when we are toasting our champagne wishes and caviar dreams) that we matter to God. That is when we should matter to each other as well. —*Gary Hall*

# Defining fences

*Are not two sparrows sold for a penny?*
*Yet not one of them will fall to the ground*
*apart from the will of your Father.*
—Matthew 10:29

The sparrow hopped over a concrete barrier that divided a ten-foot-wide graveled area from a well-manicured lawn. A twelve-foot-tall chain-link fence topped with sharp razor wire marked the other side of the graveled area and divided it from another well-manicured lawn.

The sparrow hopped around for a minute, through the fence, and back into the graveled area. It hopped some more, traveling through rolls of coiled concertina wire, seemingly oblivious to the fact it was heading into a prison. Finally, it crossed the space between the fences and hopped back into the prison visiting area where I was sitting with my wife.

"Look," I said. A few hops down around our feet, in and around the picnic table, then back through the fence and graveled area, and the outside fence until it was hopping around in the "free world."

The sparrow didn't seem to recognize the implications of the fence. It seemed as content to hop inside the fence as it did outside the fence. In fact, it was clear that the essence of its being—its sparrowness, if you will—was not defined by which side of the fence it hopped on.

Then I noticed that the sun shined on the bird on both sides of the fence; the wind ruffled its little brown, gray, and black feathers on both sides. And, the little sparrow sang on both sides, too. The fence wasn't a defining force in the sparrow's life and that day it became less of one in mine.

What fences define you? —*Bo Cox*

# Last stand in the favorite season

Rain: falling hard, straight down in vertical lines that look like they could last all day. I wouldn't mind in the least; we've been needing a good soaking.

I am over my brief period of mourning for the passing of summer. It never lasts for long; I have always been in the happy position of thinking that whatever time of year I'm in is my favorite of all. So now I am all about autumn, excited about the leaves changing and my husband's surprising September harvest of figs, an achievement in New Jersey. My own New Jersey lemon grove doubled its yield, if I do say so myself: four actual lemons this year, up from last year's two.

The roses that can rebloom are doing so, and those irises with the same capacity are gathering their forces to follow suit. One of these days the autumn-blooming crocus will appear, utterly unannounced: how a plant manages to produce a large flower straight from the ground, without offering so much as a leaf beforehand, is an annual mystery.

I guess sometimes you just wake up on a morning and everything is changed, our cat Ben will think as he walks carefully across the patio to see what's what. He will be right about that: some days give no sign at their beginning that a world will have ended and another one begun by the time they are over.

September 10. Tomorrow morning there will be a community observance over by the train station here in town, one of many in small commuter towns along the train line. Off to work went our friends and neighbors, as usual, picked up a paper and coffee and just made the train, as usual. Got to work a few minutes early, as usual. And then "usual" came to an end for some of them, never to be seen again.

Every season we have really is the best one. The favorite season. It might as well be. Because anything can happen.

—*Barbara Cawthorne Crafton*

# *Towering strength*

*For you have been my refuge,*
*a strong tower against the enemy.*
—Psalm 61

I lived in New York City on September 11, 2001. I have thought a lot about towers in recent years.

In ancient Palestine, towers protected the people from marauders. Their presence was a visible reassurance of safety. It is no accident that strong towers provided the biblical writers with metaphors for God's loving and steadfast protection of his people.

In our day, towers are more likely to take the form of skyscrapers and office buildings. Such towers are all too vulnerable, as we learned that September morning. In light of that day, the psalmist's metaphor sounds ironic. But many who witnessed the destruction in New York City and at the Pentagon, who lost loved ones there and in Pennsylvania, and who flocked for refuge to area churches perhaps recognized that for all the vulnerability of man-made towers, God's own towering presence as shield and guide seemed all the more secure and sure.

I am reminded of the prayer that concludes the healing service in the Prayer Book, a fitting complement to Psalm 61:

> *The Almighty Lord, who is a strong tower to all who put their trust in him, to whom all things in heaven, on earth, and under the earth bow and obey: Be now and evermore your defense, and make you know and feel that the only Name under heaven given for health and salvation is the Name of Our Lord Jesus Christ. Amen.*

—Roger Ferlo

# *Love your enemies*

I was working in the yard one afternoon when Kay ran out of the house to exclaim, "Pat, there is some scary stuff going on in England!" Sure enough, the plot of some two dozen British, middle-class al-Qaeda operatives to blow up ten aircraft full of innocent people was lighting up the airwaves. My first reaction was raging anger. "Enough!" I thought out loud. "Round up all those people who want to hurt others and drop them all on a deserted island." Then I remembered my Lord extending his bottomless love even to those who conspired to murder him. Never has so much love been expressed from such a horrible place as that cross on the trash heap called Calvary.

How can we love like Jesus? We can't, unless Jesus fills us with himself. Perhaps that is why the feeding of the five thousand is the only miracle chronicled in all four gospels. Like those people on that grassy hillside, we are famished for righteousness. We are famished for forgiveness. We are famished for love until Jesus feeds us with his own body.

Jesus uses his disciples to seat and feed the multitude, even though they think the task impossible. Only Jesus can put into our hands and our hearts what others really need from us. Remember, too, it is a seemingly insignificant boy who emerges from the ravenous crowd to offer Jesus the five loaves of bread and two fish to feed the crowd. Christ will transform our paltry offerings into the sumptuous fare this wounded world needs.

Next time we walk up to the altar rail, let us remember that it suits Christ to feed us with himself so that we will feed others, both friends and enemies, with his transforming love. —*W. Patrick Gahan*

# *Late summer*

My father, if he were alive, would be astonished. I'm peering through his ancient Bausch & Lomb binoculars, the old leather strap smelling like a relic from the Civil War. Through the lenses I'm watching one of my neighbors, a broad-winged hawk. This majestic bird keeps vigil in the treetops, huge claws clutching a branch, intense eyes surveying his kingdom. Far off I hear the thin, piercing whistle of his mate. Perhaps she's hunting for a chipmunk or a snake. I'm blessed. Hawks are usually seen from afar. This pair has found a home outside my front door.

As a child, I didn't share my dad's passion or patience for bird-watching. But now my day isn't complete until I've checked on the local raptors. Soon they'll wing their way to the Florida Keys or Central America. I'll miss them. But natural wonders will still abound, for all creation is "very good" (Genesis 1:31), all year 'round.

In proclaiming the truth of the Incarnation, we profess that God lived and died as one of us in Jesus. This has led many to the anthropocentric presumption that Christianity is solely about God and humankind. True, it is the death and resurrection of Jesus that most fully invests our life with meaning, joy, and hope. But the rest of creation is not merely staging for the dramatic play "God's Mighty Acts in Human History." Our faith is rooted in a reverence for creation that compels us both to thank our Creator for this bountiful planet that sustains and enchants us, and to care for it as responsible stewards.

For now, as summer begins to melt into autumn, I encourage you to go outdoors. Find a park or other green place. Smell the heady fragrance of late summer. Close your eyes and listen to the symphony of God's tiny kingdoms. Gaze up at the wheeling planets and stars. Creation is dancing all around—and within—you. —*Charles F. Brumbaugh*

# *Sheep*

Have you ever been asked, as a party game or conversation starter, to select which animal you would like to be?

I go for something beautiful and exotic, like a tiger; or unusual, like a unicorn; or at least amusing, like a monkey. Never would I choose to be a sheep! I think of sheep as dumb, plodding, and boring. Isaiah says, "All we like sheep have gone astray," and preachers sometimes say, "We nibble ourselves lost." Well, none of that for me, thanks. If I'm going to be lost, I want to lunge forward fully into it, with flair.

Since Jesus identified himself as the "good shepherd" (John 10), there have to be sheep. Surely Jesus chose this metaphor for a reason. What is it that he finds so appealing about sheep? Suddenly I have a flash of a photo of my husband, taken when he was about two years old, on a farm in Indiana, with his arm around the neck of a big, woolly sheep. It softens my heart.

Sheep do have good qualities. Sheep pay attention to the voice of their leader. They are willing to be protected, which is hard for many of us; humans like to deny that we need help. Sheep will follow the path their leader takes. They recognize and respect their shepherd, and are not easily deceived into following a stranger, who may have evil intentions. Their ability to accept love when it is offered to them is no small accomplishment. In return, they give their love and loyalty. Although sheep tend to wander off, with the shepherd's tending they travel in a flock, so they are never alone.

Maybe it's not so bad to be a sheep! —*Lee Krug*

# *Unreal city*

Twice in his celebrated poem *The Waste Land*, T. S. Eliot quotes another poet, Baudelaire, in referring to the fever of life as an "unreal city." Eliot wanders along the crowded and impersonal streets of London overcome by the impression that the movement and push he observes around him is just meaningless sound and fury, an *unreal city*.

When you succumb to the wound of enlightenment, you start to see things as they are—reality. What you thought was solid you now recognize as transitory. It is like the grass of the field, which Jesus said "today is alive and tomorrow is thrown into the oven" (Matthew 6:30). Little that you saw and trusted before stands up to scrutiny.

Enlightenment wrecks your worldview. When the roof caves in, much of what you thought you knew you really didn't know, and you realize there is a whole lot you don't know at all.

Literary scholars say that Eliot wrote *The Waste Land* in response to an overwhelmingly painful first marriage that included the acute mental illness of his wife. Thus the phrase "unreal city" is a sort of enlightened response to his suffering. This is no different from the "dying to self" of which Christ, Saint Paul, and Saint John all spoke.

If you have been shocked, by events, into *awareness*—enlightenment, if you will—the flimsy falseness of much of what you thought and saw now confronts you. This is the way to God, finally—the negation that allows for affirmation. But the old has to die first.
—*Paul F. M. Zahl*

# *Too much structure*

Laws and rules are important to civilized life. Anarchy may appeal to some, but without enforceable order, civilization cannot be maintained; the strong rule, the weak are preyed upon, and society eventually crumbles. We need some structure in order to function.

Of course, too many laws, too strictly enforced, are just as bad. "Anything that is not forbidden is permitted" is a far healthier ideal than "anything that is not permitted is forbidden." Rules should aid and protect us, not trip us up. The structure is not the end-all and be-all.

The law of Moses was intended to give people a framework for living, to bring them closer to God, to let them live in peace with their fellows and remain separated from the various other peoples who surrounded them. The psalmists praise the law: "Give me understanding, and I shall keep your law; I shall keep it with all my heart" (Psalm 119:34).

But it had become too restrictive by the time of Christ; the structure had become the focus, rather than the message. So much time and energy were spent parsing the rules that people forgot why those rules were there in the first place. Over and over, Jesus cuts to the chase: love your neighbor as yourself, turn the other cheek, pray for those who persecute you.

We can't be perfect, at least in this world, but we can strive for perfection; we can do our best to live according to Christ's law, loving those who hate us, giving alms to those who ask us, helping all who need our help, and remembering the One who came to save us.
—*Sarah Bryan Miller*

# *Bless the dern fog*

"Dern the dern fog." We were stumbling along a mountain trail, straining to see farther than fifty feet beyond the ends of our noses, when I remembered a bit from *Huckleberry Finn*—Huck and Jim on their raft in a thick morning fog. A disembodied voice from a nearby barge grumbles, "Dern the dern fog."

Brenda and I had arrived in the evening at the Monastery of Montserrat, set among jagged peaks and weird rock formations in the Pyrenees Mountains. We had planned a full day's hike to outlying hermitages and cave shrines. I anticipated glorious mountain vistas.

So when we woke to a thick blanket of fog, I felt personally offended, and my sense of injury grew as we started out. "Dern the dern fog." But deciding eventually it was wiser to bless than curse, I admonished myself to focus on what *was* visible along the path—small wildflowers, the shapes of leaves, the texture of the earth. I exerted my senses of smell and hearing, and tried to perceive in my imagination the fullness of this spectacular place that I couldn't see very well.

Seven centuries ago, an anonymous mystic wrote of the hiddenness of God in a classic treatise on prayer, *The Cloud of Unknowing.* "If you hope to feel and see God, it must be within this darkness and this cloud." One must, so to speak, bless the dern fog.

Paying attention to what was close at hand, I began to see small beauties I'd have otherwise overlooked. And from time to time the fog blew away and gave glimpses of the landscape that aided my imagination during the longer periods when everything was obscured.

"Now we see through a glass darkly," Paul wrote, "but *then* face to face." If I ever get back to Montserrat in full sunlight, I'll remember the foggy day as a blessed foretaste. —*Bruce Birdsey*

# *"Don't worry, be happy"*

It has been many months since I began a day without some degree of financial worry. As a church's development director, I saw the recession starting three months before the Bear Stearns collapse and nine months before anyone in Washington dared to use the word "recession." As a self-employed writer and church consultant, my stomach never stops churning.

My morning prayers haven't been petitions for wealth. I have prayed for peace—for my family, especially—and I have asked God's help in providing for my family's needs. Mostly, I have given thanks. Specific thanks for a child, for time to write, for kindness, for my wife. Whether the bills are piling up or under control, I am grateful for God's precious gift of family.

Years ago, a friend offered her personal theology in the words of a pop song: "Don't Worry, Be Happy." I disagreed at first, but I came to understand her determination not to let life—and soon her husband's debilitating illness—get her down. She was a survivor, not a Pollyanna. Deep down, I have a special place in my heart for survivors. For people who do what it takes to put food on the table, to hold their heads high, to make the world even marginally a better place.

I admire the immigrant families who run small fruit-and-vegetable stands on the sidewalks near my home, who stand outside all day long, in all weather, to make their start in America. I hope that I have even half as much courage and pluck.

Financial stress takes its toll on many lives. I think God understands. I think God responds to our prayers for peace and humility.

Wealth probably isn't God's concern. But peace in our hearts, peace in our families, and peace in our communities matter greatly to God. —*Thomas L. Ehrich*

# *Communion Sunday*

My family abruptly stopped going to church one Sunday in 1951, when I was eight. It was Communion Sunday, which was important because it happened only four times a year. It wasn't a big church, but on Communion Sunday every pew was filled. We were fairly new but had learned to come early on this Sunday.

During the singing of the first hymn, a woman with two children about my age came down the aisle looking for a seat. They squeezed in across the aisle from us. The girl's dress looked homemade and the boy's pants were about four inches too short. I stared at them and they stared at me, as children will do.

After the hymns and prayers and sermon, the deacons started preparing for communion. One came down the aisle and quietly said to the woman that communion was only for members, so they would have to leave. Obviously shamed and embarrassed, she gathered up her pocket book and children, preparing to leave.

I looked at my father, whose face was beginning to twitch. As she started down the aisle, my father stepped into the aisle and said to the deacon, "If she's not welcome, then we're not welcome." He took my mother's arm and my hand, and we followed her out the door.

After a few weeks of Sunday services at home and reflecting on what it means to be a Christian, we started attending another church. I don't know what effect that rejection had on that woman and her daughter and the boy with short pants, but I do know the effect it had on me. Thirty years later, during my first chapel service on my first day at General Seminary in New York, as I knelt at the altar in the Chapel of the Good Shepherd, I vowed I would never deny any sacrament to any person for any reason. —*David L. James*

# Things temporal, things eternal

*Increase and multiply upon us your mercy;*
*that…we may so pass through things temporal,*
*that we lose not the things eternal.*
—The Book of Common Prayer,
Collect for Proper 12

The word "eternal" is inevitably misused and misunderstood, confused with the word "immortal." Only God is immortal, continuing unchanged forever and ever, Amen. Our lives and all human history are different. Everything we know has a beginning and an end. But within this progression, there is the possibility of the eternal.

The eternal is a new dimension that we glimpse, occasionally, when we look into the eyes of a beloved or listen to the song of the mourning dove or gaze in wonder at the beauty of a sunset. The eternal is caught in a line of poetry and the melodic line of a great symphony. The eternal emerges from the temporal. All time passes. Within it, all we know for sure is the now. The past has gone; the future may or may not happen. The eternal rises above them both, capturing the now and taking it to a new level, created by transcending all human experience. It is why we go to galleries to sit and reflect, why we read and write and hope.

The eternal is our salvation. We all long for it. Too few of us know its language or aspire to speak it. Yet we can. Where we do so, our words are the words of prayer. These are the words that pass us from the temporal to the eternal. —*Edward S. Gleason*

# *Missing Belle*

Belle the cat died nine months ago. I miss having her greet us when we return to the house, no matter how short or long our absence. The shorter the better, according to her. A long absence deserved a cool reception. I miss Belle for many reasons, not least among them our shared interest in afternoon naps. We had worked out where our spots were on the bed. After some feigned deliberation she always settled in—having circled several times—between my chest and right arm, often with a contented sigh.

After a month or two I wanted to get two kittens, but my wife wasn't ready, didn't know when she would be ready, might never be ready. The pain of loss was still too strong. I got it, but I missed having a cat.

Then came William the Orange, real name and owner unknown. For three or four years he has visited our yard in the warm months to hunt birds and chipmunks. Only this year has he approached us. He likes to be with us; sometimes he comes to the back screen door and calls for us to come out. Apparently he doesn't want anything but our company.

When cold weather sets in William will disappear for a while and we will have adopted a couple of kittens. Meantime, we're happy for his company. He rubs and winds around our legs. We give him a back rub and a scratch. Love given, love received, creation's perfect arrangement. —*Robert Horine*

# *Get well and get real*

One of my favorite cartoon characters is Ziggy, a hapless everyman who often finds himself in bizarre or unfortunate circumstances that contain a lesson or a kernel of wisdom. In one such strip, Ziggy is in a greeting card store looking at the "Get Well" selection. Next to it is a section labeled "Get Real." A humorous notion, yes, but there is also truth in these two sentiments: Get Well and Get Real.

In order to get well, especially spiritually, and in many cases physically and emotionally, we have to get real first. We must be honest about what is wrong and what needs to be made right. We have to be honest about whether we actually want to be healed, remembering that when we are healed we often have to give up our excuses. We have to take some risks.

Reinhold Niebuhr once said: "The powers of human self-deception are seemingly endless." Getting real means fearlessly acknowledging before God and ourselves what needs healing in our lives and in our hearts, and then allowing God to create something new.

—*James L. Burns*

# *Forgiveness*

Thinking through the world's critique of the church, that Christians are by nature conflict animals—that we are even defined by the conflict inherent in trying to make *you* one of *us*—we need to return to our founder.

What is never-failingly impressive in Jesus' ministry is his majoring in forgiveness and grace, rather than a frustrated demand for judgment and law. He is not there to straighten people out. He is there to forgive people whose lives have become *un*-straightened through outward circumstances or through their own deliberate fault. "God did not send the Son into the world to condemn the world, but in order that the world might be saved through him" (John 3:17). So strong is the overwhelming theme of forgiveness and absolution rooted in the ministry of Christ that he says he has nothing to say to righteous persons, everything to say to sinners (Matthew 9:13).

When I walk down Connecticut Avenue near my parish in Washington, D.C., wearing my clerical collar, I receive a few warm smiles. But I also get a lot of dirty looks and quite a few accusing stares. This is new for me. Somehow the collar has come to represent, for many people, judgment. The collar signifies intolerance.

This was not Jesus. He loved and forgave. He ended the conflict-structure of accusation and separation with words of forgiveness and unity. He gathered. He did not cast out.

Jesus' unity of approach lies in his forgiveness of sin and of sinners. There is an antidote to all this bad blood. —*Paul F. M. Zahl*

# *In Eden*

It is said that a myth is a story that may never have happened but is always true. There is no better illustration than the great myth of the Fall in Genesis 3. I doubt that a recorder could have picked up the dialogue between Eve and the snake, or that the CSI team could analyze the half-eaten apple. But I have no doubt about the truth of the story.

Notice that it makes no attempt to tell us why or how the evil snake got into the garden. The real question is not behind us in our origin, but before us in our behavior. And look at how Eve, Adam, and I behave.

We pounce on self-serving lies and treat them as gospel. "You will not die," says the snake, in the same tone I use when I tell myself that I will not gain weight, have a heart attack, get caught driving under the influence, or get in trouble with my VISA bill. Eve thinks she can eat the apple with impunity the way we think we can ignore cholesterol, postpone serious conversations, blow off disciplines, or listen to children only when it is convenient. The apple, of course, appeals to her appetites and desire for an edge in life the same way that every bit of advertising we regularly fall for appeals to us. And when lies turn out to be lies and personal exemptions evaporate, Adam, Eve, and I are ready to blame anyone else or, in the case of Eden which had only two people, everyone else.

This story that may never have happened happens every day in my life. I am just glad we call it the Fall of Adam instead of the Fall of Frank. I don't think I could stand the notoriety. —*Francis H. Wade*

# *Homes*

The cats had been waiting for us, it seemed, as we returned to our temporary home in Florence: they had arranged themselves right by the front door so that we would trip over them when we entered.

"Were you good boys for Tony?" I asked. It was a meaningless question, the feline moral vision differing so profoundly from ours. I was thinking of them when I was on the plane, imagining this house, the beautiful old table in the entrance hallway, the couches in the living room. I went on to another house in my imagination, our house back in the United States. I am in the bedroom, up in the wee hours of the morning, putting on my robe and walking carefully down the stairs to the kitchen. I am putting the tea kettle on and going out through the front garden to get *The New York Times* from the sidewalk. I wonder about the garden; it's probably a little wild by now. There will be a lot to do when we get home.

"I sleep outside," a Sri Lankan man here in Florence tells me, and those three mournful words hang between us. I have a home; he does not. I have two homes, in fact: one here and another one waiting for me across the sea. I have lots of room. "I sleep outside," he says. I ponder his need and my abundance. I have been pondering that for decades. Once in a while, I've been able to do something about it. Often, I have not. Maybe this time, too. Or maybe not.

But maybe so. There is no end to the need. It is beyond my ability to count. But each one is only one. "How do you manage to help all those people?" somebody once asked Mother Teresa. "One by one by one," she said.

Which, come to think of it, is the way we do anything we do. One by one by one. —*Barbara Cawthorne Crafton*

# The church has power

Indiana doesn't have hurricanes, but when the remnants of Hurricane Ike blew through our little community, we sustained winds over seventy miles an hour for more than six hours. To say that we were unprepared would be an understatement. By day's end, we had lost more than a thousand two-hundred-year-old trees that had graced the city. As the trees came crashing down, they took electric lines with them. The town went dark.

I was so busy checking on neighbors and congregants that I didn't eat dinner that Sunday evening. By morning I was hungry, and I wound up at a little café at the far end of the main drag, the only place that was open. As I ate, other church members appeared. We chatted, wondering what we could do. "Well, the church has power," I said. "The sign in the front yard was on when I came by earlier."

And with one voice they said, "That means we can cook!" So it began. We pooled food that needed to be used immediately out of our refrigerators, and wound up making a huge pot of chili for lunch. We set out a sign that read: FREE HOT LUNCH and served until 2:00 p.m. or until we ran out, whichever came first.

Someone said, "I just can't get going without my morning coffee." So, we agreed to serve coffee along with toast made in the oven the next morning. We flipped our sign over and printed COFFEE AND? The local radio station discovered us, then the local newspaper. Homemade jam began to appear from folks in the neighborhood. A local bakery brought a supply of doughnuts.

By week's end our little group had fed more than six hundred people.

When I had said, "The church has power," I had no idea how right I was. —*Gregory A. Russell*

# *Grace is the glue*

One of the chief wonders of *The Book of Common Prayer* is the Celebration and Blessing of a Marriage, especially the service's insight that marriage is a means and channel of grace. Again and again, the prayers and formularies speak of marriage as a grace-conveying ministry of one person to the other: "Assist them with your grace....Eternal God, giver of all grace....Give them grace, when they hurt each other....Bestow on them, if it is your will, the gift and heritage of children, and the grace to bring them up....So transformed by your grace..."

Of modern American writers I consider Eugene O'Neill the darkest. Still, his 1926 stage play, *The Great God Brown*, reveals a glimmer of hope. Putting the children to bed, Brown says, "A little paste, Margaret! A little paste, gentlemen!...A little dab of pasty resignation here and there—and even broken hearts may be repaired to do a yeoman service!" And then O'Neill records the children wide-eyed in astonishment as Brown puts his finger to his lips and says, "This is Daddy's bedtime secret for today: Man is born broken. He lives by mending. The grace of God is the glue!"

Grace is the healing agent in our badly broken and distorted world. Like the watches on our wrists and the shoes on our feet, our lives break down and need repairing. It is a broken world, and it lives by mending. I believe in the grace of God. —*Richard L. Shimpfky*

# No ordinary time

On the Gulf Coast, the long, green season of summer fits well with the long, green season we know as "after Pentecost," or ordinary time. The trees here are fully green well before we hear about flames flickering above the disciples' heads in Jerusalem, and many will stay green almost as long as our altars do, deep into the fall, some even up until Advent.

Other seasons of the church year race in rapid bursts of changing colors and themes sharply focused on Jesus' life, death, and resurrection. But even as its name suggests, this season after Pentecost softly arrives and quietly lingers like the leaves themselves, deepening over time.

And of course, that is its purpose—to dwell on that third, open-ended phrase in our proclamation of faith: "Christ has died. Christ is risen. Christ will come again." The season after Pentecost is the time in which we live, the time since the first day of Pentecost that continues to this day, the present time in which we remember what Christ has done, but also look forward to what he will do.

Ordinary time, not as in humdrum, but as in the Latin, *tempus ordinarii,* or "numbered time." Our days are numbered. But instead of merely counting them down and looking forward to time with God in the hereafter, we also are called to expect Christ in the here and now, in each and every day.

By September, some might long for a change of color in church. But this long, green season cannot be rushed any more than our long, green season of summer on the coast.

All we can do is sit back, relax, and soak up the Son who has come, who is here, who is coming. —*Jerald Hyche*

# Circling the wagons

The church is tempted to circle the wagons and worship its own security and safety. We cannot stand letting go of control, yet our faith requires it. This is one reason I love the discoveries of modern science, especially cosmology. They introduce us once more to the deep mystery that holds us in being, with all its terror and wonder. Michael R. Trimble, psychiatrist and professor of behavioral neurology, writes in *The Soul in the Brain,* "There are more stars in our galaxy than there are grains of sand on all the beaches of our world, and perhaps, more galaxies in the universe than the number of those stars." Can we stand the mystery? Can we stand *in* the mystery? Can we uncircle the wagons and continue our pilgrimage?

Living in the mystery can help us get moving. It can rescue us from the gossip or mean-spiritedness which forced us to circle the wagons in the first place. It's often the petty and silly things, things of appalling smallness, that push us into a stance of belligerent defensiveness.

Take the spreading of rumor. Some years ago Lincoln Cathedral in England went through a saga rather like the ones written about in Trollope's Barchester series of novels. In this case, it was said that the bishop, the dean, and the sub-dean didn't speak to each other. It was hilarious and tragic at the same time. The then sub-dean recalled that shortly after coming to Lincoln he had told someone at a reception that he worked for the cathedral. "Fearful place, lots of trouble going on up there," he was told. "Really," asked the sub-dean, "what kind of trouble?" "Well, the sub-dean won't speak to the archdeacon." "Hang on," said the sub-dean, "I'm the sub-dean and I'm having lunch with the archdeacon tomorrow." "So you are not sub-dean Cook?" asked the man. "No. He died twenty-seven years ago!"

That wagon train hadn't moved for decades! —*Alan Jones*

# *O gracious light*

The day's light begins to fade. Lights go on in nearby windows. Workers head home; mothers take restless children outside for one last ride in the stroller.

In this mellow time, feelings are nearer the surface. Sadness, tenderness, joy, satisfaction, worry—all swirl gently, and the borders separating them blur. I can't name that pang I felt while walking from kitchen to office.

Now is the time when those who have homes go in search of them. And those who have food prepare to eat it. And those who aren't in harm's way relax.

In the devotional for early evening, I thank God for "gracious light," both the Light that was Jesus and the light that illumines our days. I thank God for the "vesper light," the evening candle, and wonder if the day will come when I light candles before praying the hours.

This is the hour of thanksgiving. In the morning I will awaken to worry and combat it with work. Now, "as we come to the setting of the sun," I am content just to be thankful. I might have done more today. But I did what I could. And for that opportunity to work, I am thankful.

Now I pray that Jesus will "stay with me" and be my "companion in the way" in the hours ahead. As I give myself over to the time after work, I pray for calm and for hope.

The day will come when I reach an end and will not rise to another day. I hope that day is like this: a peaceful step away from worries, and a settling of my inner self to be held close by God.

"For God alone my soul in silence waits." —*Thomas L. Ehrich*

# *Watch your lips!*

One sentence has cost me a whole day. In the heat of anger or the cool of disappointment, I have issued words I wanted to retract before the last syllable was out of my lips. Accentuating the pain is the battalion of words I must later offer to make amends for my poor judgment and lack of discipline. My experience gives credence to one of the first adages we all learn: "Say something nice or say nothing at all."

James says the tongue is a fire (James 3:6). In contrast to Paul's assertion that the we give greater honor to the inferior parts of the body (1 Corinthians 12:24), James states that the tongue is a "small member yet it boasts of great exploits. How great a forest is set ablaze by a small fire!" (James 3:5) James is so alarmed at the poisonous power of our speech that he recalls how human beings at creation were made masters of all the mighty beasts on the earth, but we seem unable to tame the diminutive function of speech within our own selves. We even curse God's highest creation—our brothers and sisters! In a scathing comparison, James says the brush fires begun by our loose talk are like the ghastly inferno of hell.

Sailors learn that "loose lips sink ships." On a more personal and Christly note, undisciplined speech can sink our lives into a "hell of a mess." —*W. Patrick Gahan*

# Leave offenders with Jesus

Our parakeets Annie and Patrick, named after long-deceased relatives, lay dead in their cages. A draft must have come in, we were told. It doesn't take much for birds to get sick. Strange. Those parakeets had been in the same place for three years and nothing had happened to them—no drafts, no death. But as a kid you tend to believe the adults around you. My mother had died a few months earlier, and there was a new housekeeper. And now there were two dead birds. My brother and I grieved the birds. A lot of sadness.

Thirty-five years later, I had that housekeeper over for Thanksgiving dinner. A nice thing to do, I thought. And the mystery of the birds was revealed. They were too much work. Too many feathers to sweep up. "I couldn't be expected to clean up after them. So I got some chloroform and some cotton." Chloroform. Really. *She had killed the birds.* At night, she murdered the birds. *They were too much work.* Murder and lies, betrayal and stupidity. I forgave her eventually, although my teenagers still think of her as Lizzie Borden.

Forgiveness. If it's real forgiveness, it's never easy, despite what people say. Others have to forgive even larger sins as they grow up. Rape. Adultery. War. Genocide. There is no forgiveness, at least in my book, without the help of God. And it's a process. I recently suggested to someone who couldn't forgive her son-in-law for hurting her daughter, that she picture picking him up and literally throwing him into a room with Jesus. Leave offenders with Jesus, alone, at least in prayer. It's a start. It's better than nothing. Both for us and for those who sin against us. —*Lindsay Hardin Freeman*

# *Busy birthday*

As usual, my daughter is running from one thing to another today: teaching, coaching soccer after school, grading papers in between activities, and then teaching again. Every day she juggles a work schedule on a par with that of Oprah Winfrey or Martha Stewart, but without the support staff.

Today is her birthday. When she was small, her birthday parties included raking the fallen leaves into piles and letting the little guests take a running leap and jump in them, over and over again. Now, the crushing workload she carries doesn't allow for much celebration; that will have to wait. I call her cell phone and leave a happy birthday message on her voicemail, in which I suggest fifteen minutes with her feet up. I want her to slow down. I am also aware that she has little choice about these things; she has a family to support, and teachers don't make much money.

I am thinking of the day she was born. I got to the hospital at one in the afternoon and she arrived at four. Later that evening, she lay sleeping in her bassinet while I gazed at her, memorizing her face, her curly hair, her eyelashes, her petal skin. Suddenly she opened her mouth and yawned—a big yawn for such a little girl. I was absurdly proud: my baby could yawn! Just like a person! She had worked hard. Being born was work enough for one short day. Tomorrow would come soon enough.

We are never finished, not until it is time for us to leave. What peace we gain in life usually does not come from completion. It is not earned; it is a gift. Today I pray a birthday prayer: peace and refreshing rest for my lovely little girl, now a lovely grown woman.

None of us can labor peace into being. It comes as gift. Let it come. —*Barbara Cawthorne Crafton*

# Laborers and the harvest

*The harvest is plentiful, but the laborers are few;*
*therefore ask the Lord of the harvest*
*to send out laborers into his harvest.*
—Matthew 9:37-38

A neighboring parish sponsored a mission trip to Latin America and invited me to go along. On our first day, I was led out into a field with one other member of our team. We were told by a local church member that one day a school would be in that field. He asked us to start digging a hole for the foundation. We both agreed that the project was a pipe dream, but we dug faithfully for almost a week. It was exhausting work. When we went home, there was a hole, but not a very big one. Two years later the school opened.

There are now five buildings in that empty field, filled with students and teachers. Jesus said, "The harvest is plentiful, but the laborers are few." Sometimes it only takes a few laborers. Even one person of faith, with a vision given by God, can change the world. —*Jason Leo*

# *The ballet of perspectives*

Mother always wanted me to be smarter and more cultured than I was (and am). She never acknowledged it was a losing battle, and she never stopped trying. God bless her.

The fall I was eight, she took me to see my first ballet over the river in Cincinnati. Music Hall was a big old barn of a place with red velvet seats, ushers with perfect posture, and glittering chandeliers. Mother was determined that I should see it all and forever after know that there is more to life than could be had in our small Kentucky town, in which I was perfectly happy, mind you.

The house lights dimmed, the orchestra struck the opening chords of Tchaikovsky's *Swan Lake*, and out came the entire corps de ballet *en pointe*, feet fluttering, dancing on the very tips of their toes, arms lifted, straining to reach the heavens. No one in my little town could do that! I had never seen anything like it.

Was it a purely magical moment? Hardly.

I leaned over to my mother and whispered, with perfect eight-year-old logic, "Why don't they just get taller girls?" They were straining *so* hard to reach *something*. Obviously, the girls were too short.

Now that I am a church pastor, when I am in the midst of a long discussion with lots of people and more than one possible outcome, this little tableau occasionally flashes before my eyes. I see my mother's astonished face and imagine I can hear her doing her very best to suppress her hearty laugh. It is then that I remember that two people can see the same thing and each draw astoundingly different conclusions from the same exact evidence—even a conclusion that is absolutely wrong!

And, the wrong one may be mine. —*Gregory A. Russell*

OCTOBER 6

# *Not as a tourist*

*A stained glass window has a different fate from a painting. Because of the setting, the eye does not look at it in the same way as a collection in a museum. The eye of a man at prayer is simply part of his heart.*

—Marc Chagall, at the dedication of the synagogue
at the Hadassah Medical Center in Jerusalem,
adorned by his stained glass (1962).

Our cruise allowed only eight hours in Stockholm, so I'd mapped out a tight itinerary for what I wanted to see. It included a notable piece of statuary (at least the guidebook called it notable) in one of the great churches. Arriving a little before noon, I was met by a polite request to refrain from sightseeing until a eucharist now in progress was over.

Slightly miffed at this disruption of my efficient plan, I took a seat near the back of the nave (the congregation on this weekday morning was gathered up front) and craned my neck in search of the statue. It was nowhere in sight; with nothing else to do, I turned my attention to the liturgy. The classical structure of the eucharist made it easy to follow, even in a foreign tongue. Rather quickly, I found my entire outlook shift from sightseer to worshiper.

It was a salutary change, cooling the overheated intensity with which I'd been hustling around the city to take in its A-list sights. As I looked at the church (still not spotting the must-see statue) I began to see, really *see*, other beauties of the building. And also, of course, the beauty of holiness. Having received communion, I meandered around a little longer, found the statue (which was indeed a jewel), and left refreshed, in multiple senses of the word.

At the risk of reducing the profound to the banal, I paraphrase Job 19:27: "I shall see, and mine eyes shall behold—and not as a *tourist*." —*Bruce Birdsey*

284

# *Ornette Coleman*

With hayseeds still in the cuffs of my trousers, I arrived in New York City in 1980 to attend the General Theological Seminary. This was the first time I'd seen a person passed out on a sidewalk in a puddle of his own urine or watched the police chase a thief down the street, darting between cars and hopping fences. These sights and sounds and smells were foreign to me.

During my first week in New York, as I was walking across 14th Street in Greenwich Village, I heard the sound of a bass drum and a few instruments struggling with "Amazing Grace." I recognized the sound because my mother used to play the piano in Salvation Army churches.

Two men slowed as they walked by the struggling musicians. One was carrying a black case. He stopped and handed the case to his friend, who held it while he took out a gold trumpet. He tapped his foot, put the trumpet to his lips, and softly joined in. Soon clear, high notes with a touch of jazz filled the block, and many people began to stop. One by one the band musicians stopped playing to listen to the trumpet. When the man finished, people tried to hand him money, but he shook his head and pointed to the Salvation Army bucket.

As he put the horn back into the case, the second man said, "It's not everyone who gets Ornette Coleman to sit in on a street revival." I later learned that Coleman was one of the greatest jazz trumpeters in the world.

Over the next few years in seminary, I thought of that scene on the street as a metaphor for my trip down the Canterbury road from guilt to grace. The strict holiness of my Methodist upbringing taught me all the steps, but it was Episcopalians who taught me how to dance. —*David L. James*

# *Small gifts*

The sound of revelry on the other end of the phone line was so loud that I could barely make out what our youth pastor was saying. I had called to check on our senior high youth group and their sponsors as they were finishing their mission work in Beaumont, Texas. The entire group was deep into celebration when I finally contacted them. They had cleaned up two damaged homes and a church yard that had been badly beaten up by Hurricane Rita. Considering the magnitude of damage left by a Category 4 storm, it is hard to imagine our small youth group could make a difference. But they did, and their faithful actions will be felt by those in Beaumont for a long time to come.

Even one person can make a difference. Only an unnamed boy believes Jesus can feed the hungry multitude that has followed Jesus and his disciples to the far side of the Sea of Galilee. Philip, speaking for all twelve of the disciples, exclaims that six months' wages would not buy enough even for each person to get an appetizer (John 6:7). Andrew, however, finds a youth who offers all the food in his knapsack to assist Jesus in his effort. Andrew, like Philip, is skeptical of their rabbi's ability to feed the ravenous bunch surrounding them. Nevertheless, propelled by the singular faith of the boy, Jesus prays over his offering and distributes the food—and everyone in the crowd enjoys a satisfying meal. What's more, twelve baskets of leftovers are collected—just to add symbolic salt to the twelve disciples' collective wound of unbelief. All it took was one boy to act on his faith.

Do we believe Christ can multiply what small gifts we offer this hurting world? If so, that is something to celebrate!
—*W. Patrick Gahan*

# *Where love begins*

As a morning person, I start the day early and fully alert and then wind down from there. I don't begin to understand evening persons, who follow the opposite course. My morning station on Pandora.com is chamber baroque, meaning gentle but complex music by Corelli, Vivaldi, Telemann and the like. Good for watching the sun come up. Later in the day, I switch to self-defined stations featuring so-called New Age music by Vollenweider, Enya, and their mellow peers, for that time when my energy is at low ebb.

In my years of planning Sunday worship, I grew quickly tired of trendy rousers like "Lift High the Cross" and found myself drawn more and more to the mellow sounds of Taizé chant and Celtic songs. I once developed an unreasonable fondness for a hymn called "Now the Silence."

Some shared this mood of the "church at peace." Many wanted exactly the opposite, namely, the grand processional hymns of the "church militant" or the boisterous songs of the "church renewed." There was no right or wrong to this, but it certainly made liturgical planning a challenge. How could a single service encompass the divergent moods and needs of its participants? Somebody would always leave disappointed.

Thus goes life, as well. It's unusual when even a couple are on precisely the same page. With more people, the diversity grows exponentially. Bullies try to bend everyone else to their will. But when we are at our best, we realize that singing someone else's favorite hymn is an act of grace, and that eventually our turn will come.

Sometimes, like a morning person and evening person having their best conversations at noon, we will meet in the middle. Other times, we will simply put our mood on hold and adapt to the other. That's the point at which love begins. —*Thomas L. Ehrich*

# No longer bristling

*Now Simon's mother-in-law was suffering from a fever,*
*and they asked [Jesus] about her.*
*Then he stood over her and rebuked the fever, and it left her.*
*Immediately she got up and began to serve them.* —Luke 4:38-39

Once there was a young woman who bristled at passages like this one: "The Bible is always treating women badly. Look at the mother-in-law! She doesn't even get a name. She is healed and then immediately gets up and serves Jesus and the disciples. She's probably fretting because she has been too ill to clean, and there's nothing fit to set out for dinner, and she's a feverish mess when the prophet comes to call. Poor mother-in-law."

Most biblical women are nameless, with nonspeaking roles, mere supernumeraries in the drama of holy history. Many of those who do get a line or two are not ideal role models—Jezebel comes to mind— and one perfectly blameless but possibly too intelligent and assertive woman, Mary of Magdala, has been confused with the woman taken in adultery for no justifiable reason. Our young woman bristles at all this, so much that she aches. The world seems to have one set of rules for men and another for women. Women are second-class citizens, sidelined and patronized even in the church, where all are supposedly one in Christ Jesus.

But wait. Things have changed. We have new and more thoughtful ways of interpreting scripture. Now women can serve according to their vocations and abilities, and not just according to their chromosomes.

And now, with more maturity and less anger, our no-longer-young woman sees this passage in a different light. I was that woman; now I know that it is a privilege for each of us to serve our Lord in the best way we can. —*Sarah Bryan Miller*

# *Knowing and believing*

It is not easy to live the life of faith in the contemporary world. Not only have our work lives become more demanding and the social supports for church attendance fallen away, but the intellectual barriers to faith keep rising. How can we believe the Bible to be trustworthy, given what we know about biology, chemistry, and physics?

I used to attend a congregation that had a lot of academic scientists as members. When we said the Nicene Creed, you could hear some voices drop away during the clauses that modify or define God, Jesus, and the Holy Spirit. These men and women knew they believed in God and wanted to follow Jesus, but they were not sure they wanted to accept first-, third-, or fourth-century definitions of what that means.

Flannery O'Connor once said, "Faith is what someone knows to be true, whether they believe it or not." As an old-style Roman Catholic, O'Connor understood that knowledge is more than what we process through our conscious thoughts. For O'Connor, and for Christians historically, knowledge encompasses what we feel, perceive, and intuit through our bodies, our relationships, and our histories.

We live too much in our heads, and when we do that we treat the Bible like a set of facts to be subjected to rational analysis. But look at and listen to what's around and inside you. There is a profound way in which you know the story of God's love for humanity and Jesus' journey with and for us to be true, even if you cannot say you know it by rational means. That story speaks both in and to you, and its promptings are the most trustworthy things you can know. —*Gary Hall*

# Out with the real, in with the artificial

The window of my office looks out on a lovely garden that is part of a museum housed in an elegant old mansion. Across the street from the mansion is the entrance to a large and beautifully maintained city park. Together they comprise a wonderful oasis in a vast urban setting.

The museum garden is often the scene of various receptions: weddings, fundraisers, reunions, and the like. Often a canopy is put up, providing shade but allowing the surrounding beauty to be seen. On one occasion, however, the event planners arranged for an immense tent to be constructed. First, a wooden platform was laid over the lush lawn. Then poles and ropes went up, and a fully enclosed tent was erected. Next, a truck delivered a large portable air conditioning unit that was hooked up to the tent by an elaborate duct system. Finally, a florist arrived with potted trees and plants to be arranged inside the tent. The day of the event was a spectacular fall day. The weather was mild, the sun and blue sky brilliant, and the fall foliage at its peak. Meanwhile the patrons gathered, sipping cocktails and nibbling on hors d'oeuvres in a climate-controlled environment with rented plants.

This reception struck me as an apt metaphor for what too often passes for spirituality. In the midst of God's extraordinary and awesome mystery, love, grace, and majesty, we confine our prayers and our spirits, even our dreams, to a smaller, self-made and controlled enclosure, perhaps decorated with a few transplanted or artificial reminders of the greater reality that surrounds us but which we have blocked out of our lives. —*James L. Burns*

# "See you, Joe"

The whole family had gathered around the hospital bed for final goodbyes. Joe, the family patriarch, was in an apparent coma and had been given only a 5 percent chance of making it through the night. They had asked me to come for final prayers and comfort.

We talked with each other around the room, across the bed where Joe lay inert. People recalled how much he had meant to them, what a good dad he was, and granddad, brother, spouse, friend.

It was a typical scene that I have experienced many times, where we are present with the loved one but there is a sense that he is already gone, is no longer really there.

At some point in my ministry I decided always to treat people as if they are in fact "present," no matter what their outward appearance. The machinery of the body might not be operative—to communicate "out" or to indicate reception "in"—but at some level the person might in fact know, hear, and be aware. And so I decided to err on the side of treating people as whole and present persons, rather than dismiss them as if they were mere things.

It came time to go, and I recalled my intent. I said a prayer, touched his hand, and said "See you, Joe. See you in the morning."

"Okay," he sat up and replied. And in the stunned silence that followed, I walked out the door as if it were the most natural thing in the world. Joe was still around a number of years later, as I recall, full of himself to the last.

We are always whole and present persons, from our first breath to our last. —*Leonard Freeman*

# *Godly life*

*Almighty God, you have given your only Son
to be for us a sacrifice for sin,
and also an example of godly life…*
—The Book of Common Prayer,
Collect for Proper 15

This is the recipe for a holy life, a few code words to say: "It's all been done for you; there's nothing you need to do except live your life with gratitude, remembering the example that has been set before you."

Over the centuries great effort has been expended in writing theological positions and arguments. Some issues have been resolved and others created. Lifetimes have been devoted to making the simple more complicated. The simple, as a matter of fact, is that whatever you think you need to do, to say, or to accomplish has already been done for you. It's all over. Nothing more is needed. Jesus Christ has made it possible for you to be the person you were made to be.

Therefore, go out and live your life as if it has just been given to you to live. Don't complicate or overanalyze. Live each day as if it were your very first day, and then do it all over again, for your life is a gift from God, redeemed by Christ, and handed to you to live with and for others.

Which brings us to one last thing. Because you have been given so much—everything, in fact—remember to be the best possible person you can be, not for yourself alone, but for your neighbor, the person next to you or across town or across the globe. New life has been given to that person too, just as it has been given to you. Remember that. Go now, and do likewise. Live your life as if it were the only life you have to live for another. It is. —*Edward S. Gleason*

# *God's castle*

When faced with what she thought an insurmountable task, Teresa of Avila, the sixteenth-century Spanish Carmelite nun and mystic, began to imagine herself a different way. She said that she "began to think of the soul as if it were a castle made of a single diamond or of very clear crystal, in which there are many rooms, just as in heaven there are many mansions." She continued, "The soul of the righteous man is nothing but a paradise, in which, as God tells us, he takes his delight." Imagine that, Teresa chides us—each of us is a castle built by God.

The Jews rebuilding the temple after the Babylonian exile feel they have undertaken an insurmountable task. They are literally fainting from the agonizing press of their labor (Zechariah 8:9-13). What's more, they are receiving no wages for their efforts, so they cannot buy food. The Lord assures the people that better days are coming, that he will bless this remnant of returnees to Jerusalem and withhold the vengeance he poured out on their unfaithful forebears. Through the mouth of Zechariah, the Lord acts as a cheerleader, extolling these famished, weary people not to give in to fear of the future but to continue to lend strong hands to the task of rebuilding. After all, the real object of God's love is not the Jerusalem temple, but the hardworking, selfless people struggling there. They are being built into a mansion reflecting the glory of the Lord.

Often at burials, I read the comforting passage from John 14:2, "In my Father's house are many mansions: if it were not so, I would have told you. I go to prepare a place for you." Could it be that we are the mansion under construction? —*W. Patrick Gahan*

# Keep the candle lit

In Ireland there is a deep beautiful glen in the woods, not far from a road, a small road, as most roads in Ireland are, but a road nonetheless. The glen is a little out of sight, down the road, so you can't see it at first. A stream winds around a large flat rock. There is a solemn sense of peace about this spot, almost sacred.

It turns out it *is* a sacred spot. When the British were persecuting the Catholics, the Catholics would gather in the glen, out of sight, breaking bread and reciting the ancient prayers that had formed their faith, kept them steady, and kept them upright. They did that because they had to. They knew what Jeremiah meant when he said: "If I say, 'I will not mention him, or speak any more in his name,' then within me there is something like a burning fire shut up in my bones; I am weary with holding it in, and I cannot" (Jeremiah 20:9).

Our faith is full of those who chose not to die inside, but to proclaim in word and action the name of the Lord *as they understood him.* In Oxford, England, the author and compiler of the original of *The Book of Common Prayer,* Thomas Cranmer, was burnt at the stake in 1556 because he would not renounce his beliefs. His friends Hugh Latimer and Nicholas Ridley had met the same fate five months earlier. As Ridley and Latimer were being led to the stake, Latimer said, "Be of good comfort, Master Ridley, and play the man; we shall this day light such a candle, by God's grace, in England as I trust shall never be put out."

Sacred trust. May we strive to keep that candle lit.
—*Lindsay Hardin Freeman*

# *Broken pieces of community*

Communities teach us to be individuals. The community in which we grow up gives us its lore, customs, principles, and priorities as the raw material with which we fashion our individuality. When I think of community I picture a gathered thing, a homogeneity, some kind of a consistency that I bounced off of as a child and draw from as an adult.

But refugees, sojourners, immigrants, and the homeless remind us that communities do not always hold together. They leak sometimes. Pieces break off. Those pieces of community also teach us, form us, and give shape to our individual selves just as much as gathered communities do. They require us to define our morals.

The homeless person who asks for spare change or the refugee who appears on my TV is going to get some of my money or some of my soul. The very fact of that person will diminish my pocketbook if I respond or my spiritual status if I pretend the person is not there. The prophet Amos warned people who live well, like you and me, of the danger in which we stand before God. The danger is not in enjoying a drink or a song, but in failing to be grieved over the ruin of others. Jesus taught us with the story of the wealthy Dives, who is punished not for being prosperous but for failing to see the hurting Lazarus at his doorstep. In every case, it is nothing that the broken pieces of community do but the very *fact* of them that requires us to say who we are as human beings, as servants of God.

Hospitality is one lesson for us to apply. Generous giving that reflects God's preoccupation with the lame, the least, and the lost is another. But all of our responses begin with the simple, uneasy, and powerful requirement that we actually see them—the refugee, the sojourner, the immigrant, and the homeless. No good is possible until we do. Every good is possible when we do.
—*Francis H. Wade*

# Nothing gold can stay

Downright chilly in the house again this morning. My husband fishes out his Irish sweater and I wear socks. Kate the cat realizes that winter is coming and demands a second breakfast—she has gotten much too thin over the summer.

The plants present the most immediate task. I have been bringing them in one at a time for a couple of weeks, but now they all have to come in. I lug the large ones through the door and up the stairs. I line the kitchen window sill with begonias in bloom.

Outside the front steps, there is an enormous purple coleus in an urn. Its velvety leaves take up more than half the sidewalk. It has stopped visitors in their tracks all summer: they pause in their walk up the sidewalk to admire it.

Here is what will happen: later this month, we will get a frost. The coleus will not survive: in the course of one night, its glorious branching stems of purple leaves will wilt and hang over the side of the urn, a sad purple pour of spent velvet. A Salvador Dali coleus.

Unless. Unless I bring the urn into the house. But the thing is three feet across. Where do I put it—on the couch?

It is hard to let lovely things die, even when it is time. I could dig up all kinds of annuals and bring them in for a few weeks more of bloom, but we would have to move into a storage unit.

To everything, a season. It is in the nature of life that it comes to an end. There would be no room for new life if this were not so. It is important to the future that the past gets out of the way. I have clippings of this magnificent coleus. Over the winter, I will take more clippings of the plants that grow from these, and next spring I will plant them in the urn again. And, again, something magnificent will grow. Magnificent. Just like its grandmother.
—*Barbara Cawthorne Crafton*

# The power came on

*Come to me, all you that are weary and*
*are carrying heavy burdens, and I will give you rest.*
*Take my yoke upon you, and learn from me;*
*for I am gentle and humble in heart,*
*and you will find rest for your souls.*
—Matthew 11:28

Following a rare and severe windstorm, most of our city was without power for almost a week. At first, the inconveniences were legion and our frustration grew and grew—no electricity, no Internet, no air conditioning, no refrigerators, no electronic entertainment. But then some strange things also started to happen.

Drivers became considerate and careful, as there were no traffic signals. People hosted spontaneous parties on their front lawns to share food before it spoiled. Everywhere I looked, kids were playing outside and thoroughly enjoying themselves. Life became a little slower, a little calmer, a little more compassionate, and, in some bizarre way, a little easier.

I often wonder if the loss of power allowed us to get closer to becoming the people God created us to be, closer to the kingdom that Jesus proclaimed. The power went out, but in another way, the power came on—and in an unexpected way, we found rest for our souls. —*Jason Leo*

# *Returning to the Hungarian Bakery*

I keep hoping the Hungarian Bakery at 111th and Amsterdam will justify the fifteen-block walk. But once again I am disappointed, this time by a cheesecake that is dry.

The walk is wonderful. We pass by Latino stores, a large youth hostel in a former home for proper but indigent ladies, small restaurants of every persuasion from Ethiopian to Thai, and finally, dominating the skyline, the Cathedral of St. John the Divine.

The walk home on Broadway takes us to the Garden of Eden for vegetables, where I am in too good a mood to be irritated by an aggressive shopper who barrels into me. "Words help," I tell her. She looks mystified.

So what if the Hungarian Bakery's pastry is unsatisfactory? I am happy just being out with my bride.

God takes forbearance like that to the infinite degree. I know I must disappoint God. I suspect we all do, more than we see. God wants such good things from us and has given us such amazing capabilities to fulfill that desire. But humanity has a tragic history of turning those capabilities to unworthy purposes.

Yet God still believes in us. God still walks with us. God still shows us the beauty in creation and in each other. God still hopes for good from us.

That belief and hope are the ground of our being. They separate us from lesser creatures. They explain Jesus. If God lost faith in us, how could we live? As many times as we turn away, God still hopes for the time we will remain steadfast.

That's why we keep returning to the Hungarian Bakery. They want to do better. And so some day, they will. —*Thomas L. Ehrich*

# *Open chapel door*

Many years ago when I was young, impatient, and ambitious, I went through a time when I felt frustrated, overburdened, and without much hope. Days were endured rather than enjoyed, a miserable way to live.

The troubles were less real than perceived. Being a reporter had been a childhood dream, and by now I was pretty good at it. I had had one plum of a job and turned down a couple of others to return to the newspaper in the city I loved. I had a wife and two children. Life should have been good. And yet going to work each morning had become a test of will.

One late fall morning that I remember as cold and dark, within as well as without, I stood on a corner, hesitating to go to the newsroom. Across the street was an Episcopal church with a garden and a chapel that was open day and night. I don't recall that I knew this, but I crossed the street and entered the chapel. It was warm and it smelled of candle wax, as it still does today. Alone, I sat in a chair, not praying, but gathering myself to face the day. It helped, and stopping there in the morning became a routine. Exactly how or when intentional prayer began, I don't know, but it did—and one thing led to another, as prayer does.

On that morning nearly half a century ago, the open door, the warmth, and the silence were so inviting. I thought I had found a sanctuary, but it was a trap—what the Celtic people call a "thin place," where heaven and earth are close. God was there, and God is God. Inevitably I had to give up and, bit by bit, let go of the cold and the darkness. —*Robert Horine*

# Simple lessons

*Truly I tell you, unless you change and become like children,*
*you will never enter the kingdom of heaven.*
—Matthew 18:3

I like to take people from the treatment center where I work to a local park where we go on a recovery walk. Their instructions are to find something in nature (no pulling up live plants!) that represents where they are in their new journey.

Later, as we sit in a circle around an old fire ring, I am amazed at the insights. Having turned away from alcohol and other drugs (including nicotine) for almost two decades, I sometimes fall prey to the misconception that more is better when it comes to sobriety.

But in this circle, where people are just days away from their last binge, I am reminded that all our journeys are day-by-day exercises and their depth is measured by more than years.

In this circle, I am told that a dead piece of wood with moss growing on it is reflective of life in the midst of death; that a smooth rock and rough rock in a trembling palm can remind the holder that even the hardest can change; that a simple forked limb can illustrate the choice we have to be happy or not; and that an acorn in the hand is as valuable as the century-old oak we sit next to because of its potential.

Finally, I am reminded that the same elements that make up the lessons in the circle, the same elements that make the woods and our world, are also the elements we're made of. When I recall that my intent was to teach *them* something, I have to smile at my arrogance.
—*Bo Cox*

# *Incrementally building a life of faith*

It is deceptively simple, yet very hard. It only takes simple incremental acts of kindness.

Here's a tiny example. On October 4, 1941, the *Stuttgart Courier* published an article attacking "cases of unsuitable compassion for Jews." These cases were not unusual, the newspaper said. For instance, women from the old people's home, wearing the Star of David, would get on a tramcar, and passengers would stand to give them their seats. A small thing—given what we know about the slaughter—but offering an older woman a seat on the tramcar was an act of protest, a share in the resurrection, a participation in the kingdom. That same month in Berlin the Nazis distributed handbills saying that the Jews were to blame for everything: "Every Jew is your enemy." Think about what that sort of thing does to the imagination. What does it mean then if you give your seat to a Jewish woman on the tramcar? Your little act of kindness could start a revolution.

Later that month, on October 23, 1941, Bernhard Lichtenberg, the dean of St. Hedwig's Cathedral in Berlin, was arrested by the Gestapo because he had been offering daily prayer for the Jews and for wounded soldiers on both sides and the bombed cities. Subversive stuff! Lichtenberg was asked if he prayed for the Bolsheviks: "I haven't, but would have no objection to include daily prayers for them to heal their madness." He was imprisoned. Two years later, after ordeals and humiliations, he died on the way to Dachau. What does the life of faith look like in the light of Lichtenberg's witness or the anonymous people giving up their seats on the tramcar? *—Alan Jones*

# Jesus shows up

We started a children's service on Sundays, and it wasn't long before one older member of the church wondered aloud if Jesus ever showed up amid the chaos. Yes, I assured him, he shows up—and typical of the resurrected Christ, he comes in quite unexpected ways.

Jesus shows up in the word. No matter how clever I think I am in translating the cosmic complexities of God into stories suitable for children, some kid in the third row will inevitably interject a one-liner to steal my prophetic punch line. "Baptism is like the tree house password," one boy blurts. "When I got lost in the store, I was just like that disciple," one girl explains. And then my favorite: "Jesus is the shepherd; we're the sheep. Duh!"

Jesus shows up in the prayers. One girl strays from the script: "We pray for our moms and dads, our families and our pets." Then she looks at the boy making faces at her. "And we pray for my brother who really bugs me—he needs you, Lord."

Jesus shows up in the offering. Crumpled dollar bills. Envelopes filled out in crayon: "5 dolar$." One lonely nickel. Then there was the week someone put a red patent leather shoe in the plate. More shoes followed the next week. Holy ground, indeed.

Jesus shows up at communion. Eyes peek over the pew during the eucharistic prayer. Arguments erupt over who bears the chalice. Little hands reach up to the altar accompanied by candid conversation: "It's like a bite of God." "It tastes like plastic." "Yeah, it's real wine—and it's good!" "Yuk!" "Can we get seconds?"

We sing a song. Parents arrive. The children rush out. And it's then—standing there in the quiet, a little off-balance, a little dazed—that I lift up my own silent prayer: "Thanks, Lord, for showing up—again." —*Jerald Hyche*

# The power of forgiveness

Almost everybody believes in a generic kind of love, but because of Christ's "Father, forgive" (Luke 23:34), Christians carry a torch for a love which forgives.

To forgive is to withhold punishment when punishment is deserved. Forgiveness does not exact a penalty. It takes no retribution; it lets you go free. The desire for justice, which all people feel instinctively, recoils at forgiveness. But forgiveness does not deny the hurt caused by the offender, nor the malice behind his action. Neither does it turn a blind eye to justice. It simply *chooses* not to extract the penalty of justice.

Lars von Trier, the Danish moviemaker, regards Christian forgiveness as ridiculous, soft, and sentimental. He made a movie about Christians entitled *The Idiots*. (I think he had in mind Prince Myshkin, the hero of Dostoyevsky's novel *The Idiot*, who forgives the villain in a spectacular way at the end of that novel.) Von Trier is not the first person to accuse Christians of a forgiveness that appears saccharine and false.

But we don't see it that way. We feel forgiven, not glossed over; shriven, not patted on the head; treated as people with real problems and active consciences, not as children who are not accountable for what they do.

Anyone on the receiving end of an act of real forgiveness has been touched by a Power beyond everyday powers. Consider Jean Valjean in Hugo's *Les Miserables*. He is forgiven first, astonishingly, by Bishop Myriel, after he steals the bishop's silver. And then he is forgiven again—this time by God alone in the quiet and the silence of an appalled repentance after his second crime. The forgiveness sticks, and the rest of Jean Valjean's life is a labor of love. Like yours and mine could be. —*Paul F. M. Zahl*

# *Forgive and let go*

I've been chewing over forgiveness all week, since I stood before a judge and made a statement about the impact of learning that the cleaning lady I had trusted and befriended was a liar and sneak thief who stole family heirlooms from my home. One precious item was returned; the rest are gone forever. She got probation; she'll make a minimal monthly restitution over the course of the next year and do a few hours of unspecified community service. My next work is to forgive her.

Some think Christians should forgive quickly and easily—almost instantly—even the deepest of hurts. I have trouble with instant forgiveness for major injuries, and I suspect the New Testament writers were thinking of forgiveness primarily of other members of the church. I'm more inclined toward the Old Testament view that forgiveness should be preceded by genuine remorse.

But what if that remorse is not forthcoming? What if the guilty are sorry only because they were caught? What if the offenders don't see—or don't want to see—the injuries they've caused? What if it's too late to make amends? Then it's up to us to find a way to forgive despite it all. Anger is corrosive, but only to the one who holds on to it tightly; the guilty are not affected by our seething.

Prayer can help. Examining the issue thoughtfully, shining the light of God's Word on it, can illuminate the path we ought to take and help dry up some of the dankness of resentment. And forgiving is not the same as forgetting. Trust so painfully lost may not be regained. But I have to release my anger, for, as Paul notes in Romans 3:19, the whole world will be held accountable to God. —*Sarah Bryan Miller*

# Don't be too religious

I've been profoundly influenced by *The Parables of Grace* by Robert Farrar Capon. He asserts that God in Jesus did not come into this world to found a new religion (Christianity) or to reform an old one (Judaism), but to put an end to religion altogether!

Capon defines religion as all the ways we sinful human beings have tried to "get right with God." We seem to sense viscerally that we're alienated from God, others, ourselves, even our planet. To fix this problem, people have tried just about everything: from the horror of human sacrifice to noble endeavors—just laws, beautiful rituals, heart-rending sacrifices, self-denying disciplines, compassionate deeds. Tragically, none of these efforts has worked.

God loves us so much that he didn't send a new self-help manual with updated illustrations and diagrams. Instead, God came to us in person—in *a* person. By word and deed, Jesus showed us what a fully human being is like. And in his death and resurrection, we behold God reconciling all that's been torn asunder and making all things new.

Forgiveness, new life, hope—the very goals we could never achieve through the blood, sweat, and tears of our religious exertion (works) are the very gifts that God gives freely to all (grace).

I still have a hankering for that "old time religion." I love hearing the scriptures, singing the hymns, saying the prayers, and sharing the sacraments. I love the flowers, candles, pageants, stained glass, and vestments. For me, all these are windows to the divine.

But I'm sobered when I remember that Jesus, whenever he got annoyed or angry, was usually displeased with religious people—people so caught up in the trappings of religion that they missed the heartbeat of the living God.

Perhaps we should help each other be less religious and more Christlike. —*Charles F. Brumbaugh*

# *Faithful to the task*

Today is the day we commemorate the apostles Saint Simon and Saint Jude. Almost nothing is known of these two saints except that they were there with Jesus. They were chosen. They walked the roads and slept in the fields. They endured nearly complete confusion as Jesus taught. They saw the miraculous healings and felt the hurt looks of the unhealed as Jesus led them away from each town. They filled the baskets when the thousands were fed. They cut the palms for the entry into Jerusalem. They had their feet washed and added their voices to the hymn in Gethsemane. They saw it all unravel on Good Friday and then take an unimaginable shape on Easter Day. They felt the power of Pentecost and they joined those who told the story wherever they went. Like most of the disciples, they did not quite know what was going on between the moment of their selection and the day of their death. They just knew it was something worth doing and that the story of it was worth telling.

It is hard to reflect on the specifics of Simon and Jude because we do not know them, but what these saints teach us about discipleship is important. Disciples are not people who have everything figured out. They are people who are faithful to the task and to the story.

We could do worse than seek to be that kind of disciple.
—*Francis H. Wade*

# Jesus and the Samaritan

I have always loved the story John tells about Jesus and the Samaritan woman at the well. Like Mary Magdalene after her, she is one of the first apostles—one of the first of those "sent out"—to tell about this fabulous outpouring of what Jesus called living water. John says that many Samaritans believed because of the widow's testimony, an outrageous statement for John to make, given how deeply he and most of his contemporaries had learned to hold Samaritans in contempt. Not to mention Samaritan *women*. Nevertheless, against all cultural expectations, he has to admit that many Samaritans believed because of the widow's testimony.

We are far removed in time from those old internecine conflicts between Judeans and Samaritans. But not in spirit. The question that persists down through two millennia is this: Would we believe? If Jesus came among us in this way, what would we say? In this encounter at that sacred well, Jesus undermined and transformed the Samaritan woman's most closely guarded assumptions about her place in the world. So also with us, if we have ears to listen. If we let him, he can undermine and transform our fiercely guarded certainties—assumptions about our place in the world, about the superiority of our cultures, about the validity of my reading of the sacred text as opposed to your reading of the sacred text.

Do we really want this? Could we really endure it? Which of our sacred wells would he feel welcome to approach? Which of our sacred wells would we try to protect from him? What strangers, what enemies, would he challenge us to receive as sisters, as brothers? What strangers, what enemies would we insist to him were beyond redemption, beyond the pale of our imagined places of safety? —*Roger Ferlo*

# *The new reservation desk*

Inside the entrance to the dining room at my father's retirement center stands a reservation desk. It wasn't always there. Now, instead of showing up for dinner when they feel like it and taking their chances on crowds, residents must call first to make a reservation. Yet another bit of freedom is taken away.

Why? Crowd management is the stated reason. Personally, I think the administrators are preparing for an important transition, when Baby Boomers start enrolling at retirement centers and bring with them their desire for the best. With this desk, the center goes a bit more upscale.

It fits with the parking valet who has suddenly appeared outside, as well as the new apartment complex being built with larger and grander units. The generation that knew the Great Depression and World War II will give way to a generation born to prosperity and an attitude of entitlement—my generation.

As reservations replace freedom, I expect a bit more dressiness at dinner, drinks at the new bistro beforehand, and less likelihood that residents like my father will feel comfortable bursting into song, as he and a friend did this week in a poignant rendition of "There's a Long, Long Trail A-Winding."

Having visited my father at this center for five years, I will recognize what has been lost. When my turn comes to move in, I hope I will have the grace and courage to burst into song. At some point, life has to be about more than money and getting our way. —*Thomas L. Ehrich*

# *Feeling fragile?*

I came across a new word the other day: *fragilization*. We are feeling fragile. This feeling affects everybody. No one who's awake can look at the world and not be concerned, puzzled, even frightened. So, a pressing question for us today is, "What holds us together?" It's not money or power or prestige. What holds us together is the risk of faith in a God who holds all things in being.

Father Herbert Kelly (1860-1950), the founder of the Society of the Sacred Mission, lived in fragile times. He preached the sovereignty and priority of God in a world that saw two world wars. A student asked Kelly, "If God does everything, why should we bother?"

"Ah!" replied Kelly, "If you don't bother, you may miss your crucifixion and that would be a pity!"

Kelly, as irascible and difficult as he was, tells the truth. There is no true life without sacrifice. "Shed your blood, and I will give you the Holy Spirit!" is one of the sayings of the desert fathers. There's no getting around this. But it shouldn't make us gloomy. Rather, it is a call to adventure.

This deep and central truth drove Kelly to extremes. In October, 1917 (note the year) Father Kelly wrote this about the Church of England: "I want disendowment—I want persecution. I want a few bishops shot against a wall. Priests in crowds…You would be astonished if you knew *how* serious I was in saying that. I would gladly leave the Dissenters their endowments, and ours, churches, cathedrals, vicarages, and we— what was left of us—would walk out into the streets and talk about God." I wonder what that would be like in our own day? Where is the risk of faith? —*Alan Jones*

# She was among the saints of God

On All Saints' Day, my thoughts tend toward my mother. Although probably not a candidate for canonization, Mother was among the saints of God: she lived her faith throughout a long life filled with both difficulties and satisfactions.

Since her parents had expected a son, Mother had no name for the first two weeks of her life. Her neonatal nickname stuck: Dolly, for her strong resemblance to a Kewpie doll. Sickly at birth, she lived past infancy only because her grandparents took her in and cared for her.

When she rejoined her parents at the age of four, she was already a voracious reader; precocious, she hid from her rackety younger siblings with her books. An intelligent, sensitive girl, she had a hard life and suffered many disappointments, but her faith carried her through.

The church was important to Mother from childhood through old age, supporting her as she served it: in choirs, in altar guilds, as a Sunday School teacher, in cooking and delivering food to shut-ins, in writing cards and notes to the ill and grieving, and in regular worship.

Mother's faith helped her not only to persevere amidst life's vicissitudes; it allowed her to grow past the prejudices of her early upbringing and to see the face of Christ in all people. She was one of the most welcoming and hospitable people I have ever known. Mother was blessed with a long and happy marriage, two cherished children, four beloved grandchildren, and many friends. They filled the church at her funeral; she touched many lives with love.

On All Saints' Day, I'll think of her and of others who served God all their lives as we sing one of her favorite hymns:

*For all the saints, who from their labors rest,*
*who thee by faith before the world confessed,*
*thy Name, O Jesus, be forever blessed. Alleluia, Alleluia!*
—*Sarah Bryan Miller*

# *Cell phone saints*

My wife walked up to me like a nurse in a hospital waiting room. "It's time," she said, handing me my old cell phone and a plastic bag. "When you're done deleting the numbers, put it in there and we'll donate it."

Yes, just a phone. But no, I do not easily dismiss such terminal situations, even when they apply to inanimate objects that have held some degree of my affection. The old bed. The old car. The old chair. As with them, saying goodbye to my old phone was not so much about the object itself as it was about the life it represented—my life for a certain span, for sure, but even more so the lives that crossed my own. There they all glowed in digital and alphabetical order. And with each appeared the ultimate question: Delete?

Some—my wife's old workplace, our former favorite restaurant, the now-closed car shop—spurred a light, nostalgic memory before I easily punched "yes." But several gave me pause. The spiritual director who guided me out of the darkness. The friend who fell out of my speed dial after that falling out. The family member who died too soon.

Delete? Yes, but not before giving thanks. Delete? Yes, but not without a prayer for reconciliation. Delete? Yes, but not before a plea for their place in the communion of saints.

And then it occurred to me that they were already there, and so was I. Even as each name scrolled up and vanished, I found comfort in knowing that we would remain forever etched in that eternal communion, the one described in the catechism of *The Book of Common Prayer* as including the "whole family of God, the living and the dead, those whom we love and those whom we hurt, bound together in Christ by sacrament, prayer, and praise." —*Jerald Hyche*

# *Just bring them by the house tonight...*

One day some twenty years ago, I told the university president in our town that my children marveled at his home. When we passed it each day on the way to school and day care, they never failed to ask me, "Daddy, is that a castle?" To my amazement, the president replied, "Well, Pat, just bring them by the house tonight in their pajamas, and we will let them bump down the three flights of stairs on their rear ends!" I was astounded that the most powerful man in our community would issue such an invitation. That night at 7:00 p.m. we were there, and the laughter of my daughter and son filled the "castle." That powerful, wise yet humble man has remained one of my greatest heroes.

James addresses those who seek wisdom in order that they may become leaders in the congregation. The Epistle of James is the only New Testament book considered Wisdom Literature, which places it in the company of Job, Proverbs, and Ecclesiastes in the Old Testament. Those ancient Hebrew texts were often used to instruct people training to be rabbis. James directs those who would seek a comparable leadership role in the church to examine themselves honestly. If they are motivated at all by selfish ambition, James promises their ministry will be marked by disorder and wickedness (James 3:14-16). Double-mindedness, that is, the love of God splintered by our cravings for worldly goods and power, dilutes the would-be leaders' credibility to the level of blatant adulterers (4:1-5).

Christian leaders are marked by their sincere, single-minded devotion to Christ and his people. Anything less is a step down.
—*W. Patrick Gahan*

# *Junior Williamson*

On a fine fall day I rode with a friend up Kentucky's Mountain Parkway into the Appalachian foothills to see the woodland colors at their best. Though the season had been very dry, the reds and golds were brilliant in the November sunshine. At the Slade exit near Natural Bridge State Park, we passed the Junior Williamson Rest Area, and I thought about the man for whom it is named.

I passed this place every Sunday for three or four years on the way to Beattyville, where I celebrated the Holy Eucharist at St. Thomas Church. When the rest area opened, I wondered who Junior Williamson was. At the time, I believe, it was the only rest area in the commonwealth named for someone. I wrongly guessed he was a local political leader, perhaps deceased. It turned out that Junior Williamson was alive and well and living in Pikeville, further up the parkway near Virginia. From his home he went to Frankfort, the state capital, whenever the General Assembly was meeting and spent the whole session shining the shoes of the legislators.

One might fear the lawmakers had honored him in the same spirit of whimsy that moves them to name, say, a state bug. But it turned out that the legislators had a genuine affection and respect for Junior Williamson, who lobbied for this rest area as he shined their shoes. I wondered if from time to time, with this representative or that senator, his humble service reminded them that they, too, despite their titles and power and honors, were servants.

Looking back, I suspect that stopping regularly at Junior Williamson's legacy helped me keep my own ministry in perspective during those years. —*Robert Horine*

# The high cost of rejection

Rejection makes the world go 'round. Especially if it comes early in life, rejection wires you for a style of cautiousness, gun-shyness in relation to love, and deep-seated resentment. Rejected people have their emotional hamstrings snipped. They can also manifest primeval rage.

Almost everyone I know who is angry and prickly—the kind of person in whose company you have to mind what you say, like at Christmas dinner or wedding rehearsals—is operating from some experience of rejection. The songwriter Hal David captures this in a number from *Promises, Promises*, when he gets the hero and heroine to sing their closing duet from distinct but parallel scripts of rejection: "I'll never fall in love again."

Another example of this is found in Mizoguchi's beautiful movie from 1951 entitled *Miss Oyu*. The heroine loves her husband, but he does not love her. He is not a bad guy, but he is in love with her sister. Nothing she can do will win his love. And the picture's denouement, of heart-rejected love, is overwhelmingly poignant.

Christians have something to offer here. For us, Jesus is "despised and rejected by others; a man of suffering, and acquainted with grief" (Isaiah 53:3). God holds the rejection of life in the closest possible way to his "Sacred Heart." Our rejections are many, deep-seated, and unhealed. Healing for them is never complete in our life on earth, no matter how much love and reassurance comes to us. Isaiah got this right. We are not alone in our rejectedness, and it can be borne.
—*Paul F. M. Zahl*

# *Learning*

My father was a civil rights pioneer in the late 1940s and '50s when that was neither fashionable nor safe. One night he came home late from a long speaking trip through the border states, locked the car, and went up to bed. In the morning he discovered the car had been vandalized and his briefcase containing years of sermon outlines and speeches had been stolen. My mother cautioned us, and we walked on eggs that day.

I didn't sleep well and woke up in the middle of the night thinking I heard voices. I crept silently down the stairs and saw my father sitting in a wing chair with his Bible open on his lap. He was talking, but there was no one else in the room. I sat on the stairs watching and listening, and then every few minutes I heard him ask, "Lord, what do you want me to learn from this?"

Forty years later, my marriage shattered like crockery dropped on a stone floor. Remembering my Dad, I sat in an empty rectory with no furniture and asked, "Lord, what do you want me to learn from this?"

Fifteen years later, having remarried, I sat by the bed of my dying wife, again silently asking, "Lord, what do you want me to learn from this?"

A few years later, with no parish, priest, or bishop, I lay alone in a cardiac unit about to have my sternum split open and my heart operated on. I said the only words I knew in these situations: "Lord, what do you want me to learn from this?"

And every time the answer has been the same: "You will weep and mourn. You will have pain. But your pain will turn to joy."

That is why I am a Christian. —*David L. James*

# *Anger and fear*

*If we were to live, we had to be free of anger.*
—Alcoholics Anonymous

Everyone *knows* how harmful anger can be. A neighbor who had been harboring a hefty resentment against another neighbor recently had to have some work done on his heart. The senior member of that neighborhood, a grandma in her eighties, said this when told the news: "That anger will kill you."

I once heard a person say that holding resentments was like taking poison and waiting for the person you're resenting to die. There's another line from Alcoholics Anonymous literature that says harboring anger-based feelings like resentments can shut us off from the sunlight of the spirit.

Anger serves many purposes. Chief among them is masking fear. When angry, I ask myself what I'm afraid of, and the anger goes away once I come up with the answer. I cannot think of one time in my life when I was angry and fear was not the underlying factor. My future is brighter if I acknowledge my fear and then act, rather than ignore it and act while angry.

Finally, a bit about "justifiable anger." Much has been said about this brand of anger. The best thing I ever heard was this: "Boiling water has no idea whether it's boiling because it's sitting on a gas flame, an electric burner, or a camp fire. Even if it could figure it out, it doesn't matter because it's boiling all the same, regardless of the source. My gut is like that; it doesn't know or care *why* I'm angry; it's tied up in knots regardless of the cause." —*Bo Cox*

# In admiration of Julia

Not long ago, a nervous Latina named Julia interviewed for a job at a local pharmacy. Six months ago, fresh from the Dominican Republic, she spoke no English. Now, after hard work, she does.

On the same day, ten executives at brokerage giant Merrill Lynch were outed as recipients of extraordinary year-end bonuses totaling $209 million, even though their firm was teetering on collapse.

Whom shall we admire? Bonus winners who live in luxury beyond most imagining, who feel superior to others, whose children go to elite schools, whose success stirs young aspirants to ninety-hour work weeks, who game the systems to evade taxes? Or immigrants like Julia who come to America seeking opportunity, who live modestly while laying ground for their families' futures, who obey laws and pay taxes as the duty of citizenship?

One test of faith is whether we choose the path of greed and wealth or the path of self-denial and moderation. Little in this or any culture affirms the virtue of self-denial. The benefits of our society, from comfort to safety to freedom itself, go to the wealthy. But life, according to Jesus, goes to those who deny themselves and serve others.

We will have a better society only when we stop idolizing the wealthy and start admiring people like Julia. She will never use a front entrance on Park Avenue, but she can hold her head high in the kingdom of God.

How do we know this? It's what Jesus said: "What will it profit [the self-serving] to gain the whole world and forfeit their life?" (Mark 8:36). It feels odd to be learning this lesson in middle age. It seems so basic. But wealth is seductive, and appetite an easy star to follow. —*Thomas L. Ehrich*

# *Ubuntu*

*Ubuntu* is a Bantu word rooted in the culture of sub-equatorial Africa. It means "I am because you are." For all of its lyrical and philosophical appeal, it is not a concept I come to naturally. My growing up—and perhaps yours as well—emphasized the opposite: the importance of the individual. In my world individuals come together and make communities. The *ubuntu* idea is that communities make individuals. It is an idea I must reach for intentionally and hold onto firmly.

When I stretch toward *ubuntu*, I can first sense and then begin to understand its wisdom. The individualism I was taught to prize was never my own invention. The fact is we are all derivatives, drawing our sense of self from that which is other than our individual selves. We derive from God who creates us, Jesus who gives us value, and the Spirit that gives us purpose. We are who we are because of ancestors of both flesh and faith, mentors and tormentors, friends and foes, those we have loved and those who have loved us. I know I am because they are. And you are because we are.

*Ubuntu* does not negate the importance of our individualism. Personal discipline, stewardship, and responsibility are still at the heart of our moral life. Private joys, personal prayers, and particular peculiarities are enriched rather than diminished by the broader perspective of *ubuntu*.

The culture of individualism is strong and not without merit. But *ubuntu* is wise, and its broader perspective contains a deeper truth. We must work on it together. Together is not only what we are—together is *who* we are. —*Francis H. Wade*

# A son's cleats

As the final seconds ticked away, my eyes brimmed with tears. My son loved playing football; I loved watching him play. But this would be his last game.

As the crowd filed out, I stood near as the players knelt around their coaches. All were still. Words were spoken. After a time they arose, proudly held their helmets aloft, and then quietly walked toward the locker room.

I darted among the players searching for my son. I found him at mid-field with his senior teammates. They seemed reluctant to surrender the turf. He too was tearful. I wrapped my arms around his heavily padded shoulders. I felt childlike as I pressed my head against his chest and told him how proud I was.

Later he told me that all the seniors had left their cleats on the field that night. When I asked why, he said, "I don't know. It's tradition. I guess it meant that we left everything on the field." I understood.

But to me, it sounded like something more, as evidenced by the lump in my throat as I pictured those cleats. I knew that they weren't just a pair of shoes carelessly abandoned. They pointed to deeper realities: to the disappointment of a dream never to be fully realized; to the pride of a competitor who played his heart out; and (seen with the other pairs of cleats scattered about) to companions who were not merely teammates, but family. But perhaps more than anything else, those cleats pointed to a young man who had just passed through a door that closed behind him, and to that ineffable sense of pain/joy, loss/anticipation that he— and his father—experienced in the passing.

God is revealed daily, though often unnoticed. But the signs are everywhere. Sense with wonder and savor all that you can see, hear, feel, taste, and smell. Remember there is always more going on than meets the eye. —*Charles F. Brumbaugh*

# *Thy rod and thy staff, they comfort me*

We received word today that one of our parishioners had died at the local country club, at the age of ninety-two, while playing cards with his friends. We knew exactly where his table was, how the sun comes in at that spot from which he looked out at the lake. He was there every Tuesday. Given that everyone has to die, you really couldn't ask for a better death. To live to that age, to be surrounded by friends, doing something you love—and then just move on, move upward. No pain. Ninety-two years.

Contrast that with another parishioner I visited in the hospital last week. She's had melanoma for seven years, outliving the original prediction of five years. Now the doctors suggest she may only have six months left. They've been wrong before, but this time I suspect their prediction may be overly optimistic. She is in pain, has been for quite a while. Gallant, she has trudged through chemo and radiation, but now will probably forgo treatments.

We have no control over the fact that death will occur. If we are lucky, we will enter old age relaxing, laughing with friends—alive that morning, checking out in the afternoon. But that probably won't be the case. Death is more often a slow and painful process than a quick and easy one.

In the Great Litany, we pray not to die suddenly and unprepared. I guess the trick to both living and dying well is really found in the Twenty-third Psalm: "Yea, though I walk through the valley of the shadow of death...thou art with me; thy rod and thy staff, they comfort me."

Dying quickly at an old age sounds good. But I'll take the rod and the staff and the presence of the Shepherd any day.

—*Lindsay Hardin Freeman*

# *Go*

Jesus gave many instructions to his disciples. He told them to love, forgive, pray, listen, follow. Then, at the end of his time with them, he said, "Go."

It is a simple command, but I think I am not alone in sometimes wondering what direction I should take. I know that there is work to be done, but where am I supposed to start? A friend once advised that I consider where the needs of the world intersect with my greatest passion in life, and then go there.

I love to snow ski, and for a time had been an instructor. A teenager in our congregation was born with cerebral palsy. One day he shared that he had tried for years to ski—group lessons, private lessons, nothing had worked. I asked if he would give it one more try. It took a lot of hard work and determination, but eventually he conquered the mountain and discovered a new sport. His smile was a true reward and a sign of the kingdom. A few years later, when he was awarded the rank of Eagle Scout, he pointed to that moment as an important part of his journey.

When Jesus told his disciples "Go," I think he knew they would find a way, and that we would too. —*Jason Leo*

# *You baptize him*

It was a number of years before the stork first showed up at our house. All went well until, to our horror, we found that a staph infection was running through the hospital nursery as we were ready to take our new son home, with all the hearts-in-mouth anxiety of new parents. Instead of getting to wrap him in our arms and bring him home to the newly painted room with its well-prepared crib—mobile, rattles, cuddle toys— we were told we had to leave him at the hospital until the contagion was settled.

I turned to a nurse who had been kind and instructed her with wavering voice: "You baptize him, if anything goes wrong."

Parents have asked me through the years what exactly baptism does besides making the person a Christian. I always remember my son (who, by the way, is now a grown man, healthy and wise, thank you) and I tell them what I believe and what I touched in that moment. I tell them sacraments are God's gifts to us, moving us further into what our hearts have already come to believe.

I tell them we love this other person, and so we will be together with him for life, "until death do us part," that we are forgiven for terrible misdeeds, and can move forward anew.

I tell them their child, like my son, is a child of God, whom the Creator loves and has taken steps to protect and nurture—forever.

But in that moment of walking away, my heart needed to be sure. "Taking them in his arms he blessed them. In the name of the Father, and the Son, and the Holy Spirit, Amen."

It was a gift to me. —*Leonard Freeman*

# *"His name is John"*

Kay and I did not have to discuss the name of our third child. We both dearly loved Johnny, my younger brother by four years. I have never met anyone who didn't love him. In the most significant irony of my life, Johnny called me a week before the crash that killed both him and his pregnant wife, and told me he was naming his yet unborn child after me. I responded modestly and playfully that he should name his son after himself. "No," he retorted in a more solemn tone, "I want him to be just like my big brother." Four years later, sitting in her bed in the tiny maternity ward of the Winchester Hospital, Kay, without inquiry or hesitation, wrote out our third child's name for the Tennessee county officials: "John."

The priest Zechariah was struck mute because he did not believe the angel Gabriel's message that his aged wife Elizabeth would bear him a son to be named John (Luke 1:18-23). When Elizabeth gives birth to her son, the temple officials are surprised when she tells them his name, because it is not a family name. They turn to Zechariah for confirmation. The mute priest takes a tablet and writes, "His name is John." Zechariah regains his speech the moment he again acts on his confidence in God (Luke 1:63-64). The temple officials and the congregation are now afraid. They know that God must be up to something big in this eight-day-old child John!

Speaking the word of God to encourage the downcast exiles of Israel, Isaiah says, "Do not fear, for I have redeemed you; I have called you by name, you are mine" (Isaiah 43:1). The Lord of the entire universe knows each of us by name and will call us home, one by one.

—*W. Patrick Gahan*

# Together

*And remember, I am with you always, to the end of the age.* —Matthew 28:20

The more people I know on the other side, the more I experience this promise as a current reality. Just as I first learned about love from human beings, it has been human beings who taught me about resurrection.

Every time someone dies, the same sequence: at first, the loss is all there is to feel, unbelievable but true. I see only the death. Then some time passes, and memory enters, alternately painful and comforting, prompting tears and smiles. Gradually the life I mourn returns to my thoughts, and I can see the life as a whole, not just as preamble to the loss of it. The most important thing about the one I lost is no longer that I lost him, but that he lived in the world and graced its life.

I find that the dead are present in other ways too. These are harder to describe and impossible to prove, but walk through life and loss with open eyes and open heart, and you will sense them: moments of something that can only be called presence, other moments that seem to constitute advice, given just when you were about to do something really stupid. A deepening consistent gratitude. An awareness that you would be nothing like you are without that person having been in your life.

This is the African concept of *ubuntu*. It applies not only to the living, but also to the dead. *Ubuntu* is a description of the way life is: *I am me, only because you are you.* We form each other. I can no more disregard your existence than I can discount my own.

How lovely to think this: we *make* each other. We stand or fall together. I read Jesus' promise, made to his friends as he passes from their sight, and it sounds like normal life to me: open-hearted and open-eyed, willing to let human existence rest upon the communion of saints and not on its own lonely pedestal. *I am with you always.*
—*Barbara Cawthorne Crafton*

# *A picture of hell?*

Our culture gives us graphic images of hell, of human lostness. We see them everywhere: on TV, in the newspapers, and on the street. They challenge us to get real and sober up. Anthony Lane's hilarious review of the movie *Sex and the City* in the *New Yorker* is a reminder of the little hells we make for ourselves. Lane called the movie "Four hormonal hobbits obsessed with a ring," a joyless romp through conspicuous consumption. The message? "Don't be a mother. And don't work." It's all deeply sad. The best line? Samantha's parting shot as she dumps a guy: "I love you, but I love me more." Lane responds, "I have a terrible feeling that *Sex and the City* expects us not to disapprove of that line, or even to laugh at it, but to exclaim in unison, 'You *go*, girl.'"

It's a world of closets, delusions, and blunt-clawed cattiness. Friends of ours told me I was taking it all too seriously, but I couldn't help at least seeing a glimpse of hell. After all, hell is to be trapped in the tight little circle of the self. It seemed to fit the movie. One thing that gets in the way of our experiencing "heaven" is the notion that we can *earn* our place in the world either by obeying the rules or seeing others as rivals for things.

Unlike the message of *Sex and the City,* salvation has nothing to do with closet space. —*Alan Jones*

# Fear not

My seventeen-year-old son tells us about a new trimester course on "Fear in *Hamlet*." How timely, and how timeless. Timely, because these are frightening times, thanks to a recession, a world at war on many fronts, and predators circling around the weak. Learning to deal with fear is important. And timeless, because in the four hundred years since Shakespeare wrote *Hamlet*, the world has seen worse days than these, and we know from history and our own experience that people can survive, sometimes even thrive, amid fearsome conditions.

While Jesus often is quoted as having said things he did not say, as having strong opinions about matters to which he was actually indifferent, and as having loathed people whom he actually welcomed to his side and loved, Jesus did give a few clear commandments.

One was to love our neighbor. A second was to feed, clothe, and shelter the weak. And the third was, "Don't be afraid." All three commandments are difficult, because they take us outside ourselves and test our faith in God.

Fear can turn us not only into cowards, but also into agents of injustice and collaborators in oppression. Fear can turn us against the ones we do love and against those whom we ought to love. Fear can make us greedy. Fear can make us foolish.

Humanity's primary addiction—to control—is stoked by fear. I fear that your freedom threatens my well-being, or that your opinion threatens my certainty, or that your needs threaten my safety and comforts. So, in fear, I take away your freedom, denounce your divergent opinion, and ignore your needs.

In saying, "Don't be afraid," Jesus urged us to trust in God's mercy and providence, not in the controlling works of our hands.

—*Thomas L. Ehrich*

# *Families*

God has placed us in families. I do not look at families with a sentimental eye. They contain both the most rewarding and the most painful interactions we experience, requiring an investment of energy beyond what we give to our jobs, possessions, entertainment, good works, and everything else.

Some time ago my family had a reunion in Maine. It reminded me of a banner in our church which reads: "Different is beautiful; God bless variety." To begin with physical differences, in our assembled family one guy was 6'5" and another 5'6". Color ranged from me at the very blonde end to a black-haired daughter-in-law. Then there were the likes and dislikes, ranging from the active ones who wanted to surf in high winds to the ones who wanted to lie on the porch and watch the waves. Some of us were playful and full of antics; others were more quiet and serious. We were Catholic, Protestant, and Jewish. Some saved their money for the future; others enjoyed life now and didn't worry about later. Some sprang for lobster every night; others wondered why anyone would eat such a creature. You get the picture.

What did we all have in common? Each wanted to be accepted as a member of this family, as a branch of this vine. All wanted to be loved and not criticized, appreciated for special gifts and talents, listened to and supported.

Jesus said: "I am the vine, you are the branches" (John 15:5). If we join ourselves to him, we will draw strength from the most accepting and loving person in history. He was not naïve, suffering many hurts, but he never cut himself off from other people. I hope you look at your family with clear and tender eyes. —*Lee Krug*

# *The hermit*

I'd been told about the hermit when I arrived at the monastery to begin my retreat. But I never expected to meet him the way I did—buck naked (him, not me).

Walking in the woods that afternoon, I saw a small hut on a bank above a swift-running stream. "Maybe that's the hermitage," I said to myself, and thought of turning back, lest the holy man be offended by the approach of a stranger. As I hesitated, a stout figure in Trappist habit emerged, scrambled nimbly down the steep embankment to the creek side, stripped, and hopped into the waist-deep water.

Thus did I meet Father Marcellus, bathing *alfresco* though the month was November and his age was then eighty-seven. It was his custom to do so every day that the temperature rose above forty. "But don't tell them back at the cloister," he said, or they'd worry about his health. His ablutions finished, he invited me up and told me about his way of life.

It included making five rosaries each morning, working from about 7:00 a.m. until noon. He calculated that he'd fashioned some 15,000. He arose every midnight to say Mass, and he prayed for me from that day in 1981 until he died or became too enfeebled. Or so I surmise from his last note to me, in 1983: "I pray for you every day, that God will give you the grace to do his will in all things. Let us pray for each other and all will be well."

Father Marcellus—wonderfully genial, deeply pious, and a very voluble talker. May you go from strength to strength in the life of perfect service in our Lord's heavenly kingdom. —*Bruce Birdsey*

# *Paying attention*

How can you attend to your interior life in a world of laptops, Blackberrys, iPhones, and Twitter? With all the claims made on our attention, how can we find ways to pay attention to the things that matter?

Meditating on the great, lonely paintings by the twentieth-century American artist Edward Hopper, the writer Leonard Michaels said, "There used to be silence, solitude, and thinking....There used to be plenty of time. There used to be day and night....There used to be privacy." In the days Hopper painted, the job occupied a definable and limited part of life's energy and time. There were boundaries to what you could know and what others could know about you.

The information revolution we're living through has some wonderful benefits. We have resources that earlier generations could not even have dreamt about. And yet all this information, all this flow of work into all the areas of our lives, all this noise in our heads and in our world comes at a cost. People are rarely present to their surroundings the way they were before computers were everywhere. We can't really hear ourselves think.

Many of the classics of Christian spirituality have to do, in one way or another, with paying attention. Tools in themselves are neither good nor bad things, but used unreflectively they can rule us. Jesus knew about that. The Sabbath was made for human beings and not the other way around.

We cannot turn back the clock. We now live in a world with little silence, solitude, time, and privacy. We can no longer take these things for granted. We will only find them as we make room and opportunity for them ourselves. —*Gary Hall*

# *Thanksssss, Tommy*

It had been a wonderful pastorate. I reflected on some of the high spots of the past six years as I stood at the door after worship and greeted folks on my last Sunday there.

We now had a burgeoning Sunday school program and a strong youth group, a financially sound budget process with dramatically increased financial support, and much greater outreach participation, not to mention a congregation with a good bit more self-confidence than when we had arrived. And that confidence was deserved; they were, and are, a really good congregation. But my wife had taken a seminary professorship in a neighboring state, and now it was time to go.

Tommy and his dad were the last ones out of the building. I had been dreading this moment especially. Here were two of my favorites. We all had worked hard together. We loved and trusted one another. I could feel the tears welling up, and I was swallowing hard.

Tommy had worn his suit that day for the special farewell dinner that was to follow, the same suit he had worn in his sister's wedding earlier that year. He came over to me, extended his hand to shake mine, and with all the dignity an eight-year-old can muster, solemnly said, "Well done, good and faithful...*serpent*."

Oh, so close, Tommy! But a good reminder, that even when we have done our very best and things have gone really well, the snake is always close at hand. —*Gregory A. Russell*

# Sunset, sunrise

I recently bought a new suit and discovered I'm an inch shorter than I used to be. This is not the first time this has happened. In fact, if I were to be measured against the doorpost in the kitchen as I was as a boy, the pencil lines would be going down, not up.

In the Alaskan summer, the sun does not sink below the horizon, but circles it as it hangs low in the sky, staying in view at all times. The sun can seem to be rising toward the zenith for a few hours but then fall back toward the horizon for a while, only to begin rising again a few hours later. Similarly, I have discovered an odd inverse relation between my outward height and my spiritual stature.

When I was at my highest height, I was cocky, self-assured, and arrogant. It was not until the lines and creases formed across my face, the bones creaked, and the eyes began to fail that I became aware of a spiritual stirring not unlike the growing pains I had experienced as a teenager. It was the pain of living and losing that humbled and nurtured my soul.

Saint Paul says: "Even though our outer nature is wasting away, our inner nature is being renewed day by day" (2 Corinthians 4:16). What feeds this inner nature is the spiritual and intellectual capital one has accumulated through the years. At this point in my life I am deeply grateful for parents, friends, mentors, teachers, priests, and bishops who have made deposits into my account.

Now that I'm shrinking in the early candlelight of old age, I find I'm beginning to bud again. As the sun is setting on my body, the sun is rising in my soul. —*David L. James*

# God's abundant gifts

*Almighty and everlasting God,*
*you are always more ready to hear than we to pray,*
*and to give more than we either desire or deserve.*
—The Book of Common Prayer, Collect for Proper 22

What an impossible and unreasonable expectation! It is abundantly clear, is it not, that those who believe such things know nothing of real life? Nonetheless, impossible and wonderful things do happen. They happen through prayer, and they happen in unusual ways.

A friend of many years survived an extended stay in the hospital, where she had been sent with a life-threatening illness. She survived, and as she regained full health she and her husband discovered a new dimension to their marriage.

Two clergy visited her while she was in the hospital. One was a bishop who entered the room and grasped her left arm that held the intravenous needle and raised it, causing her pain. He prayed loud and long, concluding with a blessing complete with hand gestures that compounded her discomfort. The patient was greatly relieved when he departed.

A much younger cleric came toward the end of each afternoon to sit next to her on the left side of the bed. He reached through the protective sidebars, found her hand, and held it. Eyes closed; neither spoke. Nothing needed to be said, until the visitor said, "Amen," rose, and left.

As far as my friend was concerned, one thing and one thing alone brought her health, survival, new life: holding hands, praying in silence. What saved her life, she often said, was simple human concern and the abiding knowledge of God's presence that gives more than we desire or deserve. —*Edward S. Gleason*

# Why me?

*Some have entertained angels without knowing it.*
—Hebrews 13:2

Sometime around Thanksgiving, I took a young man to the Salvation Army to get some clothes. On the way there, he began to tell me about himself. That was helpful because he had never participated in the recreational activities at our treatment center, so I had not gotten to know him at all.

He talked of an abusive father and broken family. He told how they had no money growing up. Then he began to share his fears with me, especially his fear of participating in playground activities as a child because he wore thick glasses that, if broken, could not be replaced. That also explained why he had not participated in recreational activities at the treatment center, and it forced me to reexamine my assessment of him as merely lazy.

His eyes sparkled and he held his head a little higher as he related to me that people had told him he was intelligent (to which I agreed and told him so), and that he wanted to do something with his life.

When we got to the Salvation Army, he grew excited and almost jumped out of the van before I had completely stopped, heading toward the store with long purposeful strides. I followed him in and tagged along as he picked out his clothes.

I noticed the care with which he was selecting his three pairs of pants and shirts, his shoes and jacket, and the pride with which he carried them to the register to check out.

Tears came to my eyes and I ducked my head to gather myself together. I wasn't sure what or whom I was looking at. Nor could I answer the question: why me? —*Bo Cox*

# *Among the prophets*

The Acts of the Apostles tells us about Saint Paul's conversation with his nephew, the son of Paul's sister. Jesus healed Peter's mother-in-law, which means that Peter had a wife. Jesus and John the Baptist were cousins, which means that Jesus' brothers and sisters were John's cousins as well.

What would it have been like to share family life with people like Paul, Peter, Jesus, and John? Pretty rough, would be my guess. People who change history are generally not what we would call well-rounded, because changing history requires a particular focus and dedication.

C. S. Lewis once pointed out that the people we call well-adjusted are simply sufficiently compromised to the local norms to get along with other people.

Jesus had trouble with his family and his hometown, causing him to famously note that prophets are without honor in their home country. That may be because the people in their home country have to listen to them all the time.

We well-adjusted types get a little tired of the one-note sonatas of the world-changers. Can you imagine being at the kids' table at Thanksgiving with Jesus and John? Can you see how hard it would be to recognize God at work in someone so close? And if it was hard for them, wouldn't it be hard for us as well?

Is it possible that some of those closest to us, some of the ones we find most irritating and difficult to be with, actually have a great truth to share? I don't know that your strange cousin is a modern day John the Baptist. Your cousin may be merely strange. But God often uses the strange ones to carry great truth because the normal ones are busy doing too many other things. —*Francis H. Wade*

# Bud's miracle

From the time Bud was diagnosed with a fast-growing, inoperable brain tumor, his wife Kay, family, and friends all over the world were praying for a healing miracle. Bud went through a round of chemotherapy and radiation. On the last day of treatment he broke his ankle. After surgery he went to a rehab center.

With Kay at his side every day, Bud spent the next eleven months at the center. As time went on he became progressively disoriented and uncommunicative, and eventually didn't speak at all. Then on the Friday after Thanksgiving, Kay was at home doing her morning devotions when the telephone rang. The voice on the line said, "Where are you?" When she asked who it was, he laughed, "It's Bud!"

Kay later said that when she reached the center, "I found my old Bud, laughing and talking. God is good!" Bud went home for Christmas with Kay, their two children, and five grandchildren. The children crawled over his wheelchair up into his lap and "he adored every minute of the day." They took pictures, ate their traditional meal, and Bud went back to the center exhausted but happy.

After Christmas he began slipping away. One day Bud saw a friend who had died years earlier. "I began to realize that he was beginning to see the angels who were going to greet him in heaven," Kay explained.

Bud died on March 1. "God did give us our miracle, of spending Christmas as a family one last time," Kay said.—*Robert Horine*

# *God and computers remember*

"You've got to try Pandora.com!" said my seventeen-year-old son. "It's the best thing to happen to music in years."

So I did. I opened a free account and selected Enya, an artist I enjoy. Using a technology called "genome," Pandora began cycling through similar songs. If I pressed "thumbs up," Pandora gave me more of that style. A "thumbs down" meant "no more of that," Pandora learned.

I found it fascinating. I created an Enya Station for late afternoon (mellow time) and another called Baroque Chamber for morning.

This isn't a plug for Pandora.com, but rather a glimpse of what could be if we truly listened to each other and learned. We could read each other's signals, remember likes and dislikes, and avoid grating behaviors that happen when we aren't paying attention. People will always collide, because our personalities and needs are different. But we also can learn from experience and be more considerate.

The "genome" technology works mainly by trial and error. So could we. The difference is that computers notice and remember, whereas we often sail past another's expression of desire or need or regret.

I think of God as one who listens to us and, guided by mercy, tries to adapt—not to lose the divine identity, but to reach us in ways that we can receive. I know some people believe God knows everything in advance and remains inflexible. I see God differently, as likely to be surprised by our behaviors and willing to go out and meet us.
—*Thomas L. Ehrich*

# Stress points and still points

For years, my father has brandished a list that assigns "stress points" to various life events. Christmas, deaths in the family, divorce, job fears, parties, job losses, marriage—happy or sad, they all add stress, and stress will make you sick. I've lived through an impressive number of those top-of-the-stress-charts events in the last year or so. Furthermore, it's been a cold, brutal winter. So why am I so shocked that I'm ill?

It came upon me stealthily. I knew something wasn't right when I suddenly developed a true contralto voice, with beautiful effortless low notes that drew the surprised approval of the choirmaster. It didn't last, turning to gravel and then to almost nothing. And then suddenly I was flattened. Viral bronchitis, said the doctor. Stay hydrated, take it easy, get some rest. I spent three days in bed, drifting in and out of strange dozes, reliving lost memories, playing an odd assortment of music in my mind. (Mozart, yes; Wagner, yes; Renaissance Masses, yes; Laura Branigan's 1982 hit "Gloria"—where did *that* come from?) And then, slowly, I started to recover.

I tend to be overbooked—no, cancel that. I consistently take on too much; I'm always busy, always running, always on deadline. Nothing is harder for me than just being still. Yet nothing is more important, especially now.

At my sickest, I could say only, "Lord, have mercy." Forced to rest and deprived of my focus, I found that the simplest prayers can sometimes say the most. —*Sarah Bryan Miller*

# Safe and warm

I just bought matching shearling slippers for my husband and me. "Jeez," Norah said when she saw them. "I can't believe you guys are actually wearing those!" But we're cold these days, always wanting a blanket, a sweater, a shawl. Socks. I used to run around the house barefoot, as my teenaged granddaughters do now, but I can't stand the chill anymore. Used to go out with my neck bare and not mind. Not now. Never bothered with a hat or a scarf. But I'm too cold now. And it's been a mild fall. It works in my favor in the summer—I don't mind the heat. We have no air conditioning and don't need any.

What's happening? Does your blood slow down as you age? Does your inner thermostat get out of whack? Or maybe I'm now simply more content to nest than to trek bravely through the wind, more interested in a nice fire in the fireplace than in going out to a movie, than in going out anywhere. *In* is where I want to be.

You want to stay in, but you must go out. Life is not over yet, and there is much to do. As you go, you reflect upon what a blessing it is to have slippers, a blanket, your own bed, your own warm house, when many people who are also cold, and older than you, have none of these things.

The shower of God's love is a warm one. This is the season. They'll sell lots of slippers, wool hats, scarves, mittens. Maybe you'll buy some warm things for people you love. But get something for those sisters or brothers, too, who have no one to give them something warm and snuggly, something to shelter them from the wind and keep them warm. —*Barbara Cawthorne Crafton*

# Warm banana bread

The first morning in our new condo, there came a knock at the door.

"Good morning, Reverend Russell. I'm Mary Beth Gilbert, one of your congregants, and, I am happy to say, also one of your neighbors. No, I can't come in. I just wanted to drop this off to welcome you and Jane and say how pleased we are that you are here. I know you have a million things to do, and I have another appointment, but we will talk soon." And as quickly as she had come, she was gone, leaving not a silver bullet, but a loaf of warm banana bread with snipped apricots.

As we came to learn over the course of the next several months, this was vintage Mary Beth. In her eighties, she was a quick, tiny lady with sparkling eyes. She swam every day the pool was open and took a brisk walk around the neighborhood each morning before I was even up. She was determined, we would learn later, to keep her leukemia at bay.

Her kindness was legendary. She was an inveterate card sender, note writer, telephone caller, and giver of small gifts that reminded you she was thinking of you. It was never anything extravagant, just a little token of her good wishes. With whatever ingredients she had on hand or tools she had at her disposal, she set about making certain you knew that she cared about you.

As time grew short for Mary Beth, we had long conversations about her life. I asked her what she hoped to hear God say to her when she got to heaven. And without missing a beat, her eyes twinkled, and she said, "Ya wanna go again?"

Vintage Mary Beth, indeed. —*Gregory A. Russell*

# Can't wait

"I can't wait!" How many times have we heard that expression—especially this time of year as we approach the big day? You know the one I mean. In the spirit of excited expectation, I love to hear these words. But recently I heard someone say, "I can't wait!" with such serious conviction that instead of passing as a throw-away sound bite, it caught in my own throat like an unchangeable truth.

Sure enough, these three little words express a certain truth of our human condition, our need-it-yesterday way of life. We can't wait because we've forgotten how. And thus, we come to the reason for the season. No, not *that* season. *This* season. Advent.

Don't worry—we still can stroll the stores on Black Friday. We still can put up the tree right after Thanksgiving. And we can reply with a cheery "Merry Christmas!" to those who wish us the same. But also, at the same time, we can welcome and embrace the anticipation that is the meaning of Advent.

We *can* wait. Really, we can.

How? One way is to carve out some quiet time. Pray. Meditate. Cherish the sacredness of silence. Or read a Bible passage. There's plenty in there about waiting and all that comes with it—elation, confusion, frustration. Nice to know others can relate.

Another way is to weave such spiritual discipline into the fabric of everyday life: Give thanks for the traffic jam. Look around for more than your late lunch date. Find rest in the waiting room. Find peace in the waiting.

We can wait. And in the waiting, we can expect the God who comes to us not just on the big day, but every day. Everywhere.

Just wait. You'll see. —*Jerald Hyche*

# *Presences everywhere*

Jeannie decided one day to sort out the mess in her closet and came across some old coins in a box. There were a few pennies—and a real treasure, a silver threepenny piece brought back from England by her dad after World War II. Holding these coins in her hand, she was transported back to her childhood. There she was, standing at the counter of the local candy shop, a penny in hand, trying to decide which of the penny-treats to buy. The old silver coin took her to another memory, back to Christmas 1945 when her mom began the tradition of hiding the silver piece inside the Christmas pudding. There were screams of delight when her cousin Rob found the hidden coin in his slice. As Jeannie, now in her sixties, stood over the mess in her closet holding the silver coin, the feeling of disappointment she had experienced as a child returned to her. She had never, not once, found one of the coveted coins in her piece of pudding. The hurt was still alive.

Certain foods can stir the memory, as can pieces of music or visits to the theater. One of the most famous references to the power of an object to stir the senses and thus the memory is Marcel Proust's *Remembrance of Things Past*. All it took was the smell of those cookies, the madeleines, to unlock and unloose a vanished world.

Presences are everywhere waiting to be revealed. And when we begin to notice things—really notice them—we catch a glimpse of the presence of the One who holds all things in being. —*Alan Jones*

# *Working stiffs*

My wife and I plan an outing to Rockefeller Center, Midtown Manhattan's Art Deco masterpiece—home of Radio City Music Hall, the ice skating rink seen in movies, and occasional sightings of television stars.

I will take photographs for this week's "God in the City" essay chronicling my explorations of New York City. I might photograph the statue of Atlas on Fifth Avenue and the way it frames St. Patrick's Cathedral, or the crowds waiting to spend $38.00 for an hour on the ice.

Most likely, I will record the Rock that I actually see, namely, the underground world of hallways and shops that lead from the Sixth Avenue subway station to Fifth Avenue. In this world of marble and brass but no sunlight, thousands of workers stream past shops, banks, and restaurants, dodge tourists, pause briefly to grab a latte, and get where they need to go.

My favorite shop is Eddie's, where six Hispanic immigrants work hard at shining shoes, and the dignity of labor is manifest. Most customers are working stiffs, not "Masters of the Universe." This is a walking culture, and people need to maintain their shoes.

I think Jesus related even-handedly to all people. He showed no preference for any group. He taught what each cadre needed to hear to draw closer to God. I can imagine Jesus speaking in the temples to Mammon that are downtown. But even more so here, in this classic Manhattan shoulder-rubbing mix of all sorts and conditions, I can imagine Jesus sitting in a chair at Eddie's and asking a worker about his family. Or chatting up folks in line at an enormous underground Starbucks. Or accompanying a vagrant being shown the door. Or walking with me as I make my solitary way to work. —*Thomas L. Ehrich*

# *The queen of saints*

"Christmas is about toys," my mother often said. Even when I was well into my thirties she would fetch some odd-shaped package from under the tree, and I would open it to find a football, basketball, Frisbee, or some other piece of athletic equipment. Even if the weather was cold, snowing, raining, or sleeting, she expected me to exit my seat beneath the Christmas tree, take one of my brothers, nephews, or my eldest son Clay, and go outdoors to play. Mother would then take her place at the kitchen window and watch us contentedly. The toys, I discovered, were mostly for her.

Perhaps Luke is toying with his readers by setting the announcement of Mary's pregnancy right next to Elizabeth's. There were similarities between the two. Both stories begin with a heavenly visit from the archangel Gabriel. Nevertheless, their ages and social stature separated the two women. Elizabeth was a "somebody," an established older woman from a leading Jewish family. Mary was a "nobody," a working-class girl, likely in her early teens. Roman law and Jewish custom allowed for marriage once a girl reached age ten. But the most significant difference between Elizabeth and Mary was need. Elizabeth desperately needed God to intervene for her to bear a child in her post-menopausal state. Mary didn't need that, but weary Israel badly needed that young Galilean girl to consent to God's wishes. Thus, we honor Mary as "the Queen of Saints" because she accedes to God's wishes, boldly declaring, "I am a servant of the Lord; let it be with me according to your word" (Luke 1:38).

It is as if all creation were holding its breath to see whether she would "play along" and accept the gift. —*W. Patrick Gahan*

# *Nothing will be impossible with God*

During our parish's most recent service of Advent Lessons and Carols, I was a last-minute substitute for a lector who didn't show up. I drew the reading from the Gospel of Luke that includes Gabriel's words to Mary: "For nothing will be impossible with God" (Luke 1:37). Those words were a blessing to me.

These are frightening times on every level, from the macro to the micro, from the global economy to the backyard economy. Cutbacks and job losses work like fancy constructions made of dominos: one falls and knocks over the next, and the next, until they're smacking and clacking across the board. No one knows what's coming.

Well, no one ever knows what's coming, even when we think we do. It's easy to talk about trust and faith when things are going well, but in times like these we are forced to confront our fears and remind ourselves, "For nothing will be impossible with God."

So walk in faith. Make your annual pledge to your church, and then make good on it. Give to those in need; bring canned goods for your local food bank, where need increases as contributions dwindle. Send something to the agencies, like Episcopal Relief and Development (www.er-d.org), that work in poverty-stricken regions and countries around the world, so that their work may continue.

Here's what we do know, in Advent and throughout the church year: Jesus, the Christ, the Savior of the world, will soon be here.

For nothing will be impossible with God. —*Sarah Bryan Miller*

# Ready to hear

*Almighty and everlasting God,*
*you are always more ready to hear than we to pray...*
—The Book of Common Prayer,
Collect for Proper 22

What is more fascinating about prayer than any other single thing is that everyone does it—everyone—but no one talks about it. Why is that? Two reasons.

First, prayer is more personal than any other activity. We talk about money, which once was never mentioned in polite society; we argue about politics, endlessly; and now, we even boast about sex, describing in some detail our most intimate physical activity. But speak of prayer? Never. Prayer is the activity closest to defining our true identity: what we fear and want the most, who we really believe ourselves to be, what we know will happen in the future. We want to talk about none of this. It is bad enough to allow ourselves to think about it.

But second, if we were to speak, right out loud, we would have no idea what to say. Attempts at words fail us. How does one speak of the unspeakable? One doesn't. Prayer is too private, and it is too difficult.

So we keep silent. Which is fine, as long as we know that is what we are doing. Why is it fine? God is always more ready to hear than we are to pray. God knows what we want before we pray. God knows what we want to say, should say, cannot find the words to say, before we begin to struggle to form the words. This means that prayer is a disarmingly simple exercise that requires but one thing and one thing only: be still and enter into the presence of God. —*Edward S. Gleason*

# Ahab

Ahab was King of Israel from 869 to 850 B.C. He was a pathetic figure rendered tragic by the company he kept. His wife Jezebel's enthusiasm for the god Baal was trumped only by her aggressive concept of what we might call executive privilege.

Ahab's nemesis was the prophet Elijah, whose miraculous powers were applied with bloody force against Jezebel.

The only way the prophet and the queen could get at each other was through Ahab, whose moral and political weakness guaranteed him a miserable life and a low rating in the polls. This is not the part of Ahab's life with which I identify but it is important to know because his major cowardice provides insight into my/our minor cowardice.

During a war conference with the King of Judah (1 Kings 22) the rulers consulted various prophets about the validity of their plans. Ahab was asked whether there were any seers they had not heard from. He replied, "There is still one other by whom we may inquire, Micaiah, son of Imlah; but I hate him for he never prophesies anything favorable about me, but only disaster."

We don't have to be as foul a character as Ahab to see something of ourselves in his disdain for the sources of bad news. How often do we avoid people who do not support our views or hopes?

How many sermons, discussions, speeches, editorials, movements, or ideas have we turned off because we did not want to deal with their point of view? How many of us have stopped listening to others of us for want of "anything favorable about me"? In the Collect for the Second Sunday of Advent, we ask God to help us to heed the prophets.

The Ahab in us needs a lot of help to do that heeding.

—*Francis H. Wade*

# *Attending to God*

Theologian Diogenes Allen once remarked, "We become what we attend to." Most of the time we attend to things that seem important but do not ultimately matter. We are in perpetual danger of becoming the things that preoccupy us. Christians read scripture and make space and time for Jesus because the more we contemplate him the more we habituate ourselves to being like him.

Novelist John Updike began his creative life as an artist, and he spoke often of the visual arts and museum-going in his early writing life as a focal point for his mental and spiritual attention. He said about these early-career museum visits in New York: "I took away, in sufficient-sized packets, courage to be an artist, an artist now, amid the gritty crushed grays of this desperately living city, a bringer of light and order and color, a singer of existence."

"A bringer of light and order and color, a singer of existence"— that phrase describes both a painter and a writer. It also describes God. If "we become what we attend to," then we attend to Jesus in order to become more like him. But "attending" means not only "looking at." It also means behaving. We behave like God by trying, in our own ways, to bring light and order and color into our existence.

As you approach this day, how will you attend, not to what is worthless, but to what gives you life in God's ways? A place to start is to keep your eyes on Jesus. And as you attend to him, give expression to that creative part of you, to become, like God, "a bringer of light and order and color, a singer of existence." —*Gary Hall*

# *A shared path*

*Years ago I recognized my kinship with all living things, and I made up my mind that I was not one bit better than the meanest on the earth. I said then and I say now, that while there is a lower class, I am in it; while there is a criminal element, I am of it; while there is a soul in prison, I am not free.*

—Eugene V. Debs

I work in a state-run substance abuse and mental health treatment facility. As a state facility, we operate on a sliding scale and therefore serve a lot of people who otherwise couldn't afford to get help.

It is a privilege and an honor to assist fellow travelers as they struggle to regain their footing on this common path. In addition to liking what I do here, I also like just being here. I often find myself grinning while I am in the shower getting ready for work or making the half-hour drive there.

So it is with confusion that I encounter others who view the people we serve with disdain or contempt. Some don't realize it's a shared path, but think there are paths marked "ours" and "theirs."

We'd recently held several fundraisers so we could buy Christmas presents for the folks who would spend the holidays in treatment. I was taken aback when a fellow worker said, "It must be nice, being *them*!" I bit my lip and walked away. I didn't ask if this co-worker was envious of legal problems, custody problems, family problems, joblessness, homelessness, bad health, or the meager twenty dollars we spend at Christmas on each resident to remind them that they're human, too. We all are. —*Bo Cox*

# *I believe in the forgiveness of sins*

I went to jail today. I wasn't in trouble, but I went to see a friend who was. It's not my favorite place to go, but Christians are not given an out on this responsibility (Matthew 25:31-46). Jesus' forgiveness must be pronounced in even the bleakest of places. Stone walls, steel bars, and concertina wire may keep prisoners in, but they cannot keep forgiveness out. Our Lord extends his grace into corners where it is most needed. A simple personal inventory will remind us of that stalwart promise. We cannot imprison ourselves so deeply in sin that Christ's forgiveness cannot find us.

The fact that forgiveness finds us means that we cannot do a thing to earn it. Paul, a sinner with a notorious record of deadly trespasses himself, confessed that Christ erased our record of sin and nailed it to the cross (Colossians 2:14). When we profess that we "believe in the forgiveness of sins," we are admitting, much like those gathered at an Alcoholics Anonymous meeting, that we are powerless over the sin that has gotten hold of us. But Christ is not powerless. To accept God's forgiveness is not purely self-serving. It is the gateway to a transformed life. Once we receive Christ's pardon, we are like racehorses poised at the gate, ready to make a run at life.

If we imagine we are permanently incarcerated in the sin that hounds us, we should humble ourselves before Christ and get ready for a prison break. —*W. Patrick Gahan*

# An act of high courage
# flung in the face of life

Carl Jung called for "an act of high courage flung in the face of life." He meant that the journey toward meaning leads inward and away from the pursuit of treasure, people to possess, and conventions to keep. That's pretty much the story of Jesus.

An inner call quickly becomes a testing. Jesus' inner struggle happens in the wilderness, and then becomes an outward struggle as he confronts the powers of religion and state—an uncertainty similar to that of relating to parents, neighbors, friends, and other authority figures. Our struggles generally end in discomfort as we let go of the comfortable expectations of others and die in order that the person God intends us to be may be born.

A clergy friend once told of a mother who came to tell him that her son had finally sorted out his life and knew what he was intended to be and do. My friend, hoping to put a "notch in his recruitment gun," thought she was going to say her son was entering seminary, but the woman said her son planned to become a professional pool player.

We should take such incidents seriously. The woman's son may have been a youth who rejected the conventional, convenient, safe way in favor of the odd turn of life in strange places that bewilders most of us. When the alternative was to spend his life trapped by the conventions of others, he chose Jung's "act of high courage flung in the face of life."

This raises the question of how you and I are doing. Are we fretting away our lives in despair, or are we on the path to the kingdom of God? —*Richard L. Shimpfky*

# Reality is God's ally

Richard Rohr, the popular Franciscan writer, says many good things. One of them is that reality is God's ally.

Father Rohr means that God speaks through what is, not through what we think should be. God speaks through things as they are, things that have fallen our way, pro or con from our vantage point. God speaks through the givens.

Martin Luther's way of saying this was that "the preacher needs to preach with his feet on the ground." Don't preach concepts or ideology or mental projections. Preach from the real situation of human conflict and pain, *on the ground.*

Reality is God's ally because reality leads us to understand our limitations and the fact that we *must* be humble before God. To be humble before God is not a choice we make. Rather, humility is forced upon us. The reversals of personal planning and hoped-for futures force us to back down, to kneel down, to lie down. You had no idea what you were getting into when you married that woman. You didn't know what this particular career choice would involve in practice. Nobody led you to expect a hurricane in Galveston during *your* retirement, given the odds from past history in that section of the Texas coast. Hey, and Merrill Lynch was a sure thing and AIG a sound and secure investment.

You didn't decide to be humbled before life and before God. You were humbled. Now you can really pray. Now you can speak, the clay to the Potter. —*Paul F. M. Zahl*

# Coincidence?

The sign on the brick wall across the street read "Coincidence is God's way of acting anonymously." It stopped me cold, for I had just come out of a side door of a hospital wing, where an instinct earlier in the day had told me to go visit a particular parishioner who'd been there awhile.

As I'd walked into her room there was a flurry of activity, and a nurse told me that they were wheeling her out for an emergency surgery. I had only that moment to take the woman's hand in comfort, make the sign of the cross on her forehead, and send her off with a prayer to "bless the hearts and minds and hands of those who administer of your healing gifts, O Lord."

Good timing? Coincidence? Coincidence in arriving on time? Or coincidence in finding that sign on that wall? My experience is that coincidences abound in the spiritual life, as pointers to God's presence and action in our lives. Not as proofs, but as indicators and messages, beckoning us forward.

I arrived at another hospital room door, nudged by an inner voice that said "go visit him," just as a man died, and I could say a prayer with his family. Literally as I was coming out of that door, my next-door neighbor greeted me from the room across the hall. "Oh, Len, I'm so glad you're here," as if I'd been meant to be there. Her mother lay dying, and she asked me to come into their room and pray with them as well.

"Coincidence is God's way of acting anonymously." What coincidences in your life have felt like the touch of God's hand, an awareness of his actions beckoning you forward anonymously?
—*Leonard Freeman*

# *Giving God a run for his money*

Money is spiritual. It is spiritual first because it is the recompense we receive for using up our time, our talent, and our lives. It is spiritual because it speaks to the self at its deepest level—both its needs and desires. It is spiritual because it holds so much power.

The word "worship" comes from the Old English "worth-ship," and means quite simply that we derive our worth from what we most desire and adore. Money can easily become the thing that defines our worth. I know this personally because when I have enough money, I feel safe, secure, and empowered, and when I don't have enough, I feel fearful, anxious, and vulnerable. But I also know more deeply that God's presence or absence in my life, not money, should determine how I feel about myself.

Money is actually the only thing I know of that has enough power to give God a "run for his money." The one thing that helps me keep things in perspective is to give back to God a portion of my money every single time I receive some—first, before all the other demands and desires of my life have their say. —*James L. Burns*

# *Stigmata*

In the Metropolitan Museum of Art in New York is a Victorian painting by Jean Vibert entitled "The Missionary's Adventures." It depicts an elegant French drawing room in which various clergymen are enjoying refreshments. Two clerics are chatting on the right. On the left an abbot seated on the sofa converses over wine. In the center sits a fat cardinal who with obvious boredom listens to the central figure in the painting, a simple friar just back from the mission field who is pointing to the gaping wound in his wrist from his crucifixion.

Few of us in this country have visible scars from living our faith. But there can be a price to be paid; there are wounds. As a parish priest, I learned of a young man who refused to go along with his fraternity brothers' exploitation of women and was ostracized. I knew a builder who refused to make a dishonest bid on a big construction job and was blackballed from certain bidding for a year. A housewife in my parish ended up on the evening news when she began to speak out about redlining in our posh suburban town and eventually had to move to another city.

In 1813, Adoniram Judson was one of the first Christian missionaries to Burma. During the Anglo-Burmese War of 1824-1826, he was imprisoned by local rulers, beaten, starved, and marched across a desert with his hands and feet chained until they were deformed. When he was finally released, he went to the King of Burma and asked if he could go to a certain city to preach. The king said, "I will let twelve preachers go there to preach, but not you, not with those hands. My people will ignore your words but not your hands."

Ridicule, reduced income, rejection—these are some of today's missionaries' scars. —*David L. James*

# Seek, come, go

*Seek the truth—Come whence it may—Cost what it will*

These words are engraved in stone by the entrance to the library at Virginia Theological Seminary. They're engraved in my memory as well, for they came unbidden to me recently. I was thinking about our country (wrestling with the twin crises of war and financial upheaval), our parish theology group (chewing on new and startling ideas), Anglicans worldwide (grappling with authority and human sexuality), and my own life (as I continue to discern my path from among many options).

"What is truth?" Pilate's question (John 18:38) was a good one. Apparently it hung in the air because Jesus didn't answer it. And the question is still hanging in the air. How many of us resonate with the frustration of another John (Lennon) who sang: "All I want is the truth! Just gimme some truth!"

I find it interesting that at Virginia Seminary this hunger for truth is coupled with the mission imperative of Mark 16:15 painted over stained glass in the chapel: *Go ye into all the world and preach the gospel.*

This connection between truth and good news is beautifully captured in John's gospel prologue: "And the Word became flesh and lived among us, and we have seen his glory...full of grace and truth" (John 1:14).

Maybe this is why Jesus didn't answer Pilate or spell everything out for the religious experts. He didn't want to waste his breath throwing out yet another doctrine or rule that would just hang in the air, lifeless, or be argued over *ad nauseam*. Instead, he embodied "the way, the truth, and the life" and invited us go and do likewise.

May the love of God, once made incarnate in Jesus, be incarnate in us, that *our* lives may be a light to the world this Christmastide, and always. —*Charles F. Brumbaugh*

# Rescued

*And the Word became flesh, and lived among us,*
*and we have seen his glory, the glory as of a father's only son,*
*full of grace and truth. —John 1:14*

When I try to explain the Incarnation, I sometimes get some help from little Jermere McMillan. The two-year-old and his older brother and sister were playing in a South Alabama vacant lot one afternoon, and without warning the grass beneath little Jermere gave way, and he fell fourteen feet to the bottom of a well.

For thirteen hours, the child sat lodged and locked in the dirt and darkness at the bottom of that deep hole. Cold, confused, wet, dirty, hungry, scared, alone save for voices calling down to him from above— words of comfort and assurance, but no doubt also words he couldn't understand. And other sounds. Shouts of warning. Sirens wailing. Shovels slicing. There was only one way to save him. Rescuers had to dig a hole straight down next to the well, and then a connecting tunnel, so they could climb down and carry him out.

As the dawn broke on the next new day, a light broke through the wall of the well. A face appeared, and hands grasped little Jermere, pulled him close, then carried him up out of the hole, scratched and bruised, but alive.

Jermere's story is our story, the story of how the world fell into darkness, how we became separated from God, how we—helpless as toddlers—were hopeless to save ourselves. And how, after calling down prophetic words we couldn't understand, God dug deep in the muck and climbed down into the dank reality of our earthly existence, to pull us close and carry us out of despair and death to life again.
—*Jerald Hyche*

# The bread lady and God

On a cold and rainy day, the Friday farmers' market on 97th Street has half the usual count of vendors. For those on hand, it looks like chilly duty.

The bread lady is cheerful as usual, however. She displays her customary array of breads, pastries, and cakes. While she wraps my crumb bun and peasant round, I picture her working hard all week at kneading board and oven. In my mind's eye, that is peaceful work and lonely, like much of what we do in life as partners, parents, and workers; satisfying, perhaps, when she returns home at the end of the weekend with no unsold inventory, but frustrating when sales just don't happen.

Imagine God as this baker. Much of God's work is done in advance—"on the come," as they say in betting. God loves first, God gives first, God looks at humanity and imagines what will "sell," that is, what humanity will dare to receive. If God "baked" everything we need, we probably would run for cover. So God lays before us a love and a call that stretch us a little, but not too much.

When God extends that love, we have it in our power to accept or to walk on by, for all the reasons that people walk by: distracted, feeling poor, in a hurry, looking for something else. I have manned enough booths and church thresholds to know the wistfulness that shop owners feel. Why don't they come in? What's wrong with my product? How can I go home without having sold enough?

I marvel at the bread lady's cheerful outlook. It's good salesmanship, of course, but it's also difficult. Even more, I marvel at God's steadfastness. How many loaves will God bake while we seek other food?
—*Thomas L. Ehrich*

# Worship or follow?

*Send us out to do the work you have given us to do.*
—The Book of Common Prayer, p. 366

A long time ago I fell in love with Anglican worship. The dignity and reverence, the music, the liturgical vestments and colors, the formality and order all inspire me and make me feel as though I am closer to God. The liturgical year and the lectionary keep the birth, death, and resurrection of the Lord Jesus, as well as the beginning of the church, ever before me.

Someone once said to me, "Jesus did not come to be worshiped, he came to be followed. Worship is part of following Jesus, but it is not the whole picture." I found this a little disconcerting, but came to see the wisdom in her statement. A king needs subjects, and the transformation of the world into the kingdom will not happen if all Christians remain in their pews. I have to remind myself again and again that the most significant thing we do on Sunday mornings is to leave the church to go out and begin again the work that God has given us to do. Next Sunday our parish will volunteer at the local homeless shelter. Perhaps your parish will too. —*Jason Leo*

# A Christmas tomato

My husband had picked all the unripened tomatoes from his vines in late October and brought them into the kitchen, green and hard. Soon some of them began to ripen, and he enjoyed a daily salad of them. "Here, taste this," he would say, handing me a little red wedge. They were good—not glorious August tomatoes, but not those duplicitous produce-aisle-at-the-A&P tomatoes, either, beckoning the unwary with their bright colors and eternal flavorless shelf-life.

I watched the tomato supply. Surely the tomato season could be extended by only a few weeks at most. But Thanksgiving came and went, and still they ripened. "We were born tomatoes and we'll go out tomatoes, the way a tomato should," I think I heard them say. "We did not come all this way to rot and not be used!" My husband had a tomato on Saint Nicholas' Day and one on Pearl Harbor Day and one on Jane Austen's birthday. By Saint Thomas' Day, December 21, things were looking good for a Christmas tomato. Several promising candidates continued to ripen on top of the toaster oven.

"How shall this be?" asks practical Mary, "since I know not a man?" (Luke 1:34). But sometimes things happen in an unusual way. Christmas is usually cold and icy, and tomatoes normally ripen in the summer. But this year Christmas dawned rainy and mild, and Christmas breakfast was a rich array of sweet breads, cookies—and a crisp green salad featuring the red goodness of my husband's Christmas tomato. Things mostly happen in the usual way, but not always. It's best to keep an open mind. —*Barbara Cawthorne Crafton*

# Bravo!

Why did God choose to contact us the way he did, through the birth of a child, with flesh and blood like ours, a heart that beats like ours? If we were planning such an event, we'd probably appoint a committee and hire a public relations expert. But no. God chose the most universal human experience, that of birth. He figured everyone in the world could get the message, since we have all been born, grown up, and known both pain and joy.

Nonetheless, we find ways to distort the message. We think it is about whether or not Mary was a virgin. We think it has to do with the pomp and ceremony of the midnight Mass. We think it's about selecting the best gifts for our family and friends. We think it has to do with children and their enjoyment of the holidays. All this stuff is at best secondary, and at worst irrelevant.

Incarnation—that fancy word which means to make flesh—is really quite simple. It means that God knows what it is to be us. He is born into a family, not a privileged family which could give him the advantages of a good education, fine food and clothes, and other enrichments. To an ordinary family, no better or worse than most of ours. Bravo, God! That is real imagination!

Into whatever circumstances we have been born, we are children of God. God is one of us. No one's life is easy. It only looks that way from the outside in, never from the inside out. But God knows all about it—the sorrows, the fears, the doubts, the triumphs. The child in the manger cries. Can we ever again believe that God is silent?
—*Lee Krug*

# Happiness or joy?

*In the bleak mid-winter, frosty wind made moan,*
*earth stood hard as iron, water like a stone;*
*snow had fallen, snow on snow, snow on snow,*
*in the bleak mid-winter, long ago.* —Hymnal 1982, #112

I'm especially drawn to Christmas carols with deep hues and shadows that aren't easily bleached into jingles. They take seriously the mystery of the Word made flesh who lived and died as one of us. They take seriously the oppressive darkness that so often envelops our lives, which makes the coming of the Light all the more astonishing and wondrous. They take seriously the oft-overlooked reason that Jesus was born in the first place, because things were going so badly on this planet.

It's no accident that Christmas Day is celebrated on December 25— mid-winter, just after the solstice, when the short, dark days begin to grow longer. Jesus was born into the very heart of darkness. But "the light shines in the darkness, and the darkness did not overcome it" (John 1:5).

I don't bristle at the generic greeting "Happy Holidays!" I'm content to share the holidays with folk of good will from all faiths and none. But the word "happy" strikes me as ephemeral, a cheerful yet fragile state of mind, dependent on desirable circumstances.

I prefer the word "joy." Joy is the rich, profound intuition (often sensed despite all appearances to the contrary) that all is well and will be well. It's a well-seasoned state of mind and heart that is not overcome by adversity. Joy grants the peace that surpasses all understanding.

So when the mall clerk dutifully chirps "Happy Holidays," receive the gift gratefully and respond in kind. But my prayer for you and for all is that this Christmas season will be marked by joy. —*Charles F. Brumbaugh*

# *Peach pie*

My oldest cousin, Bob, is the black sheep of the family—married and divorced three times, and currently rumored to be living with a woman over in Bloomington. This is a matter of no small embarrassment for an otherwise pretty stable Midwest family, especially our eighty-five-year-old grandmother.

Grandma has let Bob know in no uncertain terms that she does not approve, that she thinks he's making a fool of himself, ruining the family name, and setting a mighty poor example for his two teenage sons. Bob just says, "It's my little red wagon, Grandma; I'll just have to pull it." Both of them are proud and stubborn. They have exchanged unbearably sharp words over this.

Why Bob comes home at Christmas, I'll never understand. He's definitely the odd man out. He has to feel it. Christmas happens at noon in Grandma's dining room. She still does the turkey and the ham, only recently agreeing to allow relatives to bring in a couple of side dishes. But Grandma always bakes the pies: apple, mincemeat (homemade, from her own recipe. Just don't ask. It starts with "two nice, fresh hogs' heads"), cherry, and peach. She bakes multiples of these, except for the peach, and they're always all gone, except for the peach.

The peach pie has only one slice taken from it—always only one. That slice belongs to Bob. He's the only one who eats peach pie.

Sure, it would be easier to make only three kinds of pie; we've all told Grandma that. But that's not the way Grandma reckons things. So every year there is a fresh peach pie. And every year there is just one slice taken from it. And every year Bob comes home for Christmas.

And, friends, it's not for the pie. —*Gregory A. Russell*

# *What about the angels?*

I was almost out the door when someone said, "What about the angels?" Until that moment I had handled the gathering and distribution of my parents' household goods pretty well. It was a big job. Mom and Pop had experienced lean to desperate times during the Great Depression and tended to keep anything they thought might be of future use to them or anyone else—my father's lunchbox from the 1940s, my grandfather's work shoes. Sorting things along with my wife, children, and grandchildren was sad, but the question about the angels got me. It was a business-like question about something sacred to me. And the lump in my throat wouldn't let me answer.

When I was a kid and we lived in my grandparents' old house, Christmas decorations were simple. There was the cedar tree with colored lights and icicles, when those things could be found during World War II. The ceramic angels held two red candles on the front room mantelpiece. After supper on Christmas Eve lights were dimmed, and my mother lit the candles. It was the official start of Christmas.

Soon there would be a knock at the door and visits would begin; aunts, uncles, cousins, friends, neighbors came. My mother's bourbon-aged fruitcake was served with coffee or a little wine. We sang carols around the piano. Then I went to bed, perhaps "said a prayer to the close and holy darkness," and began the interminable wait for Christmas morning.

My mother continued to light Christmas Eve candles in her new house as my children grew up. Now my daughter carries on the tradition; on the mantelpiece the angels still bear the light as angels should. —*Robert Horine*

# *What child is this?*

Our attempts to tame Christ begin at his cradle. We want to make it a sentimental scene, the innocent baby snuggled in the hay, surrounded by admirers. Rather like the welcoming of a baby or a grandbaby in our families, we rejoice in new birth, the continuation of life.

We know that the journey of a child into the world is sometimes perilous and may bring fear and trembling to those who await it. Mary, Joseph, the shepherds, and the wise men experienced a mix of fear and trembling, and joy.

We once created a roadside sign for our church that said "JESUS IS DOWN TO EARTH." And so he is. Yet he is more than just one of us. Poet Dylan Thomas writes, "Blessing on the wild child...and the splashed mothering maiden who bore him with a bonfire in his mouth and rocked him like a storm."

Never set aside the awe-fulness of the birth. This baby changed the world. When we see little children re-enacting the nativity roles, we are charmed. We also need to be shaken, to comprehend the revolutionary nature of who the infant was. The mystery of Christmas is enfolded in the manger and unfolds in the power and mystery of God connecting with us.

To kneel before the baby is, most of all, to love the God who sent him. The wild child leads us to adventures we could not otherwise imagine. —*Lee Krug*

# Christmas, in so many words

The Nativity stories in the Bible have been much discussed—why the accounts in Luke and Matthew contradict one another, why Mark lacks one and John and Paul don't mention the Nativity at all, the stories' various historically troublesome aspects, the mainstream British news media's (typically sensationalistic) little number on the archbishop of Canterbury's thoughtful comments on that very subject. Amidst all this talk, I find myself thinking of the first chapter of the Gospel of John.

No, it's not, strictly speaking, a Nativity story. There are no shepherds abiding in the fields, no angels announcing the Savior's birth, no stars leading the way, no wise men bearing symbolic gifts, no wicked kings scheming against the innocent, no reverse-Moses flight into Egypt—nothing, in fact, that would work in a Christmas or Epiphany pageant. But that does not lessen the inherent drama of the passage.

"In the beginning was the Word, and the Word was with God, and the Word was God."

I love the (sometimes self-contradicting) amalgamated account that has become "the Christmas story," love it as I loved seeing my small daughters taking on the various roles in years of pageants, love it as I love the carols of the season.

But for heart-filling theology, this is the passage that says it all, without costumes, without props, without supernumeraries. "And the Word became flesh and lived among us, and we have seen his glory... From his fullness we have all received, grace upon grace."

Thanks be to God. —*Sarah Bryan Miller*

# Singing creation

There's a story about Caedmon, the first known English poet, who lived in the seventh century and thought of himself as an ungifted cowherd—until he found his voice. According to the Venerable Bede, Caedmon saw a heavenly visitor who commanded him to sing. "But what should I sing about?" he wondered. "Sing of what you know," said the wise mentor, "sing of creation." And so he did.

Some years ago my friend David was given an unexpected Christmas present. He and his family were spending Christmas with friends who, like David and his wife Caroline, had a couple of kids. Henry was an opera singer, and after the two families emerged from Christmas midnight Mass at St. Luke's Church in Greenwich Village, Henry, with a twinkle in his eye, turned to David and said, "You certainly belted out those Christmas carols. I think I've just found the perfect Christmas present for you." Henry gave David six singing lessons with a coach from the Metropolitan Opera. You should have seen David's face, a mixture of delight and horror. "I can't waste her time. I mean, I don't have the talent." Eventually, David, with some trepidation, went for his first lesson.

The coach, a wonderful teacher, was delighted to put him through his paces, starting with scales to loosen him up and then teaching him to sing a few eighteenth-century Italian arias. These lessons changed David's life. No, he didn't start singing at the major opera houses of the world, but he did change the way he looked at himself. His life became pregnant with possibility, all because an imaginative and generous friend had dared to give him what he didn't dare claim for himself. There was no way that David on his own would have sought out singing lessons. But after he had enjoyed his amazing Christmas present, he looked at his life differently. His life became a work in progress. —*Alan Jones*

# *The innkeeper*

Early morality plays sometimes centered on a character known as Everyman. The meaning is not subtle.

Everyman was each and all of us. The Bible is full of Everyman, although it does not use that name. Consider the innkeeper in the Christmas story. Although only a bit part in the pageant, he is the perfect representation of humanity.

The innkeeper was busy. Everybody was traveling because of the census required by Rome.

Those who took hospitality seriously were hard pressed. He was a decent sort of fellow who was willing to do what he could for those in particular need. When a young couple with a baby on the way came asking for a room he didn't have, he made room for them where he could, with the animals. Having done what he could, he returned to his tasks, and did not reappear in the story of the Incarnation. Consequently he did not hear the rustle of angels' wings in his backyard nor did he notice the devotion of others. When the holy family moved on, he remained what he was: decent, busy, kind, oblivious.

Is not the innkeeper an Everyman? The world is full of good people who never connect their goodness to what God might be doing. I know scores of people who diligently go about their tasks and never look up to scan for wonder in their work.

How many times have I been in the presence of the holy and treated it as another mouth to feed or problem to solve? How often have we, as the writer of Hebrews put it, "entertained angels without knowing it"? Often enough for the innkeeper to be Everyman. —*Francis H. Wade*

# Two cities, one cross

My daughter, the young artist, was inspired a few years ago to paint a poignant Christmas scene out of her imagination. Against a blazing sunset over the desert, you see in the far distance across an open plain the tiny silhouette of a man leading a woman on a donkey. A giant star shines in the sky directly above them. They are going from the dark, diffuse profile of one city toward that of another.

When she first showed me this picture, I quickly praised her work as any good father would do—but when I looked more closely at the picture, I had some questions.

"So, who are these people?" I asked.

"Joseph and Mary," she said.

"So, where are they going?"

"To Bethlehem," she said.

I paused, careful how to phrase my next question. "Was there a cross in Bethlehem?" I asked, pointing to a large, dark cross jutting from the city's skyline.

"Is that not where it was?" she asked.

I explained that Jesus was born in Bethlehem, but the cross was in Jerusalem.

"Oh, well, it's the same thing," she said.

And then the greater truth of this young artist's expression became clear to me. All I could say was, "It certainly is the same thing. This painting is perfect."

And so it hangs on my office wall, not just because it is my daughter's, but because it reminds me of the story of Christmas all year long—and how the story of Christmas neither begins nor ends in Bethlehem, but is the story of our Savior who was born in a manger so he could grow up to be raised not to an earthly throne, but up on a cross to die. —*Jerald Hyche*

# *When is Christmas over?*

When our children were small, Christmas was the most celebrated time of the year.

Selecting the tree involved multiple inspections of many possibilities. Our own childhood ornaments decorated it, along with newer and sometimes handmade ones by the kids. Cookies were baked. Week by week, candles on the Advent wreath were lit. Opening of Advent calendars began. Along with neighbors, we went up and down our street, led by a doctor who played the trombone, singing at each house. On Christmas Eve we held a procession through our house, with candles and carols, the youngest person carrying the baby Jesus to place in the crèche. The visiting grandmother read *The Night Before Christmas,* and the father read from Saint Luke. Stockings were hung and cookies and carrots left for Santa and his reindeer. After the late Mass, weary parents returned home at 2:00 a.m. to assemble dollhouses and little garages. What a grand mix of the sacred and the secular!

A week or so after December 25, the tree comes down and the baubles and candles and wreaths are all put away for another year. Is Christmas over? Not for me: we keep a small lighted tree in our living room year-round. The hand-carved angel atop our big tree returns to its place on the wall. It came from a wood-carver in Oberammergau, and symbolizes the angel who appeared to Mary with news that would dwarf today's headlines.

Christmas is never over. It is the turning point when we are able to see God in a way we can understand—as a human being like us. Other religions have ways of connecting to God, but for us Christians it is the arrival of the baby, growing to become the man who discloses to us the face of God. —*Lee Krug*

# Things can end

For a few years, I had a hard time letting plants go. I would lug enormous woody grandmother geraniums into the house in the fall, struggling to find sunny places for all of them indoors. If I left one outside into the first frost, I felt like a murderer when I went out in the morning and saw it slumped over the side of its pot, darkened, limp, and pretty much dead.

More gardening and more years of watching what happens in a garden have changed my attitude. It's important that species survive, but every individual of every species doesn't need to survive, not every time. They have life spans. Our task is not to make them immortal, but to make their lives good while they are here, so that they can do what they came to do. After that, their delight is in their return to the earth, to enable the larger survival of everything.

Now I take cuttings and save seeds. I might bring a blooming plant or two inside for some winter color. Of course the lemon trees come in. There are some tender herbs that come indoors to spend the winter with us and to flavor and perfume our stews and roasted vegetables. But most of them give themselves back to the soil. They either lie there and decompose, get shredded for compost, or wind up in a leaf bag at the end of the driveway.

Things end. Things that don't go on forever aren't a waste of time. All your friendships don't have to endure in just the same form as when they began; it's not disloyal if some friends ease out of your present and into the place of memory. You both had a hand in making the other what you are; it may be that now the smiles of a winter's remembering are life enough. —*Barbara Cawthorne Crafton*

# Contributors

**BRUCE BIRDSEY** has served Episcopal parishes in Georgia, Pennsylvania, and North Carolina. He currently lives in Richmond, Virginia, where he specializes in interim ministry. A former journalist, he has written for both the church and secular press.

**CHARLES F. BRUMBAUGH** is priest associate at Church of the Redeemer, Cincinnati, Ohio. He has previously served Episcopal churches in Pennsylvania and Missouri.

**JAMES L. BURNS** is rector of Church of the Heavenly Rest, New York City. A native of Indiana, he previously served parishes in Tennessee and Kentucky. He has served as chairman of the board of directors of Forward Movement and has written for *Forward Day by Day*.

**BO COX** is a frequent contributor to *Forward Day by Day* and the author of *God Is Not in the Thesaurus* (Forward Movement, 1999). Paroled from an Oklahoma prison in 2003, he and his wife Debb now live near Norman, Oklahoma. He works in a state-run substance abuse treatment facility.

**BARBARA CAWTHORNE CRAFTON** is an Episcopal priest, writer, and spiritual director. She is the author of many books, and speaks and leads retreats in the U.S. and abroad. She heads the Geranium Farm, an online institute for the promotion of spiritual growth. The Farm publishes her widely-read "Almost-Daily eMo" at www.geraniumfarm.org.

**THOMAS L. EHRICH** is an Episcopal priest and president of New York-based Morning Walk Media, Inc., writer of "On a Journey" meditations and essays (www.onajourney.org), a *Forward Day by Day* author, creator of the Church Wellness Project, and a nationally syndicated newspaper columnist. He has led parishes in Indiana, Missouri, and North Carolina.

**ROGER FERLO** is director of the Center for Lifetime Theological Education at the Virginia Theological Seminary in Alexandria, Virginia. He has served as a priest in New York, Pennsylvania, and Georgia. His books include *Heaven* (Seabury, 2007) and *Sensing God* (Cowley, 2002).

**LEONARD FREEMAN** retired as rector of St. Martin's Episcopal Church, Minnetonka Beach, Minnesota, after forty years in parish, print, and television ministries. A *Forward Day by Day* author and film critic for *The Episcopalian* and *Episcopal Life*, he also has headed communications for Trinity Church, Wall Street, and the Washington National Cathedral.

LINDSAY HARDIN FREEMAN is an Episcopal priest who has served in Massachusetts, Pennsylvania, and Minnesota. The editor of *Vestry Papers*, she has written feature articles, news stories, and humor columns. Her book, *The Scarlet Cord: Conversations with God's Chosen Women*, will be published in 2010 (O Books).

W. PATRICK GAHAN is rector of St. Stephen's Episcopal Church in Wimberley, Texas. A native of Birmingham, Alabama, he has served as a prep school chaplain and as rector of St. Stephen's Episcopal Church in Beaumont, Texas. He is the author of several articles in educational and spiritual journals.

EDWARD S. GLEASON retired in 2005 after eleven years as editor and director of Forward Movement. He is the author of *Redeeming Marriage* (Cowley, 1988), *Dying We Live* (Cowley, 1990), and *New Life: Every Work That Begins Ends* (Forward Movement, 2005). He resides in Washington, D.C.

GARY HALL is dean of Seabury-Western Theological Seminary in Evanston, Illinois. He has served as priest in California, Massachusetts, Michigan, and Pennsylvania, and has taught at several academic institutions on ethics, leadership, and American literature.

ROBERT HORINE is a retired Episcopal priest living in Lexington, Kentucky. For several years he was a full-time journalist for the *Lexington Herald* and now writes a monthly column for *Interchange*, the newspaper of the Diocese of Southern Ohio. He was senior editor of Forward Movement from 1985 to 1997.

JERALD HYCHE is associate rector for discipleship and spiritual formation at St. Martin's Episcopal Church, Houston, Texas. He was formerly business editor for the Mobile, Alabama *Press Register*.

DAVID L. JAMES served as an Episcopal priest for twenty-five years. In 2004 he resigned from the church "to serve all of creation." Today he is the chaplain of Hartsdale Pet Cemetery in Hartsdale, New York, the oldest pet cemetery in the United States. He is the author of numerous articles and the book *From Loss to Hope* (Forward Movement, 2006).

ALAN JONES retired in 2009 after serving for twenty-four years as dean of Grace Cathedral, San Francisco, California. He taught at the General Theological Seminary in New York from 1973 to 1985. Among his eight books are *Seasons of Grace* (Wiley, 2003), *Soul's Journey* (Cowley, 2001), and *Living the Truth* (Cowley, 2000). He resides in San Francisco.

LEE KRUG is a psychotherapist and couples counselor in private practice. She serves as a member of the vestry and is a healing minister at Christ Episcopal Church in Hackensack, New Jersey. She is the author of Forward Movement's *Forty Days of Lent 2006* and a contributor to *Comfort Ye* (Forward Movement, 2007.)

JASON LEO is rector of Calvary Episcopal Church, Cincinnati, Ohio. He was formerly director of youth ministries for the Diocese of Southern Ohio and has contributed to *Forward Day by Day*.

CAROL MCCRAE is a clinical psychologist in private practice. She is a parishioner at St. James Memorial Episcopal Church in Eatontown, New Jersey. McCrea is also a contributor to *Comfort Ye* (Forward Movement, 2007.)

SARAH BRYAN MILLER is a licensed lay preacher, eucharistic minister, and lector at St. Peter's Episcopal Church, St. Louis, Missouri. A singer and musician, she is also the classical music critic for the *St. Louis Post-Dispatch* and has written meditations for *Forward Day by Day*.

GREGORY A. RUSSELL is pastor of the First Christian Church (Disciples of Christ) in Madison, Indiana. He has contributed to several Forward Movement anthologies, including *Comfort Ye* (2007).

RICHARD L. SHIMPFKY retired in 2004 after fourteen years as bishop of the Episcopal Diocese of El Camino Real in California. He had previously served as priest in New Jersey and Virginia. He lives in Monterey, California.

FRANCIS H. WADE retired in 2005 after twenty-two years as rector of St. Alban's Episcopal Church in Washington, D.C. He is the author of *The Art of Being Together* (Forward Movement, 2005) and has written several times for *Forward Day by Day*.

PAUL F. M. ZAHL retired as rector of All Saints Episcopal Church, Chevy Chase, Maryland, in 2009. He formerly served as dean and president of Trinity Episcopal School for Ministry, Ambridge, Pennsylvania, and as dean of the Cathedral Church of the Advent, Birmingham, Alabama. He is the author of ten books and has written for *Forward Day by Day*.

# Author Index

# Notes and Reflections

# *Notes and Reflections*

# *Notes and Reflections*

# Notes and Reflections

# *Notes and Reflections*

# Notes and Reflections

# *Notes and Reflections*